Evaluating Democratic Innovations

In the face of increasing political disenchantment, many Western governments have experimented with innovations that aim to enhance the working and quality of democracy as well as increasing citizens' political awareness and understanding of political matters.

This text is the most comprehensive account of these various democratic innovations. Written by an outstanding team of international experts it examines the theories behind these democratic innovations, how they have worked in practice and evaluates their success or failure. It explains experiments with new forms of democratic engagement such as:

- direct democracy
- deliberative democracy
- co-governance.

Drawing on a wide variety of theoretical perspectives and with a broad range of case studies, this is essential reading for all students of democratic theory and all those with an interest in how we might revitalise democracy and increase citizen involvement in the political process.

Brigitte Geissel is Professor of Political Sciences and Political Sociology at Goethe University in Frankfurt am Main, Germany, and Ash Center for Democratic Governance and Innovation, Harvard Kennedy School, USA.

Kenneth Newton is Visiting Professor at the Wissenschaftszentrum Berlin and Emeritus Professor of Comparative Politics at the University of Southampton, UK.

Evaluating Democratic Innovations

Curing the democratic malaise?

Edited by Brigitte Geissel and Kenneth Newton

Routledge
Taylor & Francis Group
LONDON AND NEW YORK

First published 2012
by Routledge
2 Park Square, Milton Park, Abingdon, Oxon, OX14 4RN

Simultaneously published in the USA and Canada
by Routledge
711 Third Avenue, New York, NY 10017

Routledge is an imprint of the Taylor & Francis Group, an informa business

British Library Cataloguing in Publication Data
A catalogue record for this book is available from the British Library

Library of Congress Cataloging in Publication Data
Evaluating democratic innovations : curing the democratic malaise? / edited by Brigitte Geissel and Kenneth Newton.
p. cm.
Includes bibliographical references.
1. Direct democracy. 2. Deliberative democracy. 3. Direct democracy—Case studies. 4. Deliberative democracy—Case studies
I. Geissel, Brigitte. II. Newton, Kenneth, 1940–
JC423.E9 2011
321.8--dc23 2011021987

ISBN: 978-0-415-66919-1 (hbk)
ISBN: 978-0-415-66920-7 (pbk)
ISBN: 978-0-203-15519-6 (ebk)

Typeset in Times New Roman
by HWA Text and Data Management, London

MIX
Paper from responsible sources
FSC www.fsc.org
FSC® C004839

Printed and bound in Great Britain by
TJ International Ltd, Padstow, Cornwall

Contents

Figures and tables

Figures

Tables

Contributors

David Beetham is Professor Emeritus, University of Leeds, and Honorary Fellow, Human Rights Centre, University of Essex. He contributed to the development of the democratic audit methodology used in the UK and internationally, and has acted as consultant to many audits overseas. He has written a guide to good democratic practice for parliaments for the Inter-Parliamentary Union, Geneva, and co-authored a guide to democracy assessment for the International Institute for Democracy and Electoral Assistance, Stockholm. Recent books include *Democracy: a Beginner's Guide* (Oneworld Publications 2005).

Ian Budge is Emeritus Professor in the Department of Government at the University of Essex. He has made major contributions both to cumulative research on democracy and to organizational developments in the discipline. His earliest research on Glasgow and Belfast focused on causes of democratic breakdown. After a period of studying elections, voting behaviour and party competition, he turned to public policy and how it might become responsive to popular preferences – a central democratic dilemma. His research covers both direct and representative democracy. He founded the Essex Summer School in Social Science Data Analysis in 1968. He was Executive Director of the European Consortium in Political Research between 1979 and 1983. Among his recent publications are (with Klingemann, Volkens, Bara and Tanenbaum) *Mapping Policy Preferences: Estimates for Parties, Electorates and Governments 1945–1998* (Oxford University Press 2001); (with Michael D. McDonald) *Elections, Parties, Democracy: Conferring the Median Mandate* (Oxford University Press 2005); and (with David McKay, Kenneth Newton and John Bartle) *The New British Politics* (Pearsons Education Limited 2007).

James S. Fishkin directs the Center for Deliberative Democracy at Stanford University where he teaches Communication and Political Science. He holds the Janet M. Peck Chair in International Communication at Stanford and is Chair of the Department of Communication. He recently wrote *When the People Speak: Deliberative Democracy and Public Consultation* (Oxford University Press 2009) as well as a number of earlier books including *Democracy and Deliberation* (Yale University Press 1991) and *The Voice of the People* (Yale University Press 1995) and (with Bruce Ackerman) *Deliberation Day* (Yale University Press 2004). His Deliberative Polling projects have provided a new method of public consultation in countries around the world ranging from the US and Canada to Britain, Italy, Bulgaria, Australia, Hungary, Poland, Brazil, Argentina, China, Thailand, Japan, Northern Ireland, Denmark and European wide. More details can be found at the Center for Deliberative Democracy site, http://cdd.stanford.edu.

Brigitte Geissel, full Professor of Political Science and Political Sociology at Goethe University Frankfurt am Main, held research and teaching positions at various universities/

institutes such as Harvard Kennedy School (USA), Social Science Research Center Berlin, Center of Excellence on Democracy at Åbo Akademi (Finland), the Universities of Münster, Berlin, and Illinois (USA) as well as the Vietnamese German University, Saigon. Her research interests include democratic innovations, new forms of governance and political actors (new social movements, associations, civil society, parties, political elites, citizens). Recent publications have been published in, for example, *Comparative Sociology*, *West European Politics*, *European Journal of Political Research.*

Hanspeter Kriesi holds the Chair in Comparative Politics at the Department of Political Science of the University of Zurich. Previously, he taught at the universities of Amsterdam and Geneva. His wide-ranging research interests include the study of direct democracy, social movements, political parties and interest groups, public opinion, the public sphere and the media. He is the director of a Swiss national research programme on the 'Challenges to democracy in the 21st century'.

Ken Newton is Emeritus Professor, University of Southampton, and Visiting Professor at the Wissenschaftszentrum Berlin für Sozialforschung (Social Science Research Center, Berlin). His recent research has been in the fields of the political media, citizenship and participation, political and social trust, and comparative government.

Dieter Rucht, retired since July 2011, was co-director of the research group 'Civil Society, Citizenship and Political Mobilization in Europe' at the Social Science Research Center Berlin and Professor of Sociology at the Free University of Berlin. His research interests include political participation, social movements, political protest and public discourse. His most recent book in English is *The World Says No to War: Demonstrations Against the War on Iraq* (joint editor with Stefaan Walgrave, University of Minnesota Press 2010). Recent publications in German are a handbook on social movements in Germany since 1945 (joint editor, Campus 2008) and a book on the media strategies and media coverage of the campaign against the G8 meeting in Heiligendamm in 2007 (joint editor, Campus 2008).

Graham Smith is Professor of Politics at the Centre for Citizenship, Globalization and Governance (C2G2) and the Third Sector Research Centre (TSRC) at the University of Southampton. He is the author of a number of academic articles, books and reports on aspects of democratic theory and practice. His most recent monograph is *Democratic Innovations: Designing Institutions for Citizen Participation* (Cambridge University Press 2009). His 2005 report for the Power Inquiry in the UK, *Beyond the Ballot: 57 Democratic Innovations from Around the World*, has been downloaded thousands of times. He is on the steering committee of the global project *Participedia* – a Web 2.0 platform for user-generated articles that describe and assess participatory governance throughout the world.

Julien Talpin is research fellow at the CNRS/Ceraps – University of Lille II. His research deals with the impact of deliberative experiences on actors, and the consequences of participation in terms of politicization, interest for politics and civic engagement. He has observed mini-publics and participatory budgets, and has recently focused on the history of deliberative practices in Europe. He recently published *Schools of Democracy. How Ordinary Citizens (Sometimes) Become Competent In Participatory Budgeting Institutions*, (ECPR Press 2011) and (with S. Wojcik) 'When the youth talk about climate change. A comparison of the learning potential of on-line and face-to-face deliberation', *Policy and the Internet,* 1(2), 2010.

Acknowledgements

This book has its origins in a conference on democratic innovation held at the Wissenschaftszentrum Berlin (WZB). We would like, first and foremost, to thank the Thyssen-Foundation for its generosity in funding the conference without which we could never even have started the work. We would also like to thank Wolfgang Merkel at the WZB for his support, help and advice, without which we could not have started or finished the work. Towards the end of the project Clare Dekker did a great deal of proofreading and editing work on the chapters in the book for which we are very grateful. Last, the contributors to this volume have been most patient in supplying their chapters, re-writing them, and waiting for the whole process of production to be wound up with all its unavoidable delays.

Ken Newton and Brigitte Geissel are especially grateful to the WZB for its hospitality while Ken has been a guest there and during Brigitte's stay as research fellow. We would like to thank the President and all the staff of the Centre for making life so pleasant, easy and productive. Particular thanks are due to colleagues in the Abteilung on Democracy: Structures, Performance, Challenges and in the Research Group Civil Society, Citizenship, and Political Mobilization in Europe for providing a working environment that is stimulating and enjoyable.

Introduction

Curing the democratic malaise with democratic innovations

Ken Newton

The democratic malaise

Democracy is a variable not a constant. It perpetually reinvents and adapts itself as political demands upon it change and as standards of democratic conduct rise. Democratic practices that were acceptable in the late twentieth century may now be poorly adapted to modern circumstances. Globalization, emerging forms of international and transnational government, a shifting balance of centralization and decentralization, the accelerating pace of economic and technological change, shifts in the role and power of the nation state, the threat of terrorism, new forms of communication, and waves of international migration and increasing social diversity all present democracy with new problems.

The past decades have also seen popular pressure for improved democratic performance. Greater affluence, rising educational standards and improved access to political information have, so the argument goes, helped to mobilize citizens and stimulate higher levels of political awareness and participation. Citizens come to expect more of their democracies: more participation, greater political accountability, greater transparency, more consultation, less corruption, more equitable treatment of minority groups, and more open and accountable government.

Since the 1970s, political scientists have detected shifts in the ways that citizens participate in politics, with a political repertoire that has expanded to include unconventional forms of protest behaviour, demonstrations, direct action and boycotts (Barnes and Kaase et al. 1979; Jennings and van Deth et al. 1990). Post-materialist theory also argues that new political values are associated with rising levels of political awareness and new, more demanding forms of political participation (Inglehart 1997; Inglehart and Welzel 2005). The trend in the United States, Britain, France and Germany over the past two or three decades is towards greater political awareness, participation and discussion (Dalton 1996: 26–7), and while citizens may be no less committed to democratic values, they are becoming more critical of the traditional institutions of democratic government and their centralized and bureaucratic ways of operating (Norris 2002). Political participation is shifting from traditional forms focusing on elections and organized by centralized and bureaucratic parties and pressure groups to more direct and individualized forms of political expression involving new parties and social movements, community groups and internet activism.

Survey evidence shows many citizens in the West are becoming more critical of their political leaders, of their main institutions of government, and of their systems of democracy. These developments are explored in depth elsewhere (see Dalton 2004) and it is enough to say here that the extensive evidence suggests that many, not all, western citizens are becoming more sceptical about their democracies, more detached from parties, less trustful of political leaders, and less supportive of their system of government and political institutions.

This is not to suggest 'a crisis of democracy'. One of the distinguishing features of democracy, and one that makes it more flexible and durable than other forms of government, is a capacity for changing itself. In this sense, democracy is a set of institutional arrangements for responding to public demands, including demands for improving democracy. Hence, it is still possible to retain a strong belief in democracy as a principle of government, while dissatisfaction with political leaders and the way democracy works in practice is growing. In western democracies at present, the overwhelming majority believe in democracy as the best form of government, but growing numbers also believe that the democratic system in their country is deficient. They believe that the cure for democracy's ills is more and better democracy.

Consequently, the past two to three decades has seen a gathering wave of democratic innovations, some pioneered by the established democracies of the West, and some introduced by new democracies that are taking a fresh look at how constitutions and practices should operate. Their list of inventions is now exceedingly long and varied, and so it is helpful to start this book by identifying and defining democratic innovations – no easy task in itself – and how the chapters that follow try to cover a ground that is neither unmanageably large nor too restrictively narrow in its scope.

The scope and nature of democratic innovation

A democratic innovation may be defined for present purposes as the successful implementation of a new idea that is intended to change the structures or processes of democratic government and politics in order to improve them. It is difficult to go beyond this vague and empty formulation because democracy itself is an essentially contested concept, and hence there is argument about what helps or hinders its improvement. Similarly, the term 'innovation' is difficult to capture in a concise manner. Innovation in public sector management has had its own dedicated journal since 1995 and was still discussing the meaning of the term six years later.[1] However, some of the general characteristics of the concept can be picked out to distinguish it from related terms such as reform, invention, modification and change.

Innovations are a special subset of changes that involve deliberate action to introduce new ways of doing things. They involve attempts to introduce methods and practices that are more than renovation, minor modification or reform of an existing system: 'To innovate is not to reform', said Edmund Burke (1991), implying that innovation is a more radical change implying a qualitatively greater potential effect than simply tinkering around with reforms. Innovation implies a discontinuity or a qualitative break with the existing state of affairs. Fitting better springs to the hansom cab was not an innovation, but the horseless carriage was; Montesquieu's tripartite separation of powers was an innovation, but widening the franchise to include more property owners was not. Nevertheless, political innovations are a matter of degree, ranging from small but discontinuous changes, to large and potentially revolutionary ones. Consequently, the exact dividing line between reform and innovation, notwithstanding Burke, is not readily seen or drawn.

Innovations are more than ideas and theories; they are ideas in action. In the natural sciences, it is one thing to develop the idea of perpetual motion, but quite another to build a working machine. In the social sciences it is one thing to argue the theory that all people are born equal, but quite another to create institutions and practices that actually promote equality. Innovations depend on ideas that can be implemented; good innovations depend on good ideas that can be implemented successfully.

Many innovations start as low-risk, small-scale experiments in communities and neighbourhoods. Pilot testing of this kind has many advantages as a first step, especially if costs are low and effects can be closely monitored over time. The small scale of some innovations, however, is not important because if they are successful they may spread across political systems and rise to higher levels of regional and national government – perhaps even to international and transnational institutions. Community policing in Chicago, participatory budgeting in Porto Alegre and the British Columbia Citizens' Assembly are three notable examples of innovations that have spread from localized beginnings. The number of generalized, high-impact innovations, however, is comparatively small. In keeping with the times, many of the most successful ones are focused on face-to-face operations within local communities and neighbourhoods.

It is often difficult to say whether an innovation has the effect of preserving the existing order by making it more effective and efficient, or whether it has succeeded in changing or even transforming the system to create something very different and ultimately better. That is, whether an innovation preserves, improves, transforms or subverts democracy is often a matter of opinion. This follows from the essentially contested nature of democracy, and makes innovations and their consequences controversial. Radical revolutionaries may dismiss most innovations as nothing more than tinkering with the system or, worse, as deliberate mystification designed to fool the general public. Pragmatists and realists who have 'accommodated to the world' may regard them as genuine progress. Perhaps the best we can do is leave the value judgements aside, while trying to assess whether a given innovation has succeeded in achieving at least some of its goals.

Lastly, democratic innovation is not a straightforward process. It has been said (Kline and Rosenberg 1986) that scientific and technological innovation is typically complex, unpredictable and disorderly, and its effects often hard to measure. Yet, scientific and technological matters are sometimes relatively simple and straightforward compared with social and political processes (Bernstein, et al. 2000). If so, democratic innovation is even more complex, unpredictable and disorderly. There are the complexities of government and political life to take into account as well as questions of values and judgements. The balance between costs and benefits can be difficult to strike, especially when effects are difficult to monitor and measure, and where some of the effects are unexpected and may appear only in the long run.

Having said all this, democratic innovation is of growing practical importance in contemporary government and politics. It has all sorts of difficulties and problems as a new field of study in political science, but it cannot be left aside for this reason. Rather, the best course of action is to try to map the field and identify its major features as the first step in developing a manageable research agenda.

Curing the democratic malaise with democratic innovations

There are different views about the origins and causes of the democratic malaise, discussed briefly at the start of this Introduction. One school of thought lays blame at the feet of ordinary citizens. Dating from Plato's belief that only philosopher kings were fit to rule, and running through the entire span of western history to modern research, it claims that large proportions of the population are unable or unwilling to play their proper citizen role because they are too ignorant, lazy or stupid. According to this approach, the democratic malaise is mainly the result of the input or bottom-up failure of the electorate to perform its citizenship role.

There is a different explanation that focuses not on the role of citizens, but on the top-down importance of leaders, political processes and democratic institutions. This school claims that citizens are more likely to support their system of government if they believe it is open and fair and protects civil liberties, if it performs well, if politicians are accountable and not corrupt, and if the system accommodates their most important interests. According to this approach, democratic malaise is as much the result of top-down, output factors associated with the performance of political leaders and institutions, as it is of bottom-up, input factors associated with the shortcomings of voters and citizens (Newton 2006; Keele 2007).

According to the citizen-centred, input theory, democratic innovation should concentrate on educating and informing citizens, and encouraging them to play a more active role in political life. According to the top-down, output approach, innovations should focus on political structures and processes, particularly on the institutions of democratic government that regulate the behaviour and performance of politicians and make them more accountable and responsive to the general public.[2]

Top-down innovation

Broadly speaking, innovations of this kind involve constitutional and governmental engineering that, in turn, require the creation of new institutions or rules of procedure and conduct. Private organizations such as parties, voluntary associations and social movements have also innovated in order to improve their internal operations and broaden their appeal. Many of the top-down forms of innovations are attempts to make the instruments of representative government work in new and better ways. In general, they can be grouped under two headings.

Vertical accountability

Vertical accountability refers to the accountability of government to its citizens. Modern innovations of this kind are often refinements of the classical mechanisms that try to ensure that governments are responsible and responsive to their citizens. Examples are: the decentralization of government; the abolition of dual mandates; term limits for elected representatives; new institutions of international and multinational government; truth and reconciliation commissions; performance-based public budgeting; new forms of quango; the greater use of courts and legal constraints on government and its agencies; transparency in government; democratic audits. Vertical innovations have also been introduced in non-governmental political organizations, particularly in parties that have tried to improve their internal democratic performance.

Horizontal accountability

Horizontal accountability is concerned with improving the checks and balances between branches of government, especially the regulation and oversight of government and public bodies (see O'Donnell 1999). It includes: parliamentary checks on the power of the executive (strengthening the powers of parliamentary committees, parliamentary ombudsmen); independent central banks; legal oversight; electoral and constitutional courts; new public management reforms; target setting and performance reviews.

One highly significant kind of horizontal innovation is concerned with citizen rights, including: freedom of information; privacy laws; ombudsmen; police integrity commissions; citizen charters; human rights; legal aid; common citizen rights across national borders and the citizen rights of resident aliens.

Some governments have set up central departments for constitutional affairs and the promotion of change, and some have created independent bodies to propose, implement and evaluate democratic innovations. These of course, bridge the distinction between top-down and bottom-up innovations, and may be classed as meta-institutions covering innovations of every kind. Private and semi-private organizations have contributed with their own ideas and innovations, especially the think tanks and new public interest organizations that research and encourage action on various aspects of government (for example, Amnesty International, Transparency International, Freedom House, International IDEA, Index on Censorship, Democratic Audit, Economist Intelligence Unit).

Some critics view government proposals for democratic innovation with scepticism or outright cynicism, claiming that they are a smokescreen to conceal lack of real change. Others doubt the effectiveness of the reforms, claiming that their merits are exaggerated, their costs too high, their benefits meagre or that they hand power to special interests groups or government agencies that are best able to exploit them for their own interests (see Smith 2005: 31; Smith 2009: 18). A third group argues that innovations within states, especially at the local and neighbourhood level, are rendered largely ineffective insofar as political power is shifting increasingly to the international level and especially to private multinational organizations (see Strange, 1996; Van Creveld 1999; Held and McGrew 1998).

Bottom-up innovation

Democratic innovations of the bottom-up kind are primarily concerned with (1) enabling those citizens who are already involved and interested to play a more proactive part in public affairs, and (2) improving the capacities, knowledge and participation of others so that they, too, can play a fuller citizenship role. Bottom-up innovations focus heavily on the inputs of citizens into the political system and owe a lot to the interest in direct democracy, which emerged in the 1960s, and later appeared in the writing on strong democracy (Barber 1984) and the post-materialist culture (Inglehart 1997; Inglehart and Welzel 2005). They differ from top-down innovations in that they seek to improve the quality and increase the quantity of mass participation and strengthen its direct-democratic nature. For practical purposes, the long and varied list of innovations of this kind can be grouped according to their primary purposes under five general headings.

Voting and elections

Concern with falling turnout and increasing voter alienation has led to suggestions and experiments with all stages of the electoral process, from voting qualifications and registration, to types of voting systems, quota rules and allocated seats for special groups. The list includes: reducing the voting age; universal citizenship; race conscious re-districting; making voter registration easier; kerbside voting and registration; electronic voting; early voting; postal voting; compulsory voting; cumulative voting; positive abstention; quota rules; shared mandates; variable thresholds; electoral quotas; reserved seats for minorities.

Information, consultation and deliberation

The wish to improve political knowledge, awareness and capacities, and to meet increasing demands for consultation between government and citizens, has resulted in many innovations, including: deliberative forums; consensus conferences; planning cells; scenario workshops; study circles; electronic notice boards and information; democracy kiosks; civics and citizenship courses; citizenship mentors; citizen panels, juries, focus groups and forums; denizen (residents, as opposed to citizens) councils; electronic means of finding others with similar political agendas and contacting others and promoting common action; consultation and interactive consultation; deliberative polling and online deliberative polling; petitions and e-petitions; shared mandates; civic service; rotating civic office.

Co-governance

Falling somewhere between direct democracy and consultation, co-governance involves direct citizen (and often organized group) involvement in the activities of the state. It includes: participatory budgeting; citizen assemblies; neighbourhood development; village and community councils; community policing experiments; and health, education and planning boards.

Direct democracy

For present purposes, direct democracy may be defined as that form of democracy in which citizen power and authority is exercised without the mediating influence of the elected representatives and officials of representative government. The list of direct democracy-related innovations includes: town meetings; referendums, initiatives and recalls; direct legislation and direct participation in rule-making; ballot propositions; and those forms of co-governance where citizens have real decision-making powers.

Electronic democracy

Electronic democracy is treated as a category in its own right because, as a means to an end, it cuts across all of the other four categories above. It attracts a great deal of attention and is claimed by some to have a power to transform the political world, and so it deserves special consideration as a separate category of innovations of its own.

There is no reason why innovations of the top-down and bottom-up kind should not be tried in tandem or alongside each other, especially if, as seems likely, democratic quality can be improved in both ways. This book, however, will concentrate on bottom-up, input innovations that try in various ways to raise the awareness, knowledge and participation of citizens in daily political life. It does so for several reasons. First, the number and variety of democratic innovations is so huge that it would be difficult to try to consider them all carefully in a single volume: the result would be superficial. Second, although the topics selected are only part of the whole field of democratic innovation, they have usually attracted the greatest interest. (A preliminary survey of the research produces a list of more than 550 publications covering e-democracy, voting and elections, consultation and deliberation, direct democracy, and co-governance.) Third, innovations that focus on bottom-up attempts to stimulate citizen political activity have been tried in many different countries and in a wide variety of circumstances, which makes it possible to evaluate their effects with a greater degree of confidence. Fourth, it is usually easier to evaluate the effects of what are often small-scale democratic experiments rather than large-scale institutional changes. For example, it is easier to estimate the impact of the trial runs of postal voting or e-voting that have been conducted in selected areas, than to evaluate the effects of administrative courts or the development of parliamentary committee systems. Moreover, innovations that focus on citizens confront some of the timeless questions of democracy. Are voters capable of making sensible decisions about politics? Are they well enough informed? How can we best overcome the problem of rational ignorance? Do voters respond favourably to being placed in the most favourable circumstances for rational deliberation?

Concentrating on citizen-centred innovations does not imply that they are more important than state or government-centred ones. In fact, it may be that some political leaders like to devote much money and time to input innovations because they distract attention from their own role in generating democratic malaise. The claim is not that bottom-up innovations are the most important form of democratic improvement, but that they are an important form that attracts a great deal of popular and government interest, with potentially big implications for revitalized democracy.

To further stake out a manageable field of work that fits without too much overcrowding within the covers of one book, we are concerned here with innovation in the public not the private sector, that is, in government and politics and in organizations that act in the public sphere and have a role in decision making and the delivery of public services. It is true that many organizational innovations have their origins in the private and commercial sectors, but there are, as many have pointed out, big differences between the public and the private, and the transfer of practices from one to the other remains a highly problematic issue. To further specify the limits of our research, we are concerned with general government bodies (international, national and sub-national) rather than public bodies concerned with particular services (agencies of government delivering education, transport or health, for example). The interest here is with general matters of government rather than citizen relations with particular public services. This is not because particular services are unimportant – far from it – but because they may have special characteristics and circumstances surrounding them that distinguish them from general relations between citizens and government.

The rest of this chapter will not describe or review citizen-centred democratic innovations in detail. That is already done comprehensively and expertly elsewhere (Smith 2005, 2009).[3] Rather, it will briefly introduce the work that follows and raise some general questions about the importance and effect of democratic innovations.

Assessing democratic innovation

The chapters that follow in this book cover a range of topics related to six general questions about democratic innovations. Most usually, each chapter considers two, three or four of these topics, because they are intertwined one with the other, yet closely associated in the real world.

Direct democracy vs representative democracy?

There is an understandable tendency in the literature on new forms of political involvement to assume that strong democracy should replace weak democracy, that deliberative democracy should supplant elite direction, and that direct democracy should render representative democracy obsolete. There is something wrong with this assumption that the new and the old are incompatible and alternative forms of government. New forms of direct democracy – whether referendums, co-governance, or citizen juries and mini-publics – are inevitably developed within and by the institutions of old forms of representative democracy. While it is the job of abstract theories to explore the abstract principles and potentials of strong democracy, deliberation and direct participation, in the real world these are set in a context of the institutions and practices of representative government – parties, pressure groups, legislatures, government institutions, the mass media and political leaders. For better or worse, the new forms are inevitably influenced, or even determined by, the old. This prompts the questions of how democratic innovations mesh with and relate to the old institutions of representative government, and whether the old forms constrain or enhance the performance of the new forms.

The reefs of cognitive incompetence

A long-established school of thought is highly sceptical about the likely success of bottom-up, citizen-centred innovations that try to increase the capacity of ordinary people to play a fuller role in political life. Plato argued that only the philosopher kings were fit to rule, Madison and Mill claimed that democracy can easily result in the tyranny of the majority, Schumpeter stated that the masses are incapable of any collective action other than a stampede (Schumpeter 1942: 283), Huntington talked of an excess of democracy bringing about a democratic distemper (Crozier, Huntington and Watanuki 1975). Most recently, Sartori (1987: 241) has argued that direct democracy will quickly and disastrously founder on the reefs of mass cognitive incompetence.[4] Evidence for this claim is provided in survey and election studies showing that unhealthily large proportions of citizens are politically lazy, ignorant and gullible, and that if they have preferences of public issues at all, these are often unstable, unclear or contradictory (Campbell et al. 1960; Converse 1964; Zaller and Feldman 1992).

Others claim that this underestimates the capacity of mass publics, and on the basis of their own empirical evidence, conclude that 'voters are not fools' (Key 1966), that a sizeable majority of citizens have a good but general sense of current political issues, that their views are comparatively stable and meaningful, and that they respond to real world events in an understandable and rational manner (see, for example, Page and Shapiro 1993: 60; Dalton 1996; Evans et al. 1996).

What do studies of democratic innovations tell us about these claims? Are modern citizen bodies capable of informed, thoughtful and public-spirited collective decision making, or is this a hopelessly utopian ideal?

Activating the inactive

Many innovations of the citizen-centred variety attempt to broaden the base of popular participation by increasing the number and variety of groups involved. Experiments with community participation, consultation and co-governance have targeted the politically detached and marginal. Some have aimed at the poorest and least well educated sections of native populations and others have concentrated on minority and immigrant groups. New forms of electronic communication have been exploited by those claiming that they have nothing less than a revolutionary potential for reaching those parts of the population that other means cannot reach. The simple question follows: what success have democratic innovations had in informing and mobilizing the groups in the population that are typically the most uninformed and inactive?

The diffusion of innovation

Can innovations from one country be transplanted to another? In this respect, political innovations differ from those in science and engineering. The internal combustion engine works irrespective of the country, its social conditions, and its political and economic climate. But political innovations that work well in one country may not travel well or thrive when transplanted to another. Similarly, innovations that work well at one level of a system, or in one institution within it, may not work well in others. For example, the Chicago community policing experiment, operating separately in each of the 285 small neighbourhoods of the city, has been successful in encouraging participation, especially among minority and disadvantaged groups, and has speeded up the implementation of new ideas and practices (Fung 2003). However, it is unlikely to be successful at a city, state or federal level, because it depends on the close social relations of small urban areas. The conclusion that it could not be effectively transferred to a higher level political unit does not detract from the success of the Chicago experience, but it does suggest that its applicability to larger political arenas is limited. Which innovations travel well across time, place and levels of the political system, and which are limited in their effectiveness to particular circumstances?

Trade-offs

Innovations can be judged according to the amount of change they produce, weighed against their costs in time, money and effort. They may be expensive or cheap and yield large or small returns. Some innovations try to produce a deep and lasting effect on a small number of people; others concentrate on large numbers of citizens, recognizing that the effects may be more superficial or short-lasting. As Beetham points out in this volume, new and old forms of politics may have different sets of advantages and disadvantages to be weighed against each other. Equally, one innovation may work at the expense of another, perhaps because it absorbs the lion's share of the resources of time, money and interest, or because its effects contradict the effects of the other. For example, an innovation designed to increase participation may reduce government efficiency, or vice versa (Dahl 1994). Equally, mass participation and the careful marshalling and monitoring of public opinion takes time, which means the decisions may be delayed. A good deal of writing on democratic innovation is concerned with improving citizen understanding of, and participation in, politics, but rather little has considered innovations that might help to increase the speed of decision making. What are the merits and deficiencies of different democratic innovations and how do they compare with the merits and deficiencies of more conventional forms of representative government?

The impact of innovations

Finally, there is a pervasive question that runs throughout all democratic innovation research: what effects do different innovations have on politics and government that add or detract from their democratic performance? Evidence is hard to come by (Rowe and Frewer 2004; Abelson and Gauvin 2006: 33), partly because there is little impact research (which requires before-and-after comparisons), partly because research trying to sort out cause and effect complexities in the real world is a minefield of problems, and partly because the initial impact of some innovations may soon wear off, while others may take a generation or more to take effect. Some innovations may be of value in themselves (such as improving citizen knowledge and understanding of politics) even if they have no measurable impact on democratic practices and behaviour (such as increasing election turnout).

Innovations may have no measurable impact for one of two main reasons. In the first place, it may be that the innovation is simply ineffective because it is incapable of producing the desired effects. Its effects may be too weak, or the logic or methods underlying it may be faulty. In the second place, it could be that some innovations might produce their desired effects, but for the actions of interested parties who succeed in negating its effects – governments, parties, bureaucrats, the mass media, or opposing interest groups. It is important to distinguish between the two possible reasons, since failure on the first count means returning to the drawing board and re-thinking the reasoning behind the innovation, while the second is a political problem that requires a different kind of response.

Equally, some innovations may have a placebo effect, caused not by the innovation itself but simply because the authorities have taken trouble to try to reach out to citizens and express an interest in their opinions. The warm and fuzzy feelings and the belief that things are getting better, even if they are not, may be what research measures, rather than any specific benefit flowing from the specific innovation. When dealing with innovation effects we must remember the Hawthorne experiments (Landsberger 1958).

In any case, the evaluation of innovations is inherently problematic insofar as there is unlikely to be universal agreement about what makes democracy better and worse (Diamond and Morlino 2004; Bühlmann et al. 2007), and hence the merits of any democratic innovation may be disputed. If 'democracy' is an inherently contested concept, then what makes it better or worse is also essentially contested. The best we can do, perhaps, is evaluate innovations against their stated aims, and leave readers to judge for themselves whether the aims are for the better or worse.

Overview of the book

New and old forms of (direct) democracy

Perhaps the first questions to ask about any democratic innovation – ones not often asked – is what relationship does it bear to conventional representative democracy and how can it help to improve it? Does it offer a way of solving the democratic malaise or improving the operations of conventional representative government? The first part of the book picks up the theme of the role of old representative institutions and practices in setting the parameters and the context for *direct-democratic innovation*. Ian Budge considers the relationship between new forms of direct democracy and traditional forms of representative democracy and the extent to which they must work in tandem to work satisfactorily. More specifically, he considers the importance of parties, legislatures and governments as mediators of direct-democratic processes and asks whether, without them, direct democracy runs the risk of majority or minority tyranny, of electoral cycling and arbitrary voting outcomes.

His theoretical analysis is well complemented by Kriesi's close empirical examination of the Swiss case – probably the best example in the world of direct democracy in practice. Switzerland's system of government mixes representative and direct principles and so Kriesi is able to analyse how they interact, what role parties and leaders play in political debate and mobilization, and how the actions of leaders and representative bodies are restrained by operations of direct democracy. He is also able to examine the impact of direct democracy on political and economic performance, as well as the extent to which citizens are able to perform the role they are allotted by theories of direct democracy. What does the Swiss case tell us about Sartori's claim that direct democracy will 'quickly and disastrously founder on the reefs of cognitive incompetence' (Sartori 1987: 120)?

In the following chapter, David Beetham focuses on new and old forms of democracy and compares their modes of citizen political engagement. The more traditional forms are campaigns such as Make Poverty History, the Countryside Alliance and the anti-Iraq war movement. The more innovative types are the citizens' forums used in the UK, and said by government to have an even more important role in the future. Citizens' juries occupy an invited space, have a closed and selected membership and are typically proactive in their contribution to policy discussions. Campaigns and demonstrations claim their own space in the political arena. They have an open and self-selected membership, and are typically reactive in the sense that they respond to government policies.

Beetham considers the advantages and disadvantages of the two forms in terms of the numbers involved, their ability to reflect a cross section of public opinion on a given issue, and their ability to mobilize the previously uninvolved. He points out that there are trade-offs between juries and campaigns in this respect. He also considers the question of whether a greater use of the proactive and representative nature of citizens' juries might help to reduce the reactive citizen campaigns and demonstrations, and whether this would be a desirable outcome from a democratic point of view. This, of course, ties in to the earlier discussion of the limitations of bottom-up innovations, given the claim that many people are unable to fulfil their citizen role.

Deliberative democracy

The theme of citizen competence is the central feature of the second part of the book, which deals with deliberative polling, deliberative democracy and mini-publics, and includes a case study of the way in which deliberation is practised within a social movement. James Fishkin investigates whether random samples of citizens can overcome their rational ignorance if they are properly and carefully briefed by impartial experts and then presented with an opportunity to deliberate calmly and reasonably with others holding different opinions. He bases his conclusions on a long series of deliberative polls carried out around the globe – from Britain, the USA and Australia to China, Bulgaria and Greece – and asks whether citizens are able to participate in discussions on an equal basis. Are they able to change their minds when presented with argument and evidence? Can they avoid the polarization of opinions that some claim characterizes group debate? And can they engage in debates about public matters in a public-spirited manner? These concerns of Fishkin's experimental studies fit neatly with the questions posed by Kriesi in his study of Switzerland.

Graham Smith broadens the scope of discussion of deliberative polls to cover a family of similar democratic innovations that he terms 'mini-publics' and which Lang (2007) terms 'randomocracies'. In addition to deliberative polls, these include the citizens' juries, examined by Beetham in this volume, as well as planning cells and consensus conferences. Just as Fishkin poses the question of the extent to which his deliberative poll participants can really deliberate, so also Smith asks: 'To what extent do mini publics live up to the expectations of deliberative democrats?' He answers this question by examining the evidence about how mini-public innovations have actually worked in practice. He then discusses how this reflects back on the theory of deliberative democracy and suggests how we can design better deliberative forums. In this way, he opens up questions that have been overlooked in the abstract discussion of deliberative theory.

The discussion of deliberative democracy continues in the following chapter with Dieter Rucht's examination of how it actually works in practice in the case of a new social movement, the Global Justice Movement – a network of loosely linked transnational groups opposed to neoliberal globalization. This concentration on particular groups of self-selected activists tackling highly controversial issues is a useful complement to the previous chapters dealing with a total population (Switzerland) or randomly selected mini-public (deliberative polls and citizens' juries). Rucht asks to what extent does discussion and debate in his new social movement live up to the pure model and in what respects does it fall short. The Global Justice Movement may be regarded as an extreme case study: if an international and multicultural group of self-selected activists and ideologues can engage in deliberation on a highly controversial topic like neoliberal globalization, then there is reason to believe that ordinary people with shared cultural understanding will be able to do so when they discuss issues that generally have a lower salience for them.

Comparing innovations

The last part turns to trade-off and impacts of new and emerging forms of democratic innovation and to the question of their impact. The effectiveness of a broad variety of innovations is considered in the chapter by Newton. The oldest are the town meetings, initiatives and recalls that are used in some states in the USA to provide their citizens with the political teeth and claws that, in theory, enable their citizens to keep politicians in line with grass roots opinion. The newest are the experiments with co-governance, mini-publics, citizen forums, and deliberative assemblies that have sprung up around the globe in the last two decades or so. The most widely used are probably the referendums and electoral quotas that are increasingly common in democracies of all kinds and ages. There is also a huge diversity of attempts to improve citizen political competence, knowledge, awareness and activity, including e-democracy and new forms of electoral democracy. In theory, all these could be important additions to the institutions and practices of conventional democratic government, but a closer look at the evidence suggests that their influence is often limited by the rules governing their operation and by the powerful social, economic and political influences that induce political indifference and inactivity in modern society.

Brigitte Geissel evaluates the impacts of democratic innovations from a comparative perspective. Geissel first sets up a framework of four criteria for the assessment that focuses on (1) input and legitimacy, (2) throughput and process, (3) output and effectiveness, and (4) democratic education and civic skills. Next, she uses these criteria to conduct a meta-analysis of direct-democratic innovations, co-governance, and deliberative procedures, choosing a wide variety of examples from Europe. In her conclusions she emphasises the strengths and weakness of different types of innovation and the need to assess the trade-offs between them. She also points to the need to take different designs into account when evaluating their effects, the need for cross-national comparisons of (more or less) success and (more or less) failure, and the need for comparative research to complement case study approaches.

Julien Talpin covers a wide range of cases in his careful assessment of co-governance, the prime ones being the Porto Alegre experiments in participatory budgeting, the Citizens' Assembly that deliberated electoral reform in British Columbia, the community policing system set up in Chicago, and decentralised planning in Kerala. In previous chapters Beetham, Fishkin and Smith raise the question of whether co-governance makes a difference to government policy – whether it has a real influence over public policy and decision making. Talpin draws out some general conclusions in his discussion of the strengths and weakness of experiments scattered across the world. He also considers the circumstances in which co-governance experiments can fail, and elaborates on five conditions that are necessary for their success.

The conclusion by Geissel reflects on the problems authors who evaluate democratic innovations have to face. It discusses the main theoretical and empirical challenges concerning the evaluation of democratic innovations: yardsticks and empirical methods. The conclusion also shows future theoretical and empirical work research on democratic innovations has to process.

Acknowledgments

The author is most grateful to Hanspeter Kriesi, Wolfgang Merkel and Graham Smith for their comments on an earlier version of this work.

Notes

1 *The Innovation Journal*, 11 August, 2001 (http://www.innovation.cc/discussion-papers/thoughts-innovation.htm).

2 The distinction between bottom-up and top-down innovations corresponds to Smith's basic categories of innovations designed to engage citizens and those designed to change institutions (Smith 2005: 2).

3 For other general accounts of democratic innovations see Held and Pollitt 1986; Renn et al. 1995; Saward 2000; Schmitter and Trechsel 2004; Wisse 2006. Reviews of topics within the general field are presented by Budge 1996; OECD 2001; Scarrow 2001; LeDuc 2003; Catt and Murphy 2003; Gibson et al. 2004; Delli Carpini et al. 2004; Kriesi 2005; Zittel and Fuchs 2007; Margolis 2007: 765–82; and the two special issues of Acta Politica 2005 on empirical approaches to deliberative democracy.

4 For a version of the argument in its most recent guise see Caplan 2007. A recent discussion of the controversy is in Kuklinski and Peyton 2009: 45–64.

References

Abelson, J. and Gauvin, F.-P. (2006) *Assessing the Impacts of Public Participation: Concepts, Evidence and Policy Implications*, Ottawa: Canadian Policy Research Networks.

Barber, B. (1984) *Strong Democracy: Participatory Politics for a New Age*, Berkeley, CA: California University Press.

Barnes, S. and Kaase, M. et al. (1979) *Political Action: Mass Participation in Five Western Democracies*, Beverly Hills, CA: Sage.

Bernstein, S., Lebow, R. N., Stein, J. G. and Weber, S. (2000) God Gave Physics the Easy Problems, *European Journal of International Relations*, March, Vol. 6 No. 1: 43–76.

Budge, I. (1996) *The New Challenge of Direct Democracy*, Cambridge: Polity Press.

Bühlmann, M., Merkel, W. and Wessels, B. (2007) The Quality of Democracy: Democracy Barometer for Established Democracies, in *Challenges to Democracy in the 21st Century*, National Centre of Competence in Research (NCCR), Working Paper No. 10a, http://www.nccr-democracy.uzh.ch/publications/workingpaper/pdf/WP10a.pdf (accessed 8 April 2011).

Burke, E. (1796) 'Letter to a noble Lord', in R.B. McDowell (Ed.) (1991) The Writings and Speeches of Edmund Burke, vol. IX, Oxford: Clarendon Press.
Campbell, A., Converse, P., Miller, W. and Stokes, D. (1960) *The American Voter*, New York: John Wiley.
Caplan, B. (2007) *The Myth of the Rational Voter: Why Democracies Choose Bad Policies*, Princeton NJ: Princeton University Press.
Catt, H. and Murphy, M. (2003) What Voice for the People? Categorising Methods of Public Consultation, *Australian Journal of Political Science*, Vol. 38, No. 3: 407–21.
Converse, P. (1964) The Nature of Belief Systems in Mass Publics, in Apter, D. (ed.), *Ideology and Discontent*, New York: Free Press.
Crozier, M., Huntington, S. P. and Watanuki, J. (1975) *The Crisis of Democracy: Report on the Governability of Democracies to the Trilateral Commission*, New York: New York University Press, 75–114.
Dahl, R. A. (1994) A Democratic Dilemma: System, Effectiveness versus Citizen Participation, *Political Science Quarterly*, Vol. 109, No. 1: 23–34.
Dalton, R. J. (1996) *Citizen Politics*, Chatham, NJ: Chatham House.
Dalton, R. J. (2004) *Democratic Challenges, Democratic Choices: The Erosion in Political Support*, Oxford: Oxford University Press.
Delli Carpini, M. X., Cook, F. L., Lomax, F. and Jacobs, L. R. (2004) Public Deliberation, Discursive Participation, and Citizen Engagement: A Review of the Empirical Literature, *Annual Review of Political Science*, Vol. 7: 315–44.
Diamond, L. J. and Morlino, M. (2004) An Overview, *Journal of Democracy*, Vol. 15, No. 4: 20–31.
Evans, G., Heath, A. and Lalljee, M. (1996) Measuring Left–Right and Libertarian–Authoritarian Values in the British Electorate, *British Journal of Sociology*, Vol. 47, No. 1: 93–112.
Fung, A. (2003) Deliberative Democracy, Chicago Style: Grass Roots Governance in Policing and Public Education, in Fung, A. and Wright, E. O. (eds), *Deepening Democracy: Institutional Innovations in Empowered Participatory Governance*, London: Verso: 119–39.
Gibson, R. K., Rommele, A. and Ward, S. J. (eds) (2004) *Electronic Democracy*, London: Routledge.
Held, D. and McGrew, A. (1998) The End of the Old Order?, *Review of International Studies*, Vol. 24: 230.
Held, D. and Pollitt, C. (eds) (1986) *New Forms of Democracy*, London: Sage and The Open University.
Inglehart, R. J. (1997) *Modernization and Postmodernization: Cultural, Economic, and Political Change in 43 Societies*, Princeton, NJ: Princeton University Press.
Inglehart, R. J. and Welzel, C. (2005) *Modernization, and Democracy: The Human Development Sequence*, Cambridge: Cambridge University Press.
Jennings, K. and van Deth, J. et al. (1990) *Continuities in Political Action*, Berlin and New York: de Gruyter.
Keele, L. (2007) Social Capital and the Dynamics of Trust in Government, *American Journal of Political Science*, Vol. 51, No. 2: 241–54.
Key, V. O. (1966) *The Responsible Electorate: Rationality in Presidential Voting 1936–60*, Cambridge, MA: Harvard University Press.
Kline, S. J. and Rosenberg, G. (1986) *An Overview of Innovation, The Positive Sum Strategy*, Washington, DC: National Academy Press.

Kriesi, H.-P. (2005) *Direct Democratic Choice. The Swiss Experience*, Lanham, MD: Lexington Books.

Kuklinski, J. H. and Peyton, B. (2009) Belief Systems and Political Decision Making, in Dalton R. J. and Klingemann, H.-D. (eds), *The Oxford Handbook of Political Behaviour*, Oxford: Oxford University Press: 45–64.

Landsberger H. A. (1958) *Hawthorne Revisited*, Ithaca, NY: Cornell University Press.

Lang, A. (2007) But is it for Real? The British Columbia Citizens Assembly as a Model of State-Sponsored Citizen Empowerment, *Politics and Society*, Vol. 35: 85–105.

LeDuc, L. (2003) *The Politics of Direct Democracy: Referendums in Global Perspective*, Toronto: Broadview Press.

Madison, J. (1787) *Federalist No. 10*. See http://en.wikisource.org/wiki/The_Federalist/10

Margolis, M. (2007) E-government and Democracy, in Dalton, R. J. and Klingemann H.-D. (eds), *The Oxford Handbook of Political Behaviour*, Oxford: Oxford University Press: 765–82.

Mill, J.S. (2006, 1859) *On Liberty*, London: Penguin Classics.

Newton, K. (2006) Political Support, Social Capital, Civil Society and Political and Economic Performance, Political Studies, Vol. 54: 846–64.

Norris, P. (2002) *Democratic Phoenix*, Cambridge: Cambridge University Press.

O'Donnell, G. (1999) Horizontal Accountability in New Democracies, in Schedler, A., Diamond, L. and Plattner, M. F. (eds), *The Self Restraining State: Power and Accountability in the New Democracies*, Boulder, CO: Lynne Rienner.

OECD (2001) Engaging Citizens in Policy-Making: Information, Consultation and Public Participation, *Puma Policy Briefing* No. 10. Paris, OECD.

Page, B. I. and Shapiro, R. I. (1993) The Rational Public and Democracy, in Marcus, G. E. and Hansen, R. L. (eds), *Reconsidering the Democratic Republics*, State College, PA: Pennsylvania University Press.

Plato (1991). *The Republic: The Complete and Unabridged Jowett Translation*. New York: Vintage Books.

Renn, O., Webler, T. and Wiedemann, P. (eds) (1995) *Fairness and Competence in Citizen Participation: Evaluating Models for Environmental Discourse*, Dordrecht: Kluwer Academic Publishers.

Rowe, G. and Frewer L. J. (2004) Evaluating Public Participation Exercises: A Research Agenda, *Science, Technology, and Human Values*, Vol. 29, No. 4: 512–56.

Sartori, G. (1987) *The Theory of Democracy Revisited*, Chatham, NJ: Chatham House.

Saward, M. (ed.) (2000) *Democratic Innovation*, London: Routledge.

Scarrow, S. (2001) Direct Democracy and Institutional Change: A Comparative Investigation, *Comparative Political Studies*, Vol. 34: 651–65.

Schmitter, P. and Trechsel A. H. (2004) *The Future of Democracy in Europe. Trends, Analysis and Reforms*, Strasbourg: Council of Europe.

Schumpeter, J. A. (1942) *Capitalism, Socialism and Democracy*, New York: Harper and Row.

Smith, G. (2005) *Beyond the Ballot: Democratic Innovations from Around the World*, London: Power Inquiry.

Smith, G. (2009) *Democratic Innovations*, Cambridge: Cambridge University Press.

Strange, S. (1996) *The Retreat of the State: The Diffusion of Power in the World Economy*, Cambridge: Cambridge University Press.

Van Creveld, M. (1999) *The Rise and Decline of the State*, Cambridge: Cambridge University Press.

Wisse, E. (2006) *Promoting Democracy: An International Exploration of Policy and Implementation Practice*, Amsterdam: Ministry of the Interior and Kingdom Relations, Department of Constitutional Matters and Legislation.

Zaller, J. and Feldman, S. (1992) A Simple Theory of Survey Response, *American Journal of Political Science*, Vol. 36: 579–616.

Zittel, T. and Fuchs, D. (2007) *Participatory Democracy and Political Participation*, London: Routledge.

Part I

New and old forms of (direct) democracy

1 Implementing popular preferences

Is direct democracy the answer?

Ian Budge

Introduction

It is perhaps paradoxical, in discussing democratic innovations, to consider procedures that were most fully realized 2,500 years ago. Direct voting on all questions of public policy by all citizens was, in fact, the form in which democracy first emerged in the fifth century BC among the Greeks – particularly exemplified by the way it was practised in the city-state of Athens. So far as the Greeks and the rest of the Ancient World were concerned, this *was* democracy. Other regimes that limited popular policy control were aristocracies, oligarchies or tyrannies. Despite its antiquity, however, the idea that citizens should debate and decide policy directly is still fiercely controversial. Any extension of popular powers in this direction is among the most radical of the changes considered in this book.

Many critics such as Mill (1861/1910), Schumpeter (1962), Sartori (1987) and perhaps most eloquently James Madison (1787–8/1911) have criticized this kind of democracy for its instability and fickleness. Athens' defeat in the Peloponnesian War has been attributed to popular susceptibility to demagogic appeals. It is not clear, however, whether any other system of decision making would have done better, and Sparta's aristocratic rulers proved totally incompetent in maintaining control after their victory over Athens.

These debates about the quality of ancient democracy have a strong modern resonance – indeed the arguments for and against direct democracy have hardly changed from then till now. This is owing to the fact that democracy as such can hardly be conceived in other terms than as a system that guarantees the translation of popular preferences into public policy. To put it more exactly (Saward 1998: 51) 'democracy … is: a necessary correspondence between acts of government and the equally weighted felt interests of citizens with respect to those acts' (see also May 1978). It is hard to conceive of a more effective way of implementing this correspondence than allowing all citizens to vote on public policy in line with their felt interests. Institutionalizing such direct policy voting then makes popular approval of policy *necessary*, as required by the definition. Anything less detracts not just from direct democracy, but – according to its supporters – from democracy itself.

It is necessary to stress this point in order to appreciate the strong moral imperative that gives movements for direct democracy their driving force. Unlike the incremental reforms and technical modifications discussed elsewhere in this book, the impetus behind direct democracy comes not primarily from a concern for technological or other improvement of existing forms, but from moral passion. If you are a true democrat, you must in the end be a direct democrat. Anything less is a sell-out.

Most critics and opponents of direct democracy actually accept that it constitutes the ideal embodiment of democracy. John Stuart Mill is quite typical here. In *Representative Government* (1861/1910: 216–18), he accepts that 'the ideally best form of government is that in which the … supreme … power … is vested in the … community; every citizen ... having a voice'. But he then dismisses the possibility of direct democracy on grounds of practicability – in a single sentence! 'But all cannot, in a community exceeding a single small town, participate personally …'. Hence, we need to have representative government.

Mill ignores Switzerland, which, as Kriesi's chapter explains, even then had federal referendums. This is fairly typical of arguments against direct democracy: broad assertions are made that, on closer examination, turn out to be controvertible, to say the least, but which hardly ever *are examined* closely. It is this that renders Kriesi's chapter, as well as his previous work (Kriesi 2005) particularly valuable, as he does closely analyse the workings of the most advanced direct democracy in the world today, in light of the general theoretical points that have been made about it (see also Geissel in this volume).

Most critics of direct democracy are more negative than Mill. While accepting that it is indeed, in principle, the most complete embodiment of democracy, they argue against it on grounds of its accompanying dangers: the tyranny and instability of popular majorities; the inability of the populace to make wise decisions (better leave decisions on policy to the better educated or to bigger stakeholders); even, in the case of the Marxist and neo-Marxist left, the inability of citizens to see where their real interests lie, or to formulate their true preferences (false consciousness). Such criticisms of popular participation rapidly acquire a general anti-democratic flavour, however, because of the close connection between direct democracy and democracy as such. If citizens are incapable of making wise policy decisions, why should they even be allowed to choose the decision makers, as they are underrepresentative forms? Most critics are, of course, basically arguing for some kind of system that balances popular participation with expertise. But it is hard to keep blunderbuss assertions about popular incapacity from being generalized, as we shall see below.

While the arguments about direct democracy have hardly changed over the millennia, they *should* have changed – if only to take cognizance of modern developments that have made the contrast with representative forms less sharp. After the defeat of popular attempts to take over power in the medieval communes, direct democracy languished as a concrete political arrangement. When democracy re-emerged as a practical aspiration in the nation-states of the nineteenth century, it took a representative form, where an elected parliament rather than the people directly debated and decided policy.

The emergence of political parties, however (which from the late nineteenth century dominated both general elections and legislative and executive bodies), brought representative democracy closer to direct popular policy voting, though in a new form. Parties competed by offering alternative policy programmes (packages of policies) to the electorate. Voters could choose the programme they preferred overall and express their choice by voting for the party that supported it. Party discipline then ensured that its representatives in parliament would support the package.

This transformation of representative democracy into party democracy gave the initiative to parties in formulating the policy alternatives for which electors voted. Often these were regarded as too narrow or even indistinguishable from each other, either because parties had been corrupted and bought by sectional interests (as asserted by the American Progressives in the early twentieth century) or because they were embedded in the capitalist system to an extent that precluded them from offering truly radical alternatives (according to neo-Marxist and Green critics of the late twentieth century). The rise of new and local issues often made the broad packages offered by parties seem inadequate or insensitive to concerns felt by particular groups of citizens. Ecological issues, in particular, remained off the main agenda.

Under these circumstances, an obvious solution to the stultifying effects of party control and elite dominance seemed again to be direct popular voting on policy, with increasing emphasis on the power to initiate such a vote if a sufficient body of opinion wanted it.

Does direct democracy provide a solution for the current democratic malaise? In this chapter we first of all examine arguments for and against direct democracy. Arguments for are powered by the fact that the best way to ensure democracy, that is 'a *necessary* correspondence between acts of governance and the equally weighted felt interests of citizens with respect to these acts' (Saward 1998: 51), is direct popular voting on each policy. Arguments against stem from distrust of what popular majorities might do, especially to unpopular minorities such as Jews, Gypsies, Muslims or immigrants. This discussion then forces us to examine the various kinds of direct democracy on offer, contrasting, in particular, unmediated with mediated forms (see also Geissel in this volume). Contrary to many preconceptions, direct popular policy voting does not necessarily involve sweeping away of parties and parliaments, though the desire to do so is often a powerful motivating force for advocates of 'people power'.

The general conclusion drawn in this chapter, and supported by Kriesi's stress on the guidance provided to popular voting in Switzerland by parties and other institutions, is that many of the critical arguments against direct democracy are valid against its unmediated forms, but not against its mediated forms. The latter do give a more direct and unhampered expression to the popular will than representative democracy, while still providing procedural safeguards for minorities. We shall consider the implications of this position in our conclusions. One of them is that the contrast between modern forms of direct and representative democracy is overdrawn, as the latter usually involves voting on party policy packages as well as on candidates and government competence. This may pave the way for a new democratic synthesis that combines direct policy elections (that is, initiatives and referendums) with general elections in the areas that are appropriate for them – not unlike modern Swiss practice as described by Kriesi.

Pros and cons of direct democracy

As already noted, direct democracy, in the sense of the people voting directly on the questions parliaments now vote on, has a driving appeal in the sense of forming the most obvious institutionalization of democracy itself. If the object is to reinforce the 'necessary link' between popular preferences and public policy, how better than to have the latter directly decided by the citizens? Opponents generally accept this argument, but argue against direct voting on three broad grounds: difficulty/impossibility of achievement (especially since we already have policy voting on overall government programmes); incapacity of citizens to make detailed policy decisions; and instability of decisions (as one popular majority succeeds another). Various forms that these objections take, together with counter-responses, are summarized in Table 1.1.

1 The most general objection to direct democracy, and the killer argument for most of the nineteenth and twentieth centuries, is the impossibility of gathering all the citizens of any modern state together for discussion and voting on policy proposals. This only works as a criticism in the contemporary context if one considers face-to-face discussion the only legitimate form of debate, and discounts the referendums and initiatives traditionally carried on in Switzerland through the press and postal ballots. With the development of the electronic media, capacities for interactive discussion are obviously increased – indeed as the introduction to this book makes clear, the possibilities are almost unbounded. Many countries, perhaps most, now have referendums of one form or another, with postal ballots and discussion in the media, accompanied by private blogs and chat rooms, with two- or multi-way discussion between individuals. Deliberative theorists (for example, Dryzek 2000) or advocates of 'deep' participation (Barber 1984) may object that much of this debate is superficial and does not rest on the deep personal engagement that face-to-face discussion produces. The latter, however, has other disadvantages (dominance by powerful or forceful individuals, fudged compromises and so on). More impersonal forms of discussion avoid this and are perfectly capable of stimulating the 'deliberations we have with ourselves'. On balance, it seems that modern developments offer citizens more than adequate opportunities for developing and stabilizing their issue preferences, and also easy facilities for registering their votes. The argument against direct democracy, in terms of the feasibility of its preconditions, now looks the most outdated of these in the table and really can be totally dismissed for the twenty-first century.

Table 1.1 Criticisms of direct democracy with responses to them

	Criticisms	*Responses*
1.	It is impossible to have direct debate and voting in modern democracies	Even postal ballots and the print media, let alone two-way communication devices, allow interactive debate and voting among physically separated citizens
2.	General elections already let citizens choose between alternative governments and programmes, hence there is no need for direct policy voting	Many issues are not discussed at general elections so if the people are to decide they need to vote on them directly. Moreover such elections primarily choose governments, which voters may do on non-policy grounds
3.	Ordinary citizens do not have the education, interest, time, expertise and other qualities required to make good political decisions	Politicians do not necessarily show expertise and interest either. Participation expands citizen capacities. Citizens currently spend a lot of time informing themselves about politics through TV and radio
4.	Good decisions are most likely to be produced where popular participation is balanced by expert judgement. This is representative democracy where citizens can indicate the general direction policy should take, but leave it to be carried out by professionals	Expertise is important but not infallible. In any case it can inform popular decisions. Modern representative (party) democracies are heavily imbalanced against popular participation
5.	Those who vote against a particular decision do not give their consent to it, particularly if the same people are always in the minority	The problem is general and not confined to direct democracy. Voting on issues one by one gives minorities more voice
6.	No procedure for democratic collective decision making can be guaranteed not to produce arbitrary outcomes. What seems like a strong majority may be destabilized by setting out the alternatives another way	Such problems are generic to democratic voting procedures. Voting on dichotomous questions one by one (the usual procedure in popular policy consultations) does, however, eliminate cyclical voting and guarantees a stable majority for one side or the other
7.	Without intermediary institutions (parties, legislatures, governments) no coherent, stable or informed policies will be made. Direct democracy undermines intermediary institutions including parties	Direct democracy does not have to be unmediated. Parties and governments can and do play the same role as in representative (party) democracies today

2 Even though direct policy voting, with its associated discussion and campaigns on one side or the other, may be technically quite easy, there are still costs involved, which could be quite heavy in terms of money and time – both public and individual. A more subtle variant of the feasibility argument is that moves towards direct democracy are costly and unnecessary, because citizens are already empowered to vote on policy in general elections. That is, they can already choose between alternative party governments in terms of their medium-term policy programme. In some ways, voting on a general programme gives voters an opportunity for control over a range of policies rather than discrete single ones. Thus, voting in representative elections (which in actual fact are now party elections) might even empower electors more than direct policy voting in referendums and initiatives.There is something in this latter argument, as we recognise below in our comments about synthesizing direct and representative democracy. However, it is also specious in suggesting that representative elections ascertain citizen preferences as well as direct votes on policy. This is for two reasons:

a General elections mix all sorts of other considerations with policy ones in choosing a government – competence and attractiveness of candidates, for example. True, the parties also present a policy programme for government as one basis for choice. If elected, they will even claim a 'mandate' for effecting any policy contained in the programme. The mass of voters, however, may well have chosen the party on non-policy grounds. Thus, general elections are far from providing a 'necessary connection' between popular preferences and public policy. And even when voters do choose on general policy grounds, this does not mean they have endorsed the party stand on every last issue contained in the programme.

b This point is strengthened if we consider the 'paradox of the platform' (Brams 1976) illustrated in Table 1.2.This shows electors' preference orderings over alternatives 'a' and 'b' (the positions put forward on each issue [*x*, *y* and *z*] by the political parties A and B). Party B wins in a programmatic election with pure policy voting, because three out of five voters (voters 1, 2 and 3) prefer its policy on two out of the three issues covered by the programmes. Had referendums been held on each issue separately, however, three out of five voters on each issue prefer policy 'a' and would have voted for it. A direct policy vote thus records citizen preferences more sensitively than an overall, programmatic vote – an additional fact that tells against the argument that general elections sufficiently record citizens' policy preferences.

All this is not to say that general elections should be totally abolished. There is indeed room for a synthesis of general and policy-specific elections (see below). But the former urgently need to be supplemented by the latter, if citizen preferences are to be transmuted accurately into public policy.

3 A key point in debates about direct democracy is whether citizens really have the capacity to formulate clear public preferences in the first place, and to apply them intelligently to decide between, and vote on, policies. That is

Table 1.2 Party B wins on its overall programme even though a majority opposes its position on each specific issue

	Issues		
Voter	*x*	*y*	*z*
1	a	b	b
2	b	a	b
3	b	b	a
4	a	a	a
5	a	a	a

Note: a and b are different alternatives on each issue x, y and z, which are the positions endorsed by political parties A and B respectively.

why, the argument goes, citizens need intermediaries or representatives to do it for them. This argument is often buttressed by pointing to the allegedly bad decisions to which referendums and popular initiatives have led, from the launch of the ill-fated Syracuse expedition by Athens in 413 BC, to Proposition 13 limiting taxes in California in 1978. Kriesi's chapter takes care of the assertion that direct democracy produces bad policy, with its summary of research that indicates that it produces *better* results in comparisons of American states and Swiss cantons with more and less initiatives and referendums (see also Geissel in this volume).

Doubts about the ability of citizens to generate informed or even stable preferences about policy have been touched on by Converse's (1964) findings about citizen 'non-attitudes' on public matters. These started from the observation that while aggregate issue preferences remained stable over time (see also Marcus and Hanson 1993) individuals' opinions did not – and indeed seemed to vary almost randomly around their over-time mean. Forty years of debate on this point have, however, led to a consensus that the variation follows from the different circumstances under which repeat issue questions are asked and which are uppermost in the individual's mind at the time (Zaller 1992: 54). The effect of political debate and party campaigning is to produce a more informed consensus on which aspects of the issues *are* salient, so that citizens can make good judgements of what their preference actually is and what their vote ought to be.

In point of fact, democracy itself – not just direct democracy – would be in a bad way if we could not rely on citizens making informed judgements and good decisions, as a result of free political debate. If we cannot rely on their good sense in judging their own interests, even in general elections, we must turn to philosopher kings, experts or unelected politicians – who individually, however, may be no wiser than many ordinary electors. Democracy puts its trust in the aggregate and considered judgements of its citizens.[1] Criticisms of the electorate's ability to do so rapidly lead us to doubt not just direct, but representative democracy (cf. Budge. 1996: 59–83).

4 A better argument is the one about balance. Citizens can take very broad decisions but are not qualified to decide technical ones. Counter-arguments range from ones that ask why non-expert politicians are better qualified to decide than non-expert citizens to the observation that many important policies have technical aspects but these can be ventilated in popular as well as parliamentary debate and a general decision then made on their merits.

5 Balance and compromise are also considerations in dealing with minorities. A traditional fear expressed with regard to direct voting is majority tyranny. Without safeguards or intermediaries, the majority may well steamroller minorities. Of course, this fear has also been expressed with regard to democracy generally and is the reason for entrenched constitutional provisions or requirements for super-majorities on certain issues. These can co-exist with direct voting just as they do with parliamentary voting. One point to note, however, is that voting issue by issue is less likely to lead to one clearly defined minority being consistently defeated than is package voting, where the defeated minority has to wait for the next general election to overturn the previous decision.

6 The effects of a tyrannical majority may be compounded by certain features of majority voting that could lead to arbitrary decisions being taken that are not even desired by the real majority. The argument takes its start from the well-known voting cycle phenomenon (Condorcet 1785; Arrow 1951) illustrated in Table 1.3.

Succinctly put, the theorem states:

> a rational individual who prefers A to B to C must prefer A to C … it is always possible that majority rule is intransitive (i.e. irrational). In the simplest case, if voter 1 prefers A to B and B to C, voter 2 prefers C to A and A to B, and voter 3 prefers B to C and C to A, there is a majority for A over B, a majority for B over C, and a majority for C over A. Transitive individual preferences lead to an intransitive social ordering, otherwise known as a cycle.
>
> (McLean 1991: 506)

This cycle implies first that the majority decision would be overturned on another vote (so it is not a true majority decision) and secondly that it is not a real reflection of majority wishes, but dependent on the order in which alternatives were voted on.

It is easy to see how this pattern of voting – where rational individual voting leads to non-rational and unstable aggregate outcomes – might generalize over large populations, and how it could occur often enough to cast doubt on the pretension of any popular vote to reflect true majority opinion (McLean 1989: 123). It would be equally likely, on the basis of these arguments, to reflect an arbitrary placement of topics on the agenda, or even deliberate manipulation of it, rather than a true majority opinion.

Table 1.3 Voting circles: consistent individual preference orders giving rise to cyclical and unstable majority choices

Preference ordering of policies or candidates A, B and C	*Classic case of the paradox (% of electors)*	*Less extreme case of the paradox (% of electors)*
A → B → C	33.3	22.2
A → C → B	0	11.1
B → C → A	33.3	22.2
B → A → C	0	11.1
C → A → B	33.3	22.2
C → B → A	0	11.1
% choosing A over B	66.6	56.5
% choosing B over C	66.6	56.5
% choosing C over A	66.6	56.5

Note: A, B and C represent three policy alternatives or candidates. The arrow → represents preferences between alternatives. Thus A→ B → C stands for A is preferred to B is preferred to C.

Riker (1982) generalizes this argument into a claim that we can never know whether a true majority exists among the population, as the majority that emerges is always 'constructed' by procedures. Hence, liberalism – a series of checks, balances and entrenched rights – is better than majority voting, even for representative elections. It may be observed that this argument, if correct, again tells against democracy in *any* of its forms. The argument – and the very possibility of voting cycles – only holds, however, insofar as the decision space is neither unidimensional nor separable (that is, each dimension is discussed and voted on separately). Insofar as decisions are made on unidimensional left–right priorities, or on issues voted on individually, one by one, a true majority is guaranteed. This is because there is always a middle position mathematically on a single line, which has to be included in a majority to make it the majority. Referendums of course do generally take the form of issues being voted on one by one, as we saw from the 'paradox of the platform' (Brams 1976) discussed above.

7 Parties impose additional constraints on the dimensionality of decision space and thus enhance the probability (already high) that stable, 'real' majorities will emerge (Niemi 1969). A telling criticism of direct democracy is, therefore, that it necessarily dispenses with intermediary institutions like parties, legislatures and governments. The shifting majorities that emerge under such circumstances then produce ill-considered policies, which are subject to sudden reversals as the majority collapses or comes under the influence of different demagogues.

This seems a valid criticism of unmediated direct democracy and that is certainly the kind of set-up that many radicals yearn for: a direct and undiluted expression of the popular will, uncontaminated by wheeling and dealing and party fixes. However, we have already made the point that the kind of informative debates necessary for fixing and defining individual preferences themselves depend on protagonists like political parties taking up the issues, and focusing and defining them. In order to assess the force of criticisms of direct democracy as essentially unstable, therefore, we have to ask if an unmediated form is the only one that direct policy voting can take. We have already suggested that, in practice, parties often intervene in referendums or sponsor initiatives for their own ideological or office-seeking purposes. In the next section, we ask whether this is a valid expression of direct democracy or a perversion of it, and whether, therefore, the criticism of shifting preferences and unstable majority tyranny applies to direct democracy as such, or simply to particular manifestations of it.

Varieties of direct democracy: mediated versus unmediated forms

Many of these criticisms of direct policy voting are based on the idea that it dispenses with mediating institutions such as parties, and with the rules and procedures that, for example, guide legislative debate. This removes the constraints that produce compromise and stability and overstrains the capacity of citizens to make good decisions by, in effect, placing them in a vacuum. In turn, this promotes decisional instability by favouring the emergence of a new majority concerned to correct the mistakes, or counter the imbalances produced by the previous one.

Certainly, the idea of unmediated voting that 'lets the people speak' is one that has inspired many supporters of direct democracy, who would be very unhappy to think that intermediaries like political parties were needed to guarantee the quality of preferences and end decisions. Equally clearly, their ideal of doing away with political structures opens itself to many of the criticisms made above. In most countries and popular consultations, policy voting is not unmediated: parties and other groups participate and courts, governments and legislatures may all decide the wording of questions, lay down rules for the conduct of the campaign and even take sides in the referendum campaign.

All this underlines the point that direct democracy is as synonymous with party and other mediation as with a lack of it. Rules and procedural constraints may be more or less present in referendums and initiatives, but are never entirely absent. Therefore, insofar as the criticisms in Table 1.1 are focused on unmediated direct democracy, they are possibly valid – but for that form of direct democracy only, not for direct democracy as such.

Conceptually, the same point may be made by considering the base definition of direct democracy – which has surely to be the electorate voting on questions that, in traditional representative democracy, parliament votes on. How the vote is held clearly affects the concrete form that a particular direct democracy takes. But it is clear that both mediated and unmediated forms fall under the definition. The only requirement of direct democracy is that the people vote on individual

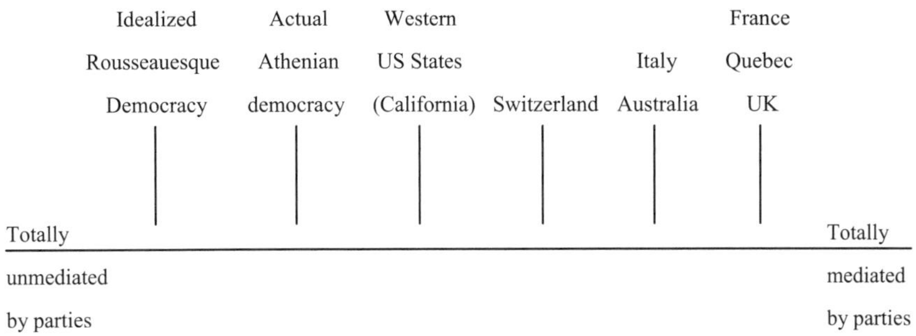

Figure 1.1 Different kinds of direct democracy

policies. How they organize themselves to vote does not affect the fact that this is direct democracy.

Looking at the extent of party mediation under various forms of direct democracy cautions us against identifying it exclusively with an unmediated form. This is shown in Figure 1.1.

Even in ancient Athens, crude party organizations were present in the form of political clubs (Bonner 1967: 45, 61): they were the most effective way for statesmen like Pericles and Demosthenes to ensure their majority in the Assembly and thus maintain stability and continuity in public policy – the functions of the political party in all ages.

This contrasts with the idealized Rousseauesque account (Rousseau 1762/1993) where the popular will has to be unmediated to be pure. California is the modern example that approaches closest to unmediated direct policy voting. But even there, parties and party-affiliated groups intervene. Lupia and Johnson (2001: 191–210) argue that this is necessary for 'competent voting' and point out that even in California voters are pretty adept at spotting which groups support which side and making inferences from this about the political import of proposals. Other American states see greater party intervention on important proposals (Magleby 1984: 88, 94), a tendency that becomes the norm in countries like Italy and Switzerland.

All this is to make the obvious point that procedural rules are necessary for votes, even popular votes, to be held. We would not expect a representative democracy to function without a constitution (written or unwritten), presiding officers, rules of procedure and debate. No more should we expect a direct democracy to do so. Just as representative democracies may have more or less regulation of these matters, so may direct democracies. To California, with its relative absence of detailed regulation of referendum campaigns, we can contrast Quebec, with a whole branch of law devoted to the few referendums that have been held, but regulating them in detail (see also Geissel in this volume).

Most criticisms in Table 1.1 apply particularly or exclusively to unmediated and relatively unregulated forms of popular policy voting. As such, they may have a high degree of validity. However, the solution under direct democracy as under representative democracy is not to abandon it altogether, but to strengthen procedures in order to deal with these dangers, and to encourage mediation rather than discourage it. This may put off many advocates of participatory or discursive democracy who wish to let the people speak unmediated. But if direct democracy consists in deciding individual policies through popular votes, mediation is quite consistent with it.

Combining direct and representative (programmatic) democracy: an emerging synthesis?

In the modern world, direct and representative democracy have come together, through the pervasiveness of policy voting and the political parties' role in organizing it. Of the two, representative democracy has come the longer way, no longer based on individual representation, but rather on programmatic voting with the successful party as guarantor of the programme. Direct democracy has continued to differentiate itself as direct voting on individual policies, most often policies not central to ongoing party politics, or else exceptional decisions that transcend normal party divisions.

We can see this better by examining actual practice in contemporary democracies. Popular policy votes tend to be held disproportionately in five areas: 1) changes in the constitution, 2) territorial questions covering secessions or extensions of the national territory, devolution and autonomy, 3) foreign policy, 4) moral matters such as divorce, abortion and homosexuality, and 5) ecology and environment (including local campaigns for protection of particular features, or in opposition to the siting of a power plant). In Swiss cantons and American states, fiscal matters are increasingly voted on, usually involving tax limitation and restrictions on the size of government (for recent surveys of content matter see LeDuc 2003).

Policy voting thus tends to take place either on issues of a certain level of generality – constitutions or foreign policy measures like trade liberalization that will have a long-term effect – or in areas that fit uneasily into the general left–right division of party politics and that might indeed provoke internal party splits, like moral and ecological matters. The closest that policy votes come to influencing the current political agenda is on fiscal matters. Even tax limitation has a long-term rather than an immediate effect, however. Almost never is a vote held, for example, to 'prioritize unemployment now', 'stop inflation', 'end the war', 'reduce prison population' and so on.

Several factors contribute to this pattern of policy consultation. First and perhaps most importantly, governments do not want to put their central policies to a referendum. So, where they have control over their timing and initiation, voting will not cover issues central to left–right conflicts – only off-issues that might split the party. New and opposition parties have generally also mobilized to put such issues on the agenda and not to refight continuing party battles.

A party-based explanation is only one part of the answer, however, since the same pattern occurs also in fairly unregulated popular initiatives where parties have less control. It is probable that electors themselves, and even interest groups, see no point in taking up matters that have already been part of the general election debate, and have already put into office parties that are pursuing them as part of a mandate. As we have stressed, so-called representative elections are heavily focused around medium-term policy plans, so it is natural that parties should be left to get on with them at least in their first years in office (and it often takes time to organize a referendum or initiative).

In this way, a certain division of labour seems to be emerging spontaneously between general, programmatic, elections and direct policy voting on individual issues. Where issues are linked together and form an integral part of the activity of governments, usually within the traditional left–right framework, the parties in power are left to get on with them. Where individual issues have long-term implications and do not fit so easily into a unifying framework, they tend disproportionately to be the subject of special popular votes. The overall mix does not seem a bad way of trying to translate popular preferences into public policy and in fact approaches that advocated by Budge (1996: 181–8).

Setting parameters for a realistic debate about direct democracy

Direct policy voting is on the increase. In the latest survey, LeDuc (2003: 21–2, 152) estimates that its use extended from around 250 referendums and initiatives from 1961–80, to nearly 350 from 1981–2000 in the countries of the world, excluding Switzerland. In both the American states and Switzerland, policy votes doubled in the last twenty years compared to the preceding period. In many jurisdictions, such as the German Länder, the UK and New Zealand, direct policy voting has now been introduced for the first time.

There is little to surprise us in this trend. In a world where the majority of citizens are better educated, better off and increasingly self-confident, it is natural that they should take the promise of democracy seriously and seek to get their preferences directly enacted into public policy. The ability of democracy to make a 'necessary connection' between the two through elections is, as we have seen, its core characteristic. This is what gives direct democracy its driving force and wide appeal in the modern world: there is no better way of enforcing the link between popular preferences and public policy than by voting directly on each policy.

Of course, the groups pressing for direct voting have other motivations too. They feel that their causes – whether to reduce taxes or protect the environment – are so obviously correct that they will get majority support if they can only get them on the ballot and sweep self-serving parties away. So far, analysts have failed to find any clear evidence that direct policy voting favours particular outcomes, either in terms of its immediate outcomes or indirect influence on legislatures from the threat of an initiative. There is some evidence, however, that its presence does bring policy closer to median (majority) voter preferences – which vary of course over time and between jurisdictions (Gerber and Hug 2001: 106; see the further analyses reported in Kriesi in this volume).

As critics have pointed out, sweeping away parties and other mediating institutions brings many undesirable consequences that may lead, in the end, to popular majorities voting against their own preferences and interests. This may result from lack of the essential, if minimal, information about the wider policy implications of referendum proposals that party endorsements provide, or from shifting majorities voting against taxes in one consultation, and for public services in another.

Despite the aspirations of many of its advocates, however, direct democracy does not generally take on an anti-party or non-partisan form. It can be argued that even in the US states, established parties fought back successfully against policy proposals that threatened their central interests, as with tax cuts (Cronin 1989: 205–6). The minority Republicans also built up to their present dominance by exploiting popular initiatives, among other tactics. Elsewhere, established parties dominate referendums, and opposition and emergent parties exploit policy votes to embarrass the government and force their own recognition. Of course, the best way to fight parties is to form an anti-party party, which many proponents of extended participation and popular voting have done (for example, the German Greens and Danish Progress Party).

In terms of actual practice, therefore, direct democracy tends towards either strongly mediated or moderately mediated, rather than unmediated forms. This is hardly surprising, as it tends to take place in party-run representative democracies with a plethora of institutions – governments, parliaments, bureaucracy and courts – overseeing their processes and codifying them along the lines of fair play embodied in general elections. The American experience should not be allowed to dominate discussion, especially since weak regulation of representative as well as direct elections is the norm there. The fact that California is so often cited as an awful warning of the perils of direct democracy is down to its lax regulation, which extends even to its general elections and legislative voting. Switzerland is a much better example of its potential for improving the quality of democracy, which is explored in the next chapter.

Convergence between specific policy consultations and general election practice should not be surprising, since in the modern world they are both about policy. An essential starting point for informed academic debates on the merits of direct democracy should be that so-called representative democracy (really party democracy) is mainly about putting policy packages to electors and following through on them in government.

Our choice between direct democracy and representative democracy should not, therefore, continue to base itself on outdated contrasts between popular policy decision and representative deliberation. Rather, it should characterize itself as being between voting on individual policies and package policy voting. Put this way, it seems much less apocalyptic than has been portrayed. The two procedures cannot be 100 per cent guaranteed against producing different outcomes, but this is far from saying that they will generally do so.

In any case, decisions on the issues involved are probably best arrived at using the different procedures. Where issues are linked to each other, generally through forming part of overarching left–right divisions, decisions on one may well have consequences for the others and so are best voted on as a package to be effected over four to five years. Where issues are more discrete and have fewer mutually interactive effects, they are probably best voted on separately, especially when they do not 'fit' in left–right terms and get ignored or totally excluded in general election debate.

Happily, this division of labour seems to be evolving in actual democratic practice. In this sense, the modern expansion in specific policy voting enhances and extends the 'necessary democratic connection' between popular preferences and public policy, much more so than threatening and undermining it. For convincing proof of this we now examine the current Swiss experience in the next chapter.

Note

1 The Marquis de Condorcet (1785) actually produced a mathematical proof of this (his 'Jury Theorem'), which shows that the majority among a large number of citizens will necessarily make the right choices between two alternatives, provided only that the average citizen has a small chance (say 0.51) of being more right than wrong on the matter.

References

Arrow, K. (1951) *Social Choices and Individual Values*, New York: Wiley.

Barber, B. (1984) *Strong Democracy: Participatory Politics for a New Age*, Berkeley, CA: University of California Press.

Bonner, R. J. (1967) *Aspects of Athenian Democracy*, New York: Russell and Russell.

Brams, S. (1976) *Paradoxes in Politics*, New York: Free Press.

Budge, I. (1996) *The New Challenge of Direct Democracy*, Cambridge: Polity.

Condorcet, Marquis de. (1785) *Essai Sur L'Application de L'Analyse à la Probabilité des Decisions Rendues a la Pluralité des Voix*, Paris: Imprimerie Royale.

Converse, P. E. (1964) The Nature of Belief Systems in Mass Publics, in Apter, D. E. (ed.) *Ideology and Discontent*, London: Collier Macmillan Publishers.

Cronin, T. E. (1989) *Direct Democracy: The Politics of Initiative, Referendum and Recall*, Cambridge, MA: Harvard University Press.

Dryzek, J. S. (2000) *Deliberative Democracy and Beyond*, Oxford: Oxford University Press.

Gerber, E. R. and Hug, S. (2001) Legislative Response to Direct Legislation, in Mendelsohn, M. and Parkin A. (eds) *Referendum Democracy: Citizens, Elites and Deliberation in Referendum Campaigns*, London: Palgrave, 88–108.

Kriesi, H. (2005) *Direct Democratic Choice: The Swiss Experience*, Lanham, MD: Lexington Books.

LeDuc, L. (2003) *The Politics of Direct Democracy: Referendums in Global Perspective*, Peterborough, ON: Broadview.

Lupia A. and Johnson, R. (2001) Are Voters to Blame?, in Mendelsohn, M. and Parkin A. (eds) *Referendum Democracy: Citizens, Elites and Deliberation in Referendum Campaigns*, London: Palgrave, 191–230.

Madison, J., Hamilton, A. and Jay, J. (1787–8/1911) *The Federalist Papers*, London: Dent.

Magleby, D. B. (1984) *Direct Legislation: Voting on Ballot Propositions in the United States*, Baltimore, MD: Johns Hopkins University Press.
Marcus, G. E. and Hanson, R. L. (eds) (1993) *Reconsidering the Democratic Public*, University Park, PA: University of Pennsylvania Press.
May, J. D. (1978) Defining Democracy: A Bid for Coherence and Consensus, *Political Studies*, 26, 1: 1–14.
McLean, I. (1989) *Democracy and New Technology*, Cambridge: Polity.
McLean, I (1991) Rational Choice and Politics, *Political Studies*, 39, 496–512.
Mill, J. S. (1861) *Utilitarianism, Liberty, Representative Government*, edited by H. B. Acton (1910), London: Dent.
Niemi, R. (1969) Majority Decision-Making with Partial Unidimensionality, *American Political Science Review*, 63, 488–97.
Riker, W. (1982) *Liberalism Against Populism*, San Francisco, CA: Freeman.
Rousseau, J. J., tr. G. D. H. Cole, J. Brumfitt, P. J. C. Hall. (1762/1993) *The Social Contract and Discourses*, London: Dent.
Sartori, G. (1987) *The Theory of Democracy Revisited*, Chatham, NY: Chatham House Publishers.
Saward, M. (1998) *The Terms of Democracy*, Cambridge: Polity.
Schumpeter, J. A. (1962) *Capitalism Socialism and Democracy*, New York: Harper.
Zaller, John (1992) *The Nature and Origins of Mass Opinion*, Cambridge: Cambridge University Press.

2 Direct democracy

The Swiss experience

Hanspeter Kriesi

Introduction

Direct-democratic procedures give rise to various hopes and fears. On the one hand, people expect such procedures to make democratic ideals come true. Thus, the adherents of 'strong' or 'participatory' democracy (such as Benjamin Barber 1984) put high hopes in the extension of democratic procedures beyond representative democracy. They assume that active participation in collective political decision making will have an educative and empowering effect on the citizens and will, ultimately, create better citizens. On the other hand, fears are widespread that such procedures would ask far too much of the average citizen. Thus, Giovanni Sartori (1987: 120), one of its most vocal critics, suggests that direct democracy 'would quickly and disastrously founder on the reefs of cognitive incompetence'. Plato, in his treatise on the Republic, already called into question the Athenian direct democracy of his day and suggested that only a minority of intellectual guardians – of 'competent public policy elites', in our contemporary parlance – was fit to govern.

Switzerland is the only country where politics at all levels – including the national level – is decisively shaped by direct-democratic institutions. Thus, more national popular votes have taken place in Switzerland so far than in any other country. Therefore, the Swiss experience with direct democracy is of utmost importance – for its critics as well as for its supporters, even if the pertinence of this experience has been called into question by some of the critics. Schumpeter (1962: 267), unsurprisingly one of the greatest detractors of direct democracy, has, for example, put into question the relevance of the Swiss experience, because, as he argued, 'there is so little to quarrel about in a world of peasants which, excepting hotels and banks, contains no great capitalist industry, and the problems of public policy are so simple and so stable that an overwhelming majority can be expected to understand and to agree about them'. In Switzerland, he suggested, direct democracy could be an effective mechanism of political decision, 'but only because there are no great decisions to be made'.

Admittedly, this was in the early forties. Today, it would probably be difficult to find a serious political theorist who would doubt the relevance of Switzerland for the evaluation of the implementation of direct-democratic procedures.

Contemporary Switzerland is a complex, highly developed modern society, closely integrated into the world economy, and characterized by the coexistence of multiple linguistic cultures and an exceptionally high share of foreigners in the resident population. If Switzerland is a relatively small country and in many ways a special case – among other things precisely because of the importance of the direct-democratic procedures for political decision making – it certainly no longer represents the backward province Schumpeter was making it out to be.

In this chapter, I start out with a brief presentation of the key direct-democratic institutions of Switzerland. Some, even superficial, knowledge of these institutions is indispensible for understanding how direct democracy may be able to function under contemporary conditions. Next, I would like to give an idea of the utilization and the success of the available instruments. Third, I shall present some empirical results about the ways citizens are making their choices in direct-democratic campaigns and about the role the political elites play in pre-structuring their decisions. To conclude, I would like to draw attention to the (largely favourable) economic and social consequences of these procedures in the Swiss context.

The direct-democratic institutions of Switzerland

Institutions define the rules of the game. We should keep in mind that the direct-democratic institutions come in different varieties, with different logics attached (see Budge and Geissel in this volume). One variant is the populist, unmediated form of direct democracy, which best corresponds to the practice in the member states of the US. When the populist and progressive reformers of the late nineteenth century introduced direct-democratic procedures in the US, they did so, above all, to restrict the power of political parties and their political machines, which were in control of the state parliaments at the time (Cronin 1989: 50–7; Bowler and Donovan 1998; Smith and Tolbert 2001: 740, 2004: 112ff.). In the US, the popular initiative, still today, is primarily used by social movements and interest groups to circumvent the state parliaments controlled by the parties. This is possible because the popular initiatives are submitted to the popular vote without the intervention of the state governments and their parliaments. By contrast, the Swiss variety of direct democracy is much more organized and more tightly controlled by the political elites. Both government and parliament have an important role to play in the preparation of the proposals submitted to the voters.

Broadly speaking, we can classify Swiss direct-democratic institutions according to two criteria:[1]

- The source of a proposition: elite or citizens.
- The initiation of the vote: required by the constitution or demanded by the citizens.

Combining the two criteria allows us to classify the three basic direct-democratic institutions at the federal level – the popular initiative, the compulsory and the optional referendum (see Table 2.1).[2] According to the source of the

Table 2.1 Classification of direct-democratic institutions

	Source of proposition	
Voted required by	*Government*	*Citizens*
Constitution	Compulsory referendum	—
Citizens	Optional referendum	Popular initiative

proposition, we can distinguish initiatives from referendums: initiatives are propositions 'from below', formulated by organizations representing groups of citizens, while referendums concern propositions 'from above', that is, legislative acts proposed by the government and adopted by parliament. Accordingly, initiatives and referendums follow entirely different logics. The initiative has an agenda-setting function. It launches a public debate on a given issue and puts the issue on the political system's agenda. An initiative qualifies for a vote if it is signed by 100,000 citizens (roughly 2 per cent of the current number of citizens) within a period of 18 months. The text of an initiative, which is formulated by the group of citizens who launch it, has to be thematically focused on a single issue, and it may not conflict with international law. Otherwise, there are hardly any requirements to be fulfilled. At the federal level, the popular initiative is only possible for constitutional amendments. In the cantons, however, there is also the legislative initiative that allows a group of citizens to propose a specific piece of legislation. In contrast to the practice in the US, the government and the parliament discuss the text of the initiative before it is submitted to the popular vote, and usually provide it with a voting recommendation that almost always recommends its rejection. Government and parliament also have the option of formulating a direct counter-proposal, which will be submitted to the vote together with the initiative. They also have the option of formulating indirect counter proposals to initiatives proposing a constitutional change by introducing normal legislation that makes some concessions to the initiative's proposals.

The referendum, by contrast, concerns a legislative act originating from the government and intervenes only after the members of the political system have taken their decision on the piece of legislation. It comes in two basic versions, which can be distinguished on the basis of our second classification criterion: referendums are required either by the Constitution (in case of Constitutional amendments) or by a group of citizens (in case of regular legislation). Constitutional amendments are subject to compulsory referendum, while regular legislation is subject to optional referendum. Constitutional amendments are quite frequent in Switzerland, where the Constitution has been, on average, amended more than twice a year since the beginning of the 1980s. Such amendments are adopted only if they obtain a double majority – a majority of the people and a majority of the Swiss cantons, that is, the country's member states. Regular legislation, once adopted by parliament, passes into law by default, if a referendum is not required by a group of citizens within three months after its adoption by parliament.

However, if a group of at least 50,000 citizens sign a petition for a referendum, the legislative act has to be submitted to a popular vote. Legislative acts voted upon in an optional referendum require only a simple popular majority to pass into law.

The referendum has the property of a popular veto that may prevent legislation from becoming effective. This general characteristic of the Swiss referendum has, according to the well known thesis of Leonhard Neidhart (1970), fundamentally shaped political decision making in Switzerland. Neidhart's thesis refers, above all, to the optional referendum, but, analogously, it may also be applied to its compulsory variety. Given the availability of the referendum, it is always possible that a party or an interest group that does not agree with the result of the legislative process launches an optional referendum against a law adopted by parliament, that is, that an organization decides to collect the required signatures to impose a popular vote and to put in danger the result of the legislative process. As a result, the threat of the referendum hovers, like the sword of Damocles, over the entire legislative process (see also Geissel in this volume). To prevent some dissatisfied group from sabotaging a legislative project by launching a referendum against it, all organizations capable of launching a referendum have, according to Neidhart's reasoning, ended up being integrated into the political process – either in the context of extended pre-parliamentary procedures (which closely resemble 'corporatist decision-making'), or in the context of the grand coalition that has governed Switzerland since 1959. In short, according to this reasoning, as a consequence of the direct-democratic opening, the Swiss system of government has been transformed from a 'plebiscitary' into a 'negotiation democracy'.

Even if Neidhart's thesis exaggerates the importance of the referendum for the extension of the negotiating structures in Switzerland – there is, indeed, a series of additional 'institutionalized mechanisms of accommodation' that serve to impose extended negotiating structures (federalism, a two-chamber parliamentary system, a proportional electoral system, a multi-party system, to mention but the most important ones) (Germann 1994). The latent functions of the referendum have nevertheless contributed to the fact that Switzerland constitutes the paradigmatic case of a consensus democracy. Incidentally, Lijphart (1999), who introduced the distinction between majoritarian and consensus democracies, does not at all take into account the referendum in the construction of his influential typology.

Since the creation of the Swiss Confederation in 1848, direct-democratic procedures have been gradually extended. The Constitution of 1848 introduced the initiative for its total revision as well as the compulsory referendum for all other constitutional amendments. In 1874, the optional referendum was introduced, and in 1891 the popular initiative. In the course of the twentieth century, further elements were added: in 1921, the optional referendum was extended to international treaties, and in 1977 the scope of the treaties covered by the referendum was once more enlarged. Since 1949, there has been a referendum for extraordinary decrees, and in 2003, in the context of the latest total revision of the Constitution, the general popular initiative was added to the inventory of direct-democratic procedures. These are the procedures as far as the federal level is concerned. At the cantonal and local levels, the panoply of direct-democratic

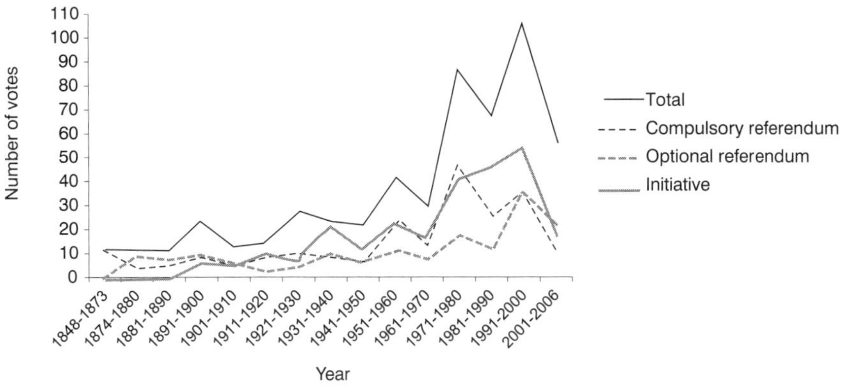

Figure 2.1 Number of popular votes – total and by instrument

Source: Kriesi and Trechsel 2008

instruments is even more elaborate, especially in German-speaking Switzerland. Thus, to give but one example, the yearly budget of the City of Berne, the Swiss capital, has to be approved by the citizens in a popular vote.

Direct-democratic practice: the use of these instruments and their success

From 1848 until the end of 2006, the Swiss citizens have voted on a total of 543 proposals at the federal level. Figure 2.1 shows the numerical development of the popular votes during the entire period. What catches the eye when looking at this figure is the enormous increase in the number of votes since the seventies. More than half of all the votes have taken place during the last thirty-five years. This indicates that the direct-democratic institutions are quite alive in Switzerland, and that their significance has considerably increased in the more recent past. On the one hand, the increase in the number of votes is a result of the increasing legislative activity in an ever more complex world; on the other hand, it results from the increasing use of the direct-democratic instruments by the citizens. Thus, the number of initiatives has increased strongly: more than two thirds of all initiatives, which have been submitted to a vote, fall in the period since the seventies.

Turning to the use of the optional referendum in particular, what strikes the observer is that of all the 2370 legislative proposals that were exposed to the optional referendum in the entire period, only 7 per cent (160 proposals) have actually been challenged by such a referendum (see also Geissel in this volume). Moreover, as Figure 2.2 shows, if the share of the proposals, against which a referendum was launched, was very high after its first introduction and again reached a peak during the thirties, it remained below average after World War II. The share of proposals that have eventually been rejected in a popular vote is even lower, and has continually decreased since the seventies. In the more recent past,

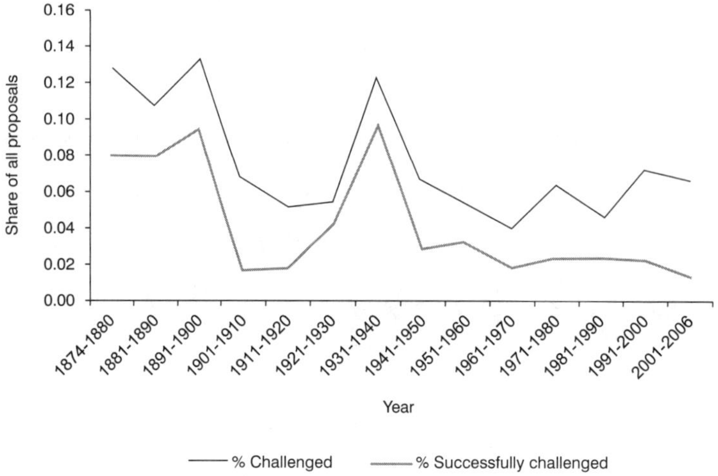

Figure 2.2 Optional referendum: share of proposals against which a referendum has been launched, and which have been attacked successfully

Source: Kriesi and Trechsel 2008

this share does not even reach 2 per cent of all legislative projects. This does not mean, however, that the optional referendum has become more or less irrelevant. As we have seen, it exerts an indirect, system-building effect by its considerable impact on the design of the decision-making processes, and it also deploys its effect in the cases where it is not used. Moreover, the optional referendum has been used, in particular, to attack some of the most important legislative projects of the more recent past.

Traditionally, the optional referendum has primarily allowed the conservatives to prevent the adoption of reform proposals (Kriesi and Wisler 1996). Thus, because of the optional referendum, the development of the Swiss welfare state has been delayed for a long time (Obinger 1998; Armingeon 2001). Since the eighties, however, the situation has changed: in the more recent past, it has been the left that has had more frequent recourse to the referendum than the right. This is a consequence of the fact that the parliament has tried to avoid far reaching social policy reforms, has only adopted minimalist modifications of the status quo, or has even contributed to welfare state retrenchment. In a period of neoliberal reforms, the optional referendum surprisingly proved to be an effective instrument in the hands of the left to prevent welfare state retrenchment (Bonoli 1999).

However, we should add that the optional referendum has become a less forceful instrument. This could already be seen in Figure 2.2, but becomes even more evident in Figure 2.3, which presents the development of the number of governmental defeats over time. As this figure shows, the optional referendum has provided the opposition with less and less success throughout the post-war period. Especially in the more recent past, that is, in the period where the left has used this instrument more frequently, its forcefulness has diminished. Conversely, the compulsory referendum, which no longer gave rise to governmental defeats

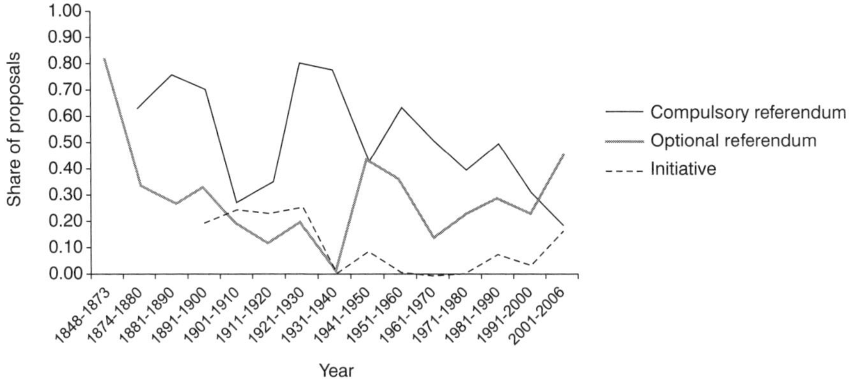

Figure 2.3 Share of governmental defeats, by instrument

Source: Kriesi and Trechsel 2008

in the thirties, has become increasingly menacing for the government and has led, in absolute, but also in relative terms, to more frequent governmental defeats than the optional referendum. As far as the initiative is concerned, it generally appears to be a rather blunt weapon. Roughly a third of the initiatives (30 per cent) have been withdrawn by their sponsors before it came to a popular vote in the first place. In the remaining cases, the electorate generally followed the recommendations of the government, who, as I have already argued, usually decides to reject the corresponding proposals. Overall, only fifteen initiatives (6 per cent) have been adopted in popular votes. As is shown by Figure 2.3, the share of successful initiatives has increased in the more recent past, admittedly based on a smaller number of initiatives submitted. After a period spanning several decades without any success, eight initiatives have been adopted since 1981.

However, in the case of initiatives, one should not deduce from their limited success at the polls that they are generally ineffective. Some initiatives have some success, even if they are not adopted in the popular vote. Their impact is often indirect, as they may influence the legislative process. Their withdrawal is often the result of such indirect effects. Thus, the initiatives of the left had a decisive impact on the reform of the old-age pension system at the beginning of the seventies, which would not have been so generous had it not been for those initiatives (Kriesi 1980).

One question that is often posed concerns the possibility of buying success at the polls. This question has been studied in detail in the US, where it has been shown that a lot of money does not necessarily mean a lot of influence with regard to the outcome of the votes. Although the investment of a lot of money may buy a certain amount of influence, the relationship between money and influence on the vote is much more complex and more limited than many critical observers care to believe. Thus, Gerber (1999) has found that economic interest groups may have the capacity to prevent the passage of propositions they oppose, but they find it very difficult to pass their own propositions. By contrast, the citizens' groups – grass-roots organizations, public interest groups or social movement organizations – are much more successful at modifying policy through the direct legislation process. Gerber was able to show that initiatives that received majority support from citizens' groups passed at a substantially higher rate than measures that received majority support from economic interest groups. Matsusaka (2004) confirmed these findings by showing that it is the large number of citizens who profit from direct-democratic procedures, rather than the few interest groups.

In Switzerland, too, the relationship in question is more complex than usually suspected, and the Swiss experience generally serves to confirm the American studies. The relationship between the overall direction of campaign expenditures and the outcome of the vote is generally weak. On the one hand, this is due to the fact that almost all initiatives – independently of the financial effort of the adversarial camps – are rejected by the citizens. Figure 2.4 illustrates this relationship by showing that the government is generally successful in the case of initiatives (that is, the initiatives are rejected), independently of the overall direction of the campaign (horizontal axis), and of its intensity (different lines are drawn for the different degrees of campaign intensity). As we have seen, the optional referendum proves to be more dangerous for the government, and the relationship between the financial effort and the success at the polls is somewhat tighter in their case. However, even then, it remains relatively weak. This has, among other things, to do with the fact that the intensive minorities, who typically launch such referendums, usually invest large sums in the voting campaign, even if their chances of success are rather limited. Only when the campaign becomes very intense, and when the government's opponents have a financial advantage in such an intense campaign, can they count upon a good chance of success, that is, they are able to block the government's proposal. In this very special case, financial investments can be decisive, as is shown in the second part of Figure 2.4.

Before concluding that it is possible to buy a vote in some cases, we should, however, not forget that the challengers of the government can often count on broad support from the bourgeois camp. The successful launching of optional referendums often leads to a fragmentation of this camp (Trechsel and Sciarini 1998). Given that this camp possesses a 'natural majority' in Swiss politics, and that it has much more financial resources at its disposal than the left, its fragmentation proves to be particularly dangerous for the governmental position. Based on my own analyses (Kriesi 2005), it is, in the final analysis, the coalitional configuration that decides on the fate of a proposition. This, however, implies that even in those cases where we find a close relationship between the overall direction of the campaign and the outcome of the vote, the financial means did not necessarily prove to be decisive.

From the point of view of the elected representatives of the Swiss political system, the picture that emerges is, therefore, anything but dramatic. Even if they are not able to completely control the direct-democratic procedures, they have succeeded in considerably reducing the uncertainty that is necessarily linked to the direct-democratic opening of the policy-making process. Conversely, from

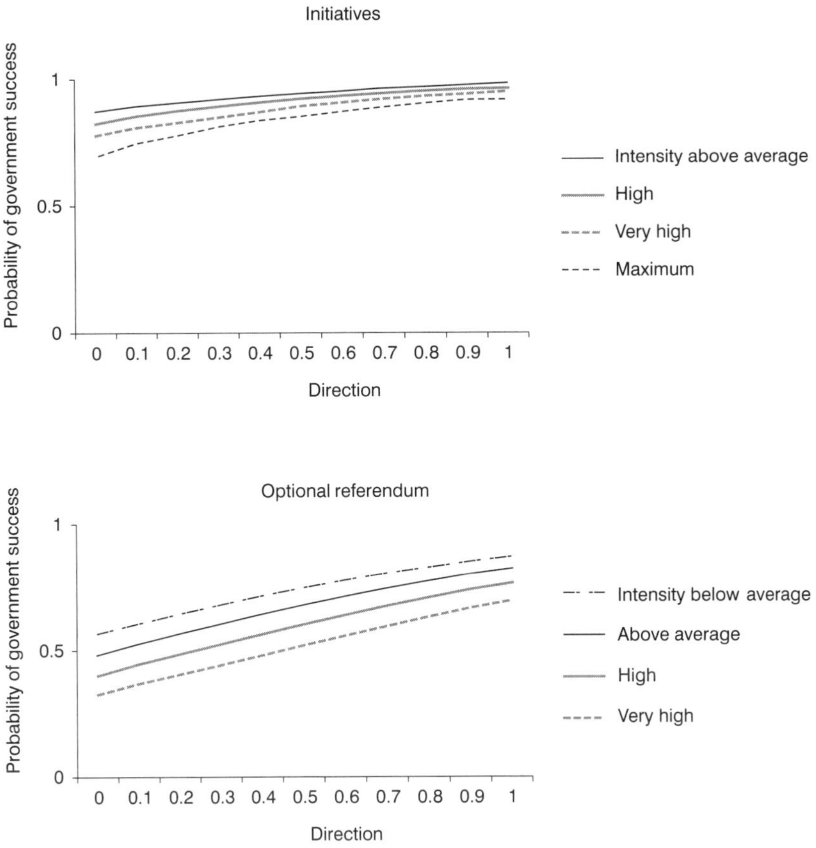

Figure 2.4 Probability of governmental success for initiatives and optional referendums (estimates based on statistical models)

Source: Kriesi 2006

the point of view of the challengers of the government and the parliamentary majority, it seems to be apparent that they are not able to modify fundamentally the procedures of representative democracy. But they may get a hearing for their cause at all levels of the policy-making process and if they don't get a fair hearing, they may sometimes successfully appeal to the general electorate.

The opinion formation and the decision of the citizens

Given the key role of the political elites in the direct-democratic process in Switzerland, we already have a partial answer to the question of how the citizens are able to make reasonable choices at the polls, even if they are politically relatively uninformed. The political elites define the options, which they submit to the citizens' vote; they form the coalitions that oppose each other in the campaign preceding the vote; and the mobilization of these coalitions supplies the heuristic cues and the systematic arguments that the citizens use for opinion formation during the campaign. The remaining question is whether the citizens are capable of properly using the information supplied to them by the elites, and whether they are able to arrive at a choice that reflects their own preferences.

According to my own study of roughly 150 popular votes, I have come to rather optimistic conclusions in this regard. First of all, the share of the electorate that is moderately to fully aware of the proposals submitted is rather high. The overall average for the 217 federal propositions of the period 1981–2004 reaches a level of no less than 73 per cent. It is true that there are exceptions to this high level of awareness. In almost 10 per cent of the cases, a majority of the electorate was quite unaware of the issues in question. Moreover, the level of awareness has been decreasing over the years, from an average of 80 per cent in the 1980s to an average of 69 per cent in the 2000s. However, citizens who actually participate in the vote prove to be significantly more competent than the electorate overall. This means that the most incompetent usually do not participate in the vote. This mechanism of self-selection of the incompetent reduces in a quasi-automatic way the possibility of an unreasonable decision, which the critics of direct-democratic procedures are so much afraid of. Even if it is true that more intense campaigns mobilize a larger number of voters from all camps, that is, that they also mobilize voters who are usually rather uninformed, the participation of those who are little interested and uninformed remains limited even in such campaigns. This results from a self-correcting mechanism whereby particularly intense campaigns that mobilize large numbers of citizens also serve to raise the general level of issue-specific competence in the electorate at large – in turn, implying that, in such cases, the group of uninformed voters becomes relatively small.

Those members of the electorate who actually participate in the vote have – following a well known theory of social psychology (the so called 'dual process theory', Stroebe 2007) – basically two possibilities for arriving at their choice: either they rely on *heuristic cues* such as voting recommendations by parties, trust in the government or defence of the status quo, which allow them, in a short-cut way, to arrive at approximately reasonable decisions. Or they may more systematically rely on the arguments promoted by the adversarial camps. In the real world of opinion formation and decision making in direct-democratic campaigns, however, the two analytically distinct ways of deciding are not so sharply distinct. On the one hand, the effective use of heuristic cues presupposes a certain amount of political knowledge. Thus, one has to know about the general positioning of the political parties in order to be able to make effective use of their recommendations. On the other hand, some of the arguments that are used by the political elites in the course of the campaigns are hardly distinguishable from heuristic cues. Thus, the decision of voters who rely on the often all too simplistic arguments that are promoted in the campaign, will not be much different from a purely heuristically determined decision.

Even if the two paths are not always as clearly distinct as the theory would have it, the results of my study with regard to the citizens' capacity to arrive at reasonable decisions are nevertheless quite clear-cut. The citizens turn out to

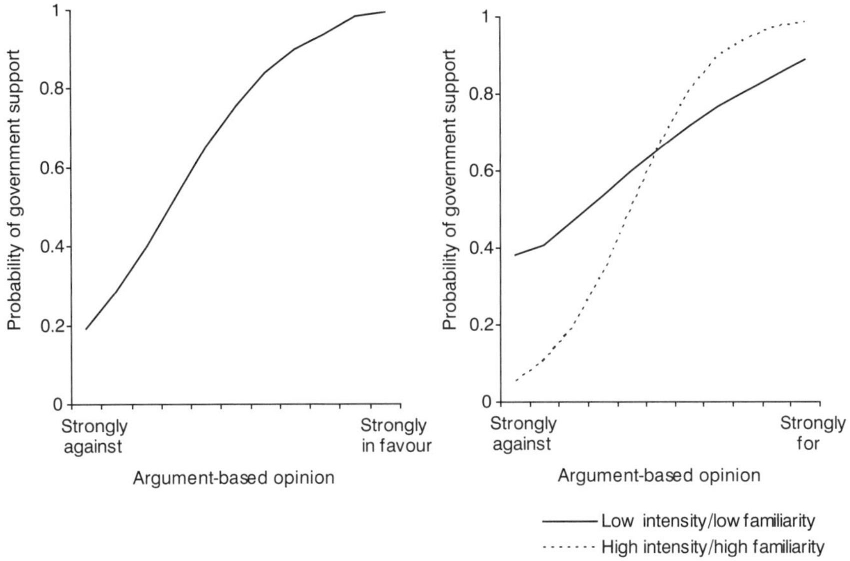

Figure 2.5 Probability of governmental support, as a function of argument-based opinions

Source: Kriesi 2005

be less minimalist than usually assumed: my study confirms the generally great importance of argument-based decisions. It measures argument-based opinions on the basis of a set of questions about the most important arguments exchanged during the campaigns preceding the vote. A voter's overall argument-based opinion score corresponds to his or her positioning on the central conflict dimension of the campaign-specific debate (which is operationalized by the first factor resulting from a factor analysis of the opinions on the campaign-specific set of arguments). The great importance of argument-based voting is illustrated by Figure 2.5, which shows the general relationship between argument-based opinions and the voting choice, that is, the support of the government's position: the more strongly citizens support the arguments in favour of the government's position, the more strongly they also decide in favour of the government's position at the polls – and vice versa. The relationship is rather tight, which means that we can explain roughly 40 per cent of the variance of individual voting decisions on the basis of the voters' opinions about the arguments that were prevalent during the campaign.

The importance of arguments varies, however, from one campaign to another depending on its intensity and on the familiarity of the proposal. Compared with these two context characteristics, individual characteristics play a subordinate role for the explanation of argument-based voting. The second half of Figure 2.5 presents the maximum joint effect of the two context characteristics on the relationship. As we can see, the curve is much flatter when both the intensity of the campaign is low and the proposal is unfamiliar. This means that arguments turn out to be much more decisive in highly intense campaigns and for highly familiar propositions – especially, as the figure also indicates, as far as the challengers of the government's position are concerned. They benefit from intensive campaigns more than the government. While the campaigns are reasonably intense in the large majority of cases, a majority of cases also proves to be rather unfamiliar to significant minorities of the electorate (a third or more). Overall, roughly a quarter of the propositions was both rather unfamiliar and did not give rise to intensive campaigns. These were also the cases where the level of awareness turned out to be particularly low, with an average share of the electorate of only 59 per cent being at least moderately aware.

Systematic and heuristic strategies are to a certain extent complementary. Thus, intensive campaigns increase the relevance of both decision strategies. The two strategies are also complementary in another respect: they are used in the same context, but by different types of voters. While the voters with strong opinions – either on the side of the opposition or on the side of the government – generally decide systematically on the basis of arguments, voters with less explicit opinions, that is, ambivalent, uncertain, neutral or ignorant voters, more heavily rely on heuristic strategies. This is illustrated by Figure 2.6, which is divided into three parts. Left and right from the centre, one finds the voters with strong opinions; in the centre, those with less explicit opinions. In each part of the figure, the relationship between the level of awareness and the support of the government's position is shown for voters with different partisan orientations and different levels of trust in the government. Without going into the details of the figure, one can easily recognize that the lines for voters with strong opinions on both sides of the centre can hardly be separated from one another, which means that they all decide in roughly the same way, independently of their partisan orientation or their level of trust in the government. For the voters with less explicit opinions, by contrast, the lines for the different groups of voters are clearly distinguishable from one another, meaning that these voters more heavily rely on partisan recommendations and their trust in government – two types of heuristic cues – to arrive at their voting decisions. Since the figure refers to propositions that are supported by centre–right coalitions and opposed by the left, the trusting conservative voters support the government most, while the distrusting left voters do so least. Finally, the figure also clearly shows that, for virtually all types of voters, the lines more or less run parallel to the x-axis. This means that the level of awareness has practically no impact on the voting behaviour. Even little-informed voters are, in other words, capable of arriving at decisions that closely resemble those of their well-informed colleagues with similar preferences (that is, party orientations and levels of trust in government).

Consequences of direct democracy

In the final analysis, the question is, of course, whether and how direct democracy functions, and also whether it performs well for the economy and for the citizens' personal situations in everyday life. This question has above all been studied by economists. They have exploited the variations that exist at the cantonal

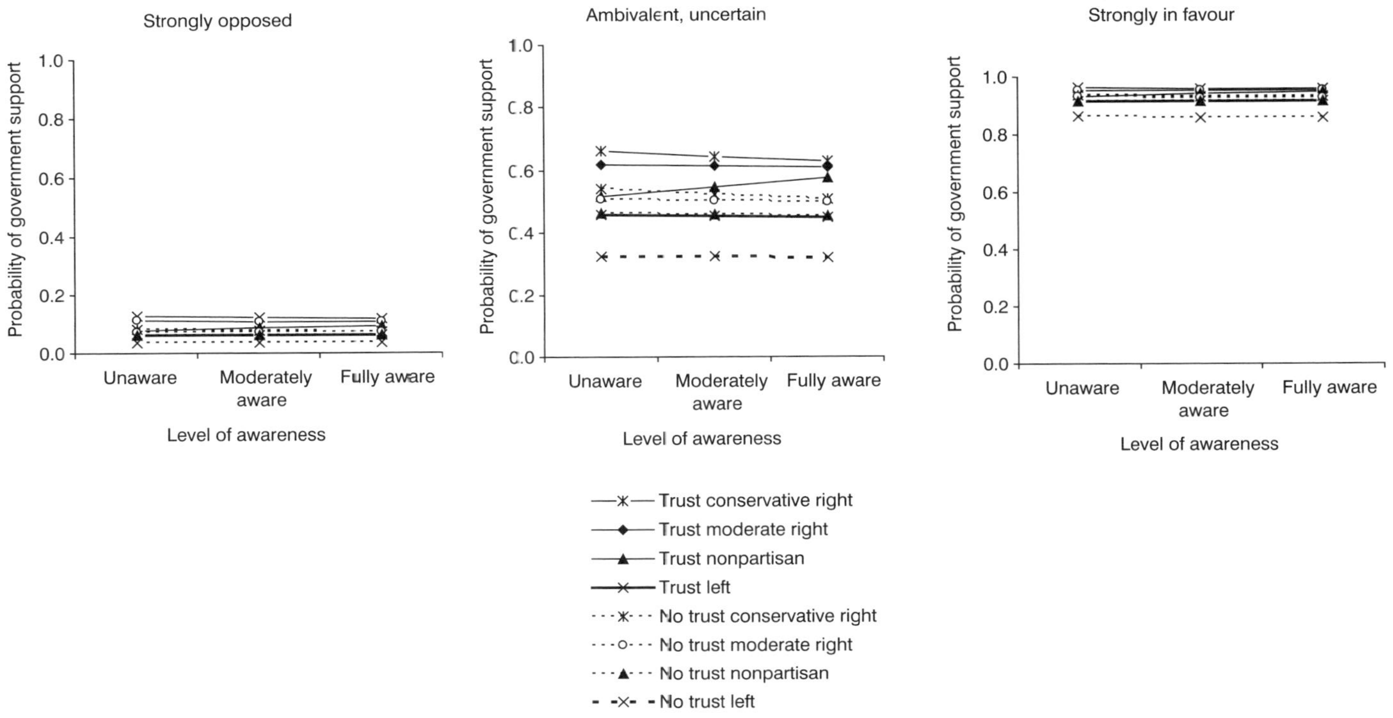

Figure 2.6 Probability of government support, argument-based opinions and level of awareness (for propositions supported by the centre-right and opposed by the left)

(regional) level within Switzerland with regard to the institutionalization of direct-democratic instruments and their practical use. Thus, in some, but not all, cantons there exist direct-democratic instruments in the area of fiscal policy that provide the citizens with the possibility of exerting a direct influence on the taxes and the expenditures of the cantonal states. Based on a comparison of the twenty-six cantons, one can draw conclusions about the consequences of direct-democratic institutions.

Such comparisons lead to the conclusion that direct-democratic institutions have mainly positive effects with regard to the economy (Kirchgässner et al. 1999; see also Geissel in this volume). Thus, they increase the macro-economic performance – the gross domestic product (GDP) per capita is higher in cantons that allow for direct-democratic interventions of the citizens in fiscal policy by as much as 3.6 per cent. Moreover, in cantons that apply the referendum in fiscal matters, the public expenditures correspond more closely to the citizens' preferences, and – *ceteris paribus* – they are also lower than in more representative systems. To the extent that they have a right to co-decide about fiscal matters, the citizens apparently deal more economically with their own tax money than their elected representatives. Cantons with elaborate direct-democratic institutions also have a lower public debt, higher tax morale and better public services. Finally, direct-democratic institutions also have a legitimating and an integrative function (Papadopoulos 1998: 156–60; 2001), and they increase the general level of life satisfaction among the citizens. The higher satisfaction with life in states with elaborate direct-democratic procedures not only results from their higher level of public performance, but also, as is argued by Stutzer and Frey (2006), is a direct consequence of the greater legitimacy of public decisions that involve such procedures. Citizens value the possibility of participating in political decision making in and of itself, independently of their implications for the performance of the state, which increases the perceived fairness of political decisions that are taken by direct-democratic procedures. Based on an original comparison of Swiss citizens and foreign residents of Switzerland, Stutzer and Frey succeed in empirically separating the effects of direct-democratic institutions on public performance from their purely procedural effects and to confirm their hypotheses. The opportunity for direct-democratic participation has, indeed, a direct effect on the general life satisfaction of the Swiss citizens. While they could not definitely confirm the positive consequences for the individuals' beliefs about their political influence, the effect on the satisfaction with life proved to be highly robust.

Conclusion

Thus, based on the Swiss experience, the direct-democratic procedures turn out to be highly attractive. On the one hand, and in line with the results of public opinion research more generally (Sniderman 1993), the Swiss experience shows that the voters, in the large majority of the propositions submitted to them, are not really overburdened by the task expected of them. This results, above all, from the pre-structuring of their choices by the way institutions are set up in Switzerland

and by the mobilizing and communicating strategies of the political elites. On the other hand, the Swiss experience also indicates that the citizens doubly benefit from direct-democratic procedures: such procedures not only increase public performance, but also the legitimacy of political decisions and, by implication, the general satisfaction of the citizens with their lives. Taken together, the Swiss experience amounts to a powerful empirical rebuttal of the arguments raised by sceptics like Sartori.

This does not mean that all is perfect in the Swiss variety of direct democracy. While the overall assessment of the Swiss experience with direct democracy lends itself to highly optimistic normative conclusions, several of the results I have presented depend on favourable conditions. Thus, citizens' decisions in the case of votes on unfamiliar propositions with little elite mobilization (about a quarter of the cases in the period studied) rely much less on argument-based opinions. There are even a limited number of propositions where the majority of the individual voting decisions cannot be explained by either heuristic or systematic considerations (Kriesi 2005). In other words, even in Switzerland, with its long experience with direct-democratic votes, the procedures do not always work as intended. Moreover, from the point of view of normative democratic theory, the self-selection of the most incompetent is not unproblematic either. If it solves the problem raised by the conservative critics of direct democracy, it raises instead a problem of social justice that has to be dealt with by measures such as civic education, or the public support of the intermediaries responsible for direct-democratic campaigns.

In my view, the lessons to be drawn from the Swiss experience are twofold. On the one hand, this experience suggests that the political elites have a very important role to play in the pre-structuration of and the mobilization for the vote. If the elites do not engage in intense campaigning preceding the vote, as was the case in the Dutch referendum on the European Union Treaty in 2005, the electorate will not be able to cast an informed vote. The elite-led debate during the campaign preceding the vote proves to be decisive for the quality of the voters' choice. On the other hand, in a properly designed direct-democratic system, the governing majority is not completely disarmed, but it does not have full control over the process either. Groups of citizens may set the agenda by imposing a vote, and the governing majority may not be able to convince a majority of the voters to adopt its preferred solution at the polls. Empowering the citizens by direct-democratic procedures implies the risk of defeat, for reasons that, most of the time, have very little to do with questions of citizen competence, but quite a lot to do with questions of pre-existing political preferences on the part of the citizens and the outcome of the political struggle among majority and opposition.

Notes

1 To be sure, there are other criteria to classify direct-democratic institutions, for example, the criterion of whether or not the direct-democratic decision is binding.

Since all Swiss votes are binding, this particular criterion is not very pertinent in our present context.

2 For each one of these three types there are different subtypes, but for our purposes it will be sufficient to distinguish among the three general categories.

References

Armingeon, K. (2001) Institutionalizing the Swiss Welfare State, in Lane, J.-E. (ed.) *The Swiss labyrinth. Institutions, outcomes and redesign*, London: Frank Cass, 143–68.

Barber, B. (1984) *Strong democracy. Participatory politics for a new age*, Los Angeles, CA: University of California Press.

Bonoli, G. (1999) La réforme de l'Etat social suisse: Contraintes institutionnelles et opprtunités de changement, *Swiss Political Science Review* 5, 3: 57–78.

Bowler, S. and Donovan, T. (1998) *Demanding choices. Opinion, voting, and direct democracy*, Ann Arbor, MI: University of Michigan Press.

Cronin, T. E. (1989) *Direct democracy: the politics of initiative, referendum and recall*, Cambridge: Cambridge University Press.

Gerber, E. R. (1999) *The populist paradox. Interest group influence and the promise of direct legislation*, Princeton, NJ: Princeton University Press.

Germann, R. (1994) *Staatsreform. Der Übergang zur Konkurrenzdemokratie*, Bern: Haupt.

Kirchgässner, G., Feld, L. P. and Savioz, M. R. (1999) *Die direkte Demokratie. Modern, erfolgreich, entwicklungs- und exportfähig*, Basel: Helbing und Lichtenhahn.

Kriesi, H. (1980) *Entscheidungsstrukturen und Entscheidungsprozesse in der Schweizer Politik*, Frankfurt: Campus.

—— (2005) *Direct democratic choice. The Swiss experience*, Lanham, MD: Lexington.

—— (2006) Role of the Political Elite in Swiss Direct-Democratic Votes, *Party Politics* 12, 5: 599–622.

Kriesi, H. and Trechsel, A. (2008) *The Politics of Switzerland*, Cambridge: Cambridge University Press.

Kriesi, H. and Wisler, D. (1996) Social Movements and Direct Democracy in Switzerland, *European Journal of Political Research* 30: 19–40.

Lijphart, A. (1999) *Patterns of democracy*, New Haven, CT: Yale University Press.

Matsusaka, J. G. (2004) *For the many or the few. The initiative, public policy, and American democracy*, Chicago, IL: University of Chicago Press.

Neidhart, L. (1970) *Plebiszit und pluralitäre Demokratie. Eine Analyse der Funktionen des schweizerischen Gesetzesreferendums*, Bern: Francke.

Obinger, H. (1998) *Politische Institutionen und Sozialpolitik in der Schweiz*, Bern: Peter Lang.

Papadopoulos, Y. (1998) *Démocratie directe*, Paris: Economica.

—— (2001) How Does Direct Democracy Matter? The Impact of Referendum Votes on Politics and Policy-Making, *West European Politics* 24, 2: 35–58.

Plato (1991). *The Republic: The Complete and Unabridged Jowett Translation*. New York: Vintage Books.

Sartori, G. (1987) *The theory of democracy revised*, Chatham: Chatham House Publishers.

Schumpeter, J. A. (1962) *Capitalism, socialism and democracy*, London: Allen and Unwin.

Smith, D. A. and Tolbert, C. J (2001) The Initiative to Party: Partisanship and Ballot Initiatives in California, *Party Politics* 7, 6: 739–57.

—— (2004) *Educated by initiative: the effects of direct democracy on citizens and political organizations in the American states*, Ann Arbor, MI: University of Michigan Press.

Sniderman, P. A. (1993) The new look in public opinion research, in Finifter, A. W. (ed.) *Political science: the state of the discipline* II, The American Political Science Association: 219–45.

Stroebe, W. (2007) Strategien zur Einstellungs- und Verhaltensänderung, in Jonas, K., Stroebe, W. and Hewstone, M. (eds) *Sozialpsychologie. Eine Einfürhung*, 5th fully revised edition, Heidelberg: Springer: 225–64.

Stutzer, A. and Frey B. S. (2006) Political Participation and Procedural Utility: An Empirical Study, *European Journal of Political Research* 45: 391–418.

Trechsel, A. H. and Sciarini, P. (1998) Direct Democracy in Switzerland: Do Elites Matter?, *European Journal of Political Research* 33: 99–124.

3 Evaluating new vs old forms of citizen engagement and participation

David Beetham

This chapter offers a different perspective on the evaluation of democratic innovations from those in the rest of the volume. Instead of an *internal* comparison, whereby innovations are assessed against one another by common criteria, such as their representativeness, deliberative range and political impact, this chapter offers an *external* comparison, against an age-old mode of citizen engagement, that of the citizen-initiated campaign or demonstration. There are two reasons for doing this. One is to test, and also extend, the criteria for assessing innovations, by including a wider range of forms of citizen engagement for evaluation. The second reason lies in the danger that, by concentrating exclusive academic attention on democratic innovations, we overlook or downplay forms of citizen engagement that may be both politically and democratically more significant.

I take it that most, though not all, of what Ken Newton in his introduction calls 'bottom-up' innovations that are the subject of this volume constitute a sub-species of a broader category that might be termed 'modes of direct citizen engagement with or participation in the decision making of public bodies and officials outside the electoral process'. The term 'direct' will exclude indirect or mediated engagement, such as takes place when citizens participate in civil society organizations and these, in turn, engage with public bodies and officials, however important this may be, indeed often supplementing or facilitating direct citizen engagement. Similarly, for the purposes of this volume, we may wish to exclude forms of direct citizen engagement that are individual rather than collective – individual contact with an elected representative or government official, submission to a parliamentary committee or government consultation, the use of redress mechanisms, and so on – on the grounds that there is no interactive or deliberative moment with other citizens involved. This distinction is, however, a fine one, since many examples of individual use of redress mechanisms have a collective dimension, for example where they involve a category of complainants or lead to a collective movement in support of an individual. We should also exclude forms of collective action that have the *unintended* consequence of influencing public decision making, such as depositors queuing outside a crisis stricken bank to cash their savings, even though this may contribute more to denuding the public finances than to the collapse of the bank itself.

Even with these exclusions, we are still left with a wide range of collective and direct modes of citizen engagement with, or participation in, the decision making of public bodies and officials outside the electoral process. My own far from comprehensive list would include:

- submission of petitions
- official consultative processes
- co-governance arrangements or partnerships
- citizens' juries, deliberative polls, consensus conferences
- campaigns and demonstrations
- membership of statutory decision bodies ('lay governance')
- citizen initiatives
- referendums
- citizen assemblies
- public or political party meetings
- television forums
- e-forums and other uses of information and communications technology (ICT) to facilitate any of the above.

In other words, innovative modes of citizen engagement, supposing we agree on what counts as 'innovative', form part of a much wider set of modes of direct citizen engagement or participation that have always been a feature of the democratic process. For this reason, it is worth considering democratic innovations in the context of the much wider set of modes of direct citizen engagement, as this chapter seeks to do.

Taking all these modes together for the moment, we can draw up a set of dichotomies to characterize or typologize them, such as:

- taking place within established structures vs outside them;
- in invited vs claimed spaces (Gaventa 2007);
- through open vs closed participation;
- with selected vs self-chosen membership;
- by proactive vs reactive engagement;
- as a one-off activity vs ongoing or recurrent one;
- involving policy or legislative formation vs implementation.

Some of these dichotomies are overlapping, and in any case they are not exhaustive.

For the purposes of this chapter, I am going to compare only two of these modes of citizen engagement – one new, one old – which stand on opposite sides of most of these dichotomies. First are citizens' juries, which form part of a wider category of 'mini-publics' (Goodin and Dryzek 2006) including similar forms such as consensus conferences and planning cells. Citizens' juries occupy an *invited space*, with a *closed* and *selected membership*, and are typically *proactive*, in the sense that they are intended to contribute to policy formation or implementation *ex ante*, even though the consultative agenda may have been preset by government or other sponsor. Second, and at the other end of the spectrum of public engagement, is the citizen-initiated campaign or demonstration that, in contrast to the citizens' jury, occupies a *claimed space*, with an *open* and *self-selected membership*, and is typically (though not always) *reactive* to the decision of a public body already taken or trailed as about to be taken. Of course, this mode of citizen engagement cannot be legislated for or form part of any deliberate programme for encouraging greater citizen involvement.

One notable feature of these two contrasting types of citizen engagement is that both were prominent in New Labour's period of office in the UK from 1997–2010. Blair's premiership from 1997 to 2007 was marked by some of the largest mass demonstrations ever seen in Britain, including Jubilee 2000 and Make Poverty History; the Countryside Alliance, campaigning against the government's neglect of rural interests in general and the proposed ban on fox hunting in particular (1998–2000); and the anti-Iraq war movement, which brought over a million people onto the streets of London in February 2003. In autumn 2000 there had been the protests against the increase in fuel taxes, which brought fuel distribution across the country to a standstill through refinery blockades. And the anti-genetically modified (GM) crops direct action campaign between 1998 and 2002 put off the introduction of GM crops for a decade. These were only the tip of the iceberg. A rough and ready count by the Democratic Audit of significant campaigns on issues of national policy under Blair came up with more than fifty, covering such issues as animal welfare, capitalism and globalization, education, the environment and transport, faith issues, farming and the countryside, justice and racial discrimination, social policy and welfare, war and weapons of destruction (Beetham et al. 2008: 58–9).

However, when Gordon Brown became Prime Minister in 2007, he recognised that the government needed to be more proactive in consulting directly with citizens on important issues of public policy. Among his first acts as premier in July 2007 was the publication of a Green Paper, *The Governance of Britain,* which recognized that action was needed 'across the breadth of the political system to restore trust in politics and in our political institutions' (Ministry of Justice 2007: 40). The Paper identified the use of citizens' juries as one mechanism for empowering citizens at the local level, and its use was also advocated in the proposed nationwide discussion on British values and a Bill of Rights (Ministry of Justice 2007: 49). In a speech to the National Council of Voluntary Organisations in September 2007, the Prime Minister announced that citizens' juries would take place on issues related to children, criminal justice and the future of the National Health Service (nine juries, one in each region, meeting simultaneously and linked by video, Brown 2007). And in a speech at a Constitution Unit conference in October 2007, the Minister of State for Democratic Renewal, Michael Wills, suggested that the use of citizens' juries might become the norm across all areas of public policy (Maer 2007b: 5). It was almost as if the use of citizens' juries in a *proactive* way was designed to pre-empt the *reactive* citizen campaigns and demonstrations that had been such a feature of the Blair era.

For all the obvious differences, then, between citizens' juries and citizen-initiated campaigns (to be explored further below), their increased incidence is symptomatic of a common phenomenon – a political class perceived to be out of touch with citizens or significant sections of them, or what Ken Newton in his introduction characterizes as a 'democratic malaise'. Both modes of citizen engagement can be seen as forms of *compensation* for perceived distortions in the representative process and in government policy making. Representation has been particularly distorted in the UK by the systems of parliamentary election and candidate selection, and the requirements of political parties and their funding. Government policy making is distorted by the huge weight and privileged status given to business and financial interests, and the resulting distortions of evidence and public communication in the treatment of major policy issues. To these 'distortions' the two modes of citizen engagement offer different forms of compensation. Citizens' juries offer a purer form of representation and deliberation, undistorted by personal, sectional or party interest, which conforms more closely to an original idealized model of the representative assembly and its deliberative processes. The citizen-initiated campaign, on the other hand, aims to bring into the public arena issues, points of view or interests that have been ignored in the decision process, or not been given sufficient weight.

So how are we now to compare or evaluate these two modes of citizen engagement, which are so different, and comparing which at first sight looks like comparing chalk and cheese? Well, one way is to use the kind of criteria that have been developed in the literature for evaluating democratic innovations, and apply them to both (Fung and Wright 2003; Beetham 2005: 130–56; Smith 2005). These criteria can be grouped into three broad categories, of which the following components can serve for our purposes (see also Geissel in this volume):

1 Participatory range
   - how representative or inclusive it is
   - what numbers of people are involved

2 Deliberative mode
   - the degree of commitment or engagement of participants
   - the range of deliberation

3 Degree of impact
   - on the participants
   - on public debate
   - on policy outcomes

One comment is worth adding on the third of these categories. Most of the literature on democratic innovations considers their impact on the participants and on policy outcomes, but ignores the potentially important aspect of their effect, if any, on public debate and opinion, however difficult this may be to gauge accurately.

Once I have briefly assessed the two modes of citizen engagement against these criteria, I shall consider a further question, which takes us to the heart of issues in representative democracy: how much notice *should* policy makers take of these forms of participation? This might be described as their comparative normative weight, which includes the criteria under (1) and (2) above, but goes beyond them, and requires locating them in an account of the norms of representative democracy.

Assessed against the above three sets of criteria, then, the citizens' jury scores highly on the representativeness and inclusivity criterion, provided its membership is selected by a method, such as stratified sampling, which guarantees a cross section of the population, including members of minority and marginalized groups. The level of commitment required from participants is high, in terms of the number of days they have to be prepared to devote to the work. The range of deliberation is also extensive, often leaving a marked impression on the participants. According to Graham Smith's review of citizens' juries, 'evidence from the UK, US and Germany suggests that citizens take their role seriously and are willing and able to deliberate on often complex and controversial issues … deliberation often leads to changes in opinions and viewpoints' (Smith 2005: 45, 54). The citizens' jury scores very low, however, on the numbers of those participating – at the most in the 20s or 30s at a time. And while there is no reason in principle why the proceedings and conclusions of a citizens' jury should not be given wide publicity, and so influence wider public debate, there is little evidence that this has happened to date in the UK. They seem to be treated by government in the same way as a privately commissioned focus group, without involving any wider citizen engagement. And it is correspondingly difficult to assess what impact they have had, or are likely to have, on policy outcomes. This assessment of impact is confirmed by Graham Smith more generally in his chapter for this volume: public awareness of the very existence of mini-publics (let alone their outputs) is very low. Commissioning bodies will simply 'cherry-pick' those recommendations or trends in opinions that support their perspective, while ignoring those that are uncomfortable.

When we turn to the citizen-initiated campaign or demonstration, we are confronted with an enormous variety between them. However, they share some typical characteristics that allow for a generic assessment against the above criteria. On national level issues, most score relatively highly on the numbers of citizens involved, and the level of engagement required; they also have the typical effect of politicizing those among the participants who previously considered themselves as 'apolitical'. Almost by definition, however, they are unrepresentative of the wider population, since they are self-selected and concentrated on a particular point of view or interest. By the same token, at first sight they lack any deliberative quality, since they are not engaged in listening to others, but in promoting a predetermined viewpoint, often at the tops of their voices. However, we should not overlook the deliberation involved in organizing a campaign and deciding which aspects of an issue to prioritize, nor the spread of supportive local groups where the level of deliberation can be quite substantial, though its range will be

Table 3.1 Comparison between citizens' jury and citizens' campaign

	Citizens' jury	*Citizens' campaign*
Representativeness	high	low
Numbers involved	low	mostly high
Commitment	high	high
Deliberative range	high	low to medium
Impact on participants	high	high
Impact on public debate	low	can be high
Impact on policy outcomes	??	??

narrow in comparison with a citizens' jury. Dieter Rucht's assessment of the levels of deliberation in Global Justice Movements – 'that the majority of these groups are more successful in reducing "hard" power and enabling deliberation than most trade unions, political parties and big non-governmental organizations' – provides a caution against writing off this dimension too readily (see Rucht in this volume).

In terms of the impact of a citizen-initiated campaign on wider public debate, much depends on the issue and levels of publicity, but it is typically much higher than that of a 'mini-public'. Even more variable is their degree of influence on public policy, which depends on the extent to which the legitimacy of a particular policy can be undermined by a campaign, or its implementation hindered. To characterize citizen-initiated campaigns as typically 'reactive' to an announced policy is not to suggest they can have no effect on it, or on future policies, even if they may not achieve their stated goal of having a policy reversed or abandoned. The campaign in the UK against the Newbury bypass road in the 1980s, for example, did not stop the bypass from being constructed, but it did influence the government's road-building programme for a decade or more.

A comparative evaluation of the two types of citizen engagement, then, can be summarised in Table 3.1.

Assessing the 'comparative normative weight' of the two modes

The comparison shown in Table 3.1 may seem rather elementary, though at least it shows that the two modes are amenable to assessment against the same criteria. More taxing is my further consideration or question: what influence *should* these modes of citizen engagement have on policy making, and how much weight *should* government, including parliament, give to them? Can we do any better in answering this question than the 'don't know' or 'it depends' represented by the question marks against their actual or empirical influence in the last row of Table 3.1?

One thing can, I think, be agreed at the outset. None of the modes of direct citizen engagement with public issues, short of a referendum open to the whole electorate, should be allowed to *decide* public policy or legislation in a system of representative democracy. However, we need to be clear why this should be so, and distinguish the good from the bad arguments (see also Budge's Table 1.1 'Criticisms of direct democracy with responses to them' in this volume).

One bad argument, because it's anti-democratic, relies on what Bernard Manin calls the 'aristocratic' dimension of representation, to the effect that representatives know more, are more intelligent or are in other ways superior to the general run of the population (Manin 1997: 161–92). This is familiar to us from J. Madison, J. S. Mill and others. So for example Mill: 'Individuals and peoples who are acutely sensible of the value of superior wisdom … will be far too desirous to secure it than to impose their opinion as a law upon persons whom they look up to as wiser than themselves' (Mill 1861: 319). This argument should rightly be given short shrift in an age when the issue is how to rescue elected politicians from a condition of widespread disrespect and mistrust. From a democratic point of view, what distinguishes representatives from the rest of the population is simply that they are assigned (and must be assigned) sufficient time, resources and access to relevant information and expertise to enable them to engage in effective deliberation and decision on public policy. Yet that is a distinction that may disappear, and does so in the case of the citizens' jury, where for a period and on a particular issue, citizens are afforded the same time and access to information and expertise that is typical to enable elected politicians to arrive at a considered judgement.

A second objection is one from the interconnectedness of policy, to the effect that all policy decisions impinge on others and cannot therefore be treated in isolation, but only by those who exercise a continuity of attention and responsibility across the whole range of government business. This can hardly be a decisive objection, however, since all policy decisions are couched as discrete issues and choices, and their relevant implications for other policy areas can be brought into the deliberations of a citizens' jury as much as they would into a cabinet or parliamentary committee.

More telling is a third argument about accountability. Any group of citizens short of the whole electorate that is given the power of decision – however representative their membership and considered their judgement may be – has no clear line of accountability to the wider citizen body. Indeed, it may serve to compromise the accountability of elected representatives or elected government. Whatever reservations we may have about the effectiveness of this accountability in practice, or the ability of the electoral process to realize it, it remains the cornerstone of a representative system. A parliamentary assembly is not just a *microcosm* of the citizen body, but also its *agent*, and is made so by the process of election. Any inadequacies in the representative body, or process of election, which frustrate this agent's accountability, ought to be addressed directly, rather than substitute for it the decisions of some other body.

It follows that the engagement and conclusions of citizens organized together around some issue of public policy should certainly carry influence with government and parliament, though not decide on that policy (see also Geissel in this volume). But how much influence should they carry? It is interesting that both Burke and Mill – the theorists of representative government most clearly associated with an 'aristocratic' conception, and with protecting the decisional autonomy of the representative – were exercised by this question. Burke, for example, wrote: 'It would be an evil more natural and tolerable, that the House of Commons should be infected with every epidemical phrensy of the people … than that it should be wholly untouched by the opinions and feelings of the people out of doors' (Burke 1834: 140). In terms of his own metaphor, while the elected assembly should not behave like a weathercock, much worse was not to be moved by the direction of the prevailing wind.

J. S. Mill, for his part, was much exercised by the relationship between representatives and their constituents, which he saw as a key issue of what he called 'constitutional morality' or 'the ethics of representative government'. While he disagreed with constituents binding their representatives *in advance* (so-called 'pledges'), nevertheless he was clear that 'a people cannot be well governed in opposition to their primary notions of right, even though these may be in some points erroneous'. And while electors should mostly defer to their representative, 'they are justified in dismissing him at the first moment' when a question arises 'involving points on which he is vitally at issue with them' (Mill 1861: 322). What might count as a 'vital issue' is of course contestable, though we can agree with Mill that a decision on peace or war would fit this category.

If both Burke and Mill, then, with their aristocratic conceptions of representation, were exercised by this question of 'constitutional morality', even more should we be with our more democratic conception. In answering it, much will depend on what I call the 'comparative normative weight' of a citizens' intervention. For example, the conclusions of a citizens' jury, provided it had a representative membership and the time and opportunity to consider all the main aspects of an issue, including expert advice and opinion, would count very high on the scale of normative weight. Would it count higher if the jury were commissioned by a government department or public body responsible for the decision, rather than by a civil society organization? If they are intrinsically of the same quality, then we are back to the question of how the conclusions of a civil society-led deliberation might be brought to the decision-makers' attention in a sufficiently convincing manner. And in practice, there would be a greater cost to government of ignoring the conclusions, if it had commissioned the citizens' jury itself. This cost is identified by the author of a UK House of Commons Advisory Note on Citizen Assemblies as a possible objection to this and other forms of government-led consultation: 'Unless proposals from consultative bodies are incorporated into policy-making, the process can be considered to be damaging to public trust as the government would be seen to "not be listening"' (Maer 2007a: 5). This is surely correct, and makes the attempt to construct a scale of comparative normative weight more than a mere philosophical exercise. The greater the 'normative weight' of the citizens' intervention, the greater one can assume the cost to government of ignoring it could be.

What, then, of the 'normative weight' of the citizen-initiated campaign or demonstration, which has no problem about being publicly heard, whether by government or other citizens? As we have seen, these typically score low on the dimensions of representativeness and deliberation and, to the extent that they do, we should conclude that they possess a lower normative weight than the average citizens' jury. Indeed, they can sometimes take the form of what Burke called 'popular phrensies', which it may be the responsibility of an elected assembly precisely to resist or counteract. Here is Richard Crossman's celebration of the role of parliament in just such a situation in 1968, when Enoch Powell's anti-immigration speech had 'unleashed the nearest thing to a mass movement since the 1930s, in comparison with which the Aldermaston marches were but a collection of liberal individuals and families drooling along the road'. 'It's in these crises', he wrote, 'that the British constitution is like a rock against which the wave of popular emotion breaks … Parliament is the buffer which enables our leadership to avoid saying yes or no to the electorate in the hope that, given time, the situation can be eased away' (Crossman 1977).

However, not all or even most citizen-initiated campaigns or demonstrations can be tarred with this brush. Indeed, they can differ enormously from one another. Elsewhere, I have attempted to construct a set of criteria by which one could assess the relative normative weight of different citizen campaigns and protest movements that took place under the Blair government (and how much notice government and parliament should correspondingly have taken of them) (Beetham 2003: 604–9). The criteria I used were:

- how important the issue was
- how far it concerned a national rather than a particular sectional interest
- the extent of the numbers involved
- whether the activists' aims were in tune with majority public opinion
- the extent and seriousness of public debate that had already taken place or was taking place around the issue.

There is not the space here to rehearse the justification for these different criteria, except to point out that the last two were attempts to cover the issues of representativeness and deliberation, on which citizen campaigns are typically weaker in comparison with juries, whereas the extent of numbers can give them much greater weight. I then used these criteria to assess the respective normative weight of four different campaigns: the protests against the increase in fuel taxes in autumn 2000; the mass demonstrations of the Countryside Alliance from summer 1998 through to autumn 2002; the anti-GM crops campaign between 1998 and 2002; the anti-Iraq war demonstrations of autumn and spring 2002–3. I came up with Table 3.2 of their relative normative weight, and compared it with what the response of the government had actually been to each of these campaigns.

By these criteria, the anti-Iraq war campaign had greater normative weight than the others. Yet, in practice, only the fuel and GM crops protests led to any significant adjustment in government policy – no doubt because the types of direct action involved proved so damaging, and because the policies gave themselves readily to a technical fix by the government. However, the Blair government paid a heavy price for ignoring the anti-war movement, not merely in reduced trust in government, but trust in the democratic process itself, not least among the important

Table 3.2 Assessment of four different campaigns

	Importance	*National vs sectional*	*Large numbers involved*	*Majority opinion pro*	*Full public debate*
Fuel price	yes	no	no	yes	no
Countryside	yes	no	yes	no	yes (hunting)
GM crops	yes	yes	no	yes	partial
Anti-war	yes	yes	yes	yes	yes

constituency of young British Muslims who took part in the demonstrations in such huge numbers. This bears out the conclusion that, the greater the normative weight of a citizen campaign, the greater the cost to government and to confidence in the democratic process of ignoring it.

Conclusion

What, then, can be concluded from this comparison between the new and the old, the innovative and the traditional? If the purpose is to increase participation, and to engage more citizens actively with issues of public policy, then democratic innovations involving mini-publics cannot compare with the traditional citizen-initiated campaign or demonstration, in the sheer numbers involved and mobilized, and the level of politicization that takes place among the previously 'apolitical'. If, on the other hand, the purpose is to provide an authoritative and undistorted assessment of a policy issue by citizens themselves, which should carry normative weight with policy makers, then mini-public forums, if well constructed and managed, have qualities that most citizen-initiated campaigns do not. However, their conclusions have to be *heard*, both by government and the public, if that normative weight is to be made to count in practice. And I have argued that, where a citizens' campaign is both representative of wider public opinion and set in the context of extensive public discussion of the issue in question, it can approach the normative weight of a citizens' jury, besides carrying the additional authority of numbers and the impact of wide publicity.

Let me address, finally, a question that directly connects the two forms of citizen engagement, old and new. If more use were made and notice taken of citizens' juries and other mini-public forums by government at the *proactive* level, then would the incidence of the *reactive* citizen campaign or demonstration noticeably decline? Intuitively this seems a plausible conclusion. It is worth citing in this context an assessment quoted by Graham Smith from the UK Royal Commission on Environmental Pollution, comparing UK with Danish experience:

> The usefulness of consensus conferences can be shown by contrasting UK and Danish experience over food irradiation. The Danish Parliament had available a very negative report by a lay panel and decided that irradiation of food should not be approved for general use. In the UK the Advisory Committee

> on Novel Foods and Processes decided that the process should be introduced. There was a hostile response from the public, and industry was unable to use plant it had installed. That outcome might well have been avoided if there had been appropriate public debate before the decision was taken.
>
> (Smith 2005: 46)

In the UK, we have moved from a Labour Government, which belatedly and perhaps only half-heartedly concluded that the use of citizens' juries and other modes of citizen consultation should be extended in potentially controversial areas of policy, to a Conservative–Liberal Democratic Coalition, which is pushing through a contentious programme of cuts in the public finances and reorganization of the health and education services without any form of public consultation whatsoever. It is hardly surprising that we are now seeing the re-emergence of mass demonstrations and direct action campaigns, beginning with students, who feel particularly betrayed by Liberal Democratic parliamentarians, many of whom owed their election in 2010 to a promise not to increase fees for university courses, which was subsequently broken. In this respect, the UK is starting to resemble the countries of the rest of Europe, such as Iceland, France and Greece, where mass protests against cuts in the public sector have been more bitter and prolonged.

From a democratic point of view, the present situation is marked by a potentially dangerous conjunction of three features:

- The necessity to reinvent the public sphere after a generation of privatization, deregulation and contempt of government.
- Chronically low levels of public confidence in the political class and institutions of representative government charged with this task.
- Widespread economic and social distress and deepening public anger at taxpayers having to pay for banking excesses, perhaps over a generation to come.

In this context, and the serious need to re-engage citizens with government, it has to be said that neither of the modes of citizen engagement considered in this chapter seem equal to the situation. Mini-publics are too small scale, and too easily restricted or ignored by government. Citizen campaigns and demonstrations, as already discussed, are primarily reactive. Where they are effective in preventing or delaying a policy, they do nothing to promote an alternative; where ineffective, they reinforce disillusion with the democratic process. That the present situation demands a reinvention of the processes of representative democracy, and new modes of citizen engagement with them, is evident. What forms will emerge best suited to this need remains an open question.

References

Beetham, D. (2003) Political Participation, Mass Protest and Representative Democracy, *Parliamentary Affairs*, Vol. 56, No. 4: 597–609.

—— (2005) *Democracy: A Beginner's Guide*, Oxford: Oneworld Publications.

Beetham, D., Blick, A., Margetts, H. and Weir, S. (2008) *Power and Participation in Modern Britain*, London: Democratic Audit.

Brown, G. (2007) Speech to the National Council of Voluntary Organisations, 3 September 2007, http://www.number-10.gov.uk/output/page13008.asp (accessed 9 April 2011).

Burke, E. (1834) *The Works of Edmund Burke*, London: Holdsworth and Ball, Vol.1.

Crossman, R. (1977) *The Diaries of a Cabinet Minister*, London: Hamish Hamilton and Jonathon Cape, Vol. 3, entry for 27 April 1968.

Fung, A. and Wright, E. O. (2003) Thinking about empowered participatory governance, in Fung and Wright (eds), *Deepening Democracy: Institutional Innovations in Empowered Participatory Governance*, London: Verso: 3–42.

Gaventa, J. (2007) Levels, spaces and forms of power, in Berenskoetter, F. and Williams, M. (eds), *Power in World Politics*, New York: Routledge: 204–24.

Goodin, R. E. and Dryzek, J. S. (2006) Deliberative impacts: the macro-political uptake of mini-publics, *Politics and Society*, Vol. 34, No. 2: 219–44.

Maer, L. (2007a) *Citizens' Assemblies*, London: House of Commons, SN/PC/4482.

—— (2007b) *Citizens' Juries*, London: House of Commons, SN/PC/4546.

Manin, B. (1997) *The Principles of Representative Government*, Cambridge: Cambridge University Press.

Mill, J. S. (1861) *Considerations on Representative Government*, London: J. M. Dent, 1910.

Ministry of Justice (2007) *The Governance of Britain*, London: CM 7170.

Smith, G. (2005) *Beyond the Ballot: 57 Democratic Innovations from Around the World.* London: Power Inquiry.

Part II

Deliberative democracy

4 Deliberative polling

Reflections on an ideal made practical

James S. Fishkin

Democratic innovations have tended to move in two conflicting directions. Some aspire to increase inclusion and some to increase thoughtfulness.[1] Ultimately, I believe the movements toward increased inclusion are supported by the value of political equality. And the movements toward increased thoughtfulness are supported by the value of deliberation. Is it possible to have both at the same time?

In what is arguably our oldest continuing democratic system, the US, the original design for the constitution was conceived by James Madison as a 'strategy of successive filtrations' of public opinion. Representatives would 'refine and enlarge the public views by passing them through the medium of a chosen body of citizens' as Madison noted in Federalist 10. This refinement of public opinion was to take place in the Senate, the Constitutional Convention, the ratifying conventions, even the Electoral College in its original form. The people would select state legislators who would select senators, states would select electors who would select the president, conventions would approve constitutional changes. This Madisonian vision spawned numerous innovations of democratic design in the name of deliberation.

But the indirect filtration of elite deliberation was soon challenged by attempts to consult the people directly. Instead of the requisite ratifying convention, Rhode Island proposed a referendum on the US Constitution so all citizens could vote on the proposal. The Federalists objected on grounds of defective deliberation. Only in a small representative body, like a convention, could arguments offered on one side be answered on another and then could all the arguments be weighed together by those making the decision. The Federalists boycotted the referendum, the Constitution was voted down and the resulting crisis was only resolved under threat of force. Connecticut threatened to invade from one side and Massachusetts from the other. Under such threats Rhode Island agreed to ratify via the required state convention.

The Rhode Island referendum was an indication of the impulse toward involving the people directly in a way that would lead to mass democracy. Progressive and later reformers led to a wave of innovations – referendums, mass primaries for candidate selection, initiatives, expansion of the franchise – which would all promote political equality. However, the result of bringing power more directly to the people has been that the people have, increasingly, less and less incentive to think about the power they are supposed to exercise. We seem to face a forced choice between politically equal but relatively less informed and thoughtful masses or politically unequal and relatively more thoughtful and deliberative elites. Our dilemma is ultimately an apparent forced choice between inclusion and thoughtfulness.

I believe the aim of escaping this dilemma provides a good agenda for possible political innovations. I will report on two strategies, which I call Deliberative Polling and Deliberation Day, both of which provide ways out. How well they do, as in all attempts at innovation, depends on empirical issues. I will try and summarize some of those here.

I will treat the combination of political equality and deliberation as the defining perspective of deliberative democracy (see also Geissel in this volume).

Concrete applications of 'deliberative democracy' raise three basic questions:

a *Who*: Who is doing the talking? How are they selected? To what extent are they a representative of some larger population?
b *How*: To what extent and in what ways does the discussion satisfy deliberative and democratic aspirations?
c *To what effect*: What difference does the discussion make? To what extent do the results have sufficient legitimacy and connections to the policy process to be implemented? Is it just talk or can it effect action?

As we have seen, policy makers who wish to consult the public face an apparent dilemma. On the one hand, if they consult mass opinion directly, they will get views that are largely uninformed. Most citizens, most of the time, in most political systems, know little about the details of public policy (Converse 1964; Luskin 1987; Delli Carpini and Keeter 1996; Kinder 1998; Price 2000). But policy elites and organized interests, which may have different interests and values, may not speak accurately for the people. Any effort to consult the public faces a parallel dilemma. Who should be consulted? How should they be selected? In open town meetings, only the passionately engaged or mobilized – unlikely to be anything like a representative sample – tend to show up. In scientific polling, random sampling can be applied to yield representative samples, but their views, on most complex policy matters, are apt to be non- or minimal attitudes, closer, in truth, to 'don't-knows' than to serious opinions (Converse 1964; 1970: 168–89; Achen 1975, 1983; Hill and Kriesi 2001; for a recent overview see Bishop 2005).

Deliberative Polling helps solve these dilemmas, increasing both political equality and deliberation, both representativeness and considered judgements. The basic idea is to assemble a random sample to discuss a set of policy or electoral issues, having first sent them carefully balanced briefing materials and then giving them the chance of questioning panels of competing policy experts or policy makers. The small groups are randomly assigned and led by trained moderators. The participants answer the same questions before and after deliberating (see Fishkin 1991; 1997 for the idea and rationale; Luskin et al. 2002 for a detailed analysis; Fishkin and Luskin 2005 for an overview). The random sampling serves equality and representativeness. The balanced information, moderated discussion and questioning of balanced panels provide good conditions for deliberation.

In theory the Deliberative Polling research programme provides a distinctive answer to the three questions with which we started. First, by using random sampling we provide an answer to the *who* question that satisfies political equality. A random sample of the mass public, particularly if its representativeness is vindicated by who actually participates, can plausibly constitute a microcosm of the whole population. And it does so by providing everyone an equal chance of participation. Second, the process embodies good conditions for this random sample to come to considered judgements. The process employs balanced briefing materials, small group discussions with trained moderators, plenary sessions with competing experts who answer questions from the small groups from different perspectives, and opportunities to reflect on the information and share competing points of view. The participants express their views in confidential questionnaires, insulated from social pressures.

Deliberative Polling's answer to our third question, *to what effect*, has usually been less clear. The results may be broadcast and taken seriously by the media and even inform the debates among policy makers, yet fall well short of determining policy. That may trouble those wishing to restrict 'deliberative democracy' to processes culminating in binding decisions.[2] We would dispute such a requirement, but, in any case, there have in fact been Deliberative Polls culminating in binding or all but binding decisions. Notably, Deliberative Polling led to the implementation of major investments by electric utility companies in Texas, instructed to follow the results by the state's Public Utilities Commission.[3] It also was recently used by PASOK, the Greek Socialist party, to choose its candidate for Mayor of Marousi (a large municipality in the Athens metropolitan area) (Fishkin et al. 2008). In addition, a series of Deliberative Polls in China have been employed to make decisions about local infrastructure and budgeting matters (Fishkin et al. 2010).

A Deliberative Poll could be evaluated in various ways. It is usually several things at once – a social science investigation, a public policy consultation, a contribution to the media and public discussion. As a public policy consultation, some reasonable criteria for evaluation would be (see also Geissel in this volume):

1. The extent to which the sample is representative.
2. The extent to which there are significant changes in opinions, particularly about policy attitudes.
3. The extent to which the changes of opinion exemplify normatively desirable processes of deliberation:
    a. In particular the extent to which the process avoids distortions from inequality.
    b. The extent to which the process avoids any predictable pattern of small group polarization.
    c. The extent to which there is a development of public spirited preferences.

d The extent to which the participants learn.
e The extent to which the learning drives the opinion change.

4 The extent to which the post-deliberation opinions or changes of opinion influence public policy.

Representative samples

With random sampling, every member of a population has an equal chance of being invited. Yet no sample is perfect. Everyone drawn into a sample cannot be reached. Everyone who is reached does not agree to participate. What sorts of bias are introduced? How can we know?

Unlike some other deliberative microcosms, the procedure in Deliberative Polling is to conduct the initial interview on first contact and then invite. This seemingly obvious and straightforward strategy produces attitudinal as well as demographic data comparing participants and non-participants. Our experience has been that there are usually very few statistically significant differences between participants and non-participants and that when they occur they are usually substantively small. This is partly because, unlike some other projects, we pay incentives for participation and employ every means possible to attract those initially drawn into the sample.

Consider the very first Deliberative Poll in Britain in 1994 on the issue of criminal justice policy. There were 869 completed initial interviews, which represented a response rate of 74 per cent. Of these, 301 attended the event, permitting attitudinal and demographic comparisons of the 301 with the 568 non-participants. We asked 102 questions, both demographic and attitudinal, in the initial questionnaire, and only fourteen showed statistically significant differences between participants and non-participants. Furthermore, most of the differences, even when statistically significant, were substantively small. While the participants were slightly more knowledgeable than the non-participants (between 7 and 11 per cent more likely to know the right answer on a battery of knowledge questions) we could truly say that we had gathered all of Britain to one room (Luskin et al. 2002).

To see the difference, consider some other efforts to apply something like random sampling to public consultation. The attraction of random sampling is that it can provide a basis for establishing a microcosm of the entire community. But everything depends on how it is done. An example of the sort of project that *appears* to employ random sampling but actually fails to provide any credible basis for its evaluation is the attempt by a group called 'America Speaks' to substitute 'random sampling' for its normal recruitment process of sheer self-selection (combined with a demographic screen selecting only some of the people who volunteer themselves). In the case of its project on health care in Maine, it sent out 75,000 postcards to randomly chosen residents in order to recruit a forum of a few hundred. They were asked to indicate interest in attending a deliberative forum about health care by sending in a response card with their demographic characteristics. Only 2,700 returned the cards and after some demographic screens were applied to these, 300 participants came on the day. Setting aside the fact that this 'sample' was supplemented by others who were recruited by stakeholder groups to make up for low numbers of young people and minorities, this design gives no confidence in any claims to representativeness. There is no data comparing the attitudes of the 2,700 who volunteered themselves with the 75,000, and no data comparing the 300 with the 2,700 or the 75,000. It is important to note that unlike Deliberative Polls, the participants in 'America Speaks' are not compensated for their time and effort. They just have to be sufficiently motivated about the issue to want to spend a whole day discussing it. Since most people are not motivated to spend much time and effort pondering policy, it seems obvious that the 300 or so who volunteered themselves from an initial list of 75,000 would not offer a credible microcosm of the views of the entire public.[4]

The lesson here is that the mere invocation of 'random sampling' is not enough to ensure representativeness. Everything depends on how it is done, what data is collected at what point and what incentives or other motivations are employed to try and attract – and enable – those initially drawn in the sample to show up. When the response rate is miniscule and there are no incentives, an initial effort at random sampling can easily transform into virtually pure self-selection.

To a lesser degree some of the same difficulties applied to the now famous Citizens' Assembly in British Columbia. A stratified random sample of 23,034 was invited via letter. 1,715 responded saying they were interested. After some demographic criteria were applied, 1,441 of these were invited to come to 'selection meetings'. 964 did so, and 158 of these were selected randomly. The issue is that we do not have any way of evaluating how the 1,715 who selected themselves compared to the initial pool of 23,034 (Citizens' Assembly on Electoral Reform 2004). How much more interested or knowledgeable about politics and public affairs, how much more skewed to one political viewpoint or another were they? Similarly we do not know anything about how the representativeness of the microcosm was affected by the other stages of selection. It is a demanding task to volunteer to give up nearly a year of one's life. How did those who put themselves forward for this opportunity compare to those who did not, or, in other words, how do they compare to the rest of the population for whom they are supposed to be a random microcosm?

Attitude change

The punchline of a Deliberative Poll is a change in policy attitudes, a change in answers to the question: what is to be done? We studied fifty-eight indices of policy attitudes in nine national Deliberative Polls conducted between 1995 and 2004. Four of these Deliberative Polls were American, four were British and one was Australian. Topics varied from US foreign policy (2003) and the US general election (2004) to Britain's future in Europe (1995) and the British General Election (1997). All samples were national with sample sizes ranging from 238 to 347. Seven of the Deliberative Polls were face to face and two were conducted online.

The first point to note is that there is a lot of change in policy attitudes. Seventy-two per cent of the fifty-eight indices show statistically significant net change comparing the answers on first contact with the answers at the conclusion of deliberations. The magnitudes of the changes are also large (Luskin et al. 2007b).[5]

A second point is that there is clearly an effect of salience. The more salient the issue to begin with, the less likely the net change. If respondents have already processed an issue, even with fairly imperfect and unbalanced deliberation in their daily lives, they are less likely to change their views. They may, in other words, have already arrived at fairly firm views. If we proxy salience by the time one knowledge scores, then there is a strong negative relationship (Luskin et al. 2007b).[6]

While there is a great deal of net attitude change, deliberation has a value even when there is no change. If the public thinks X should be done, but has not thought about the issue much, has not tested its views in comparison to alternative policies and the reasons for them, then there is an issue about how seriously, from the standpoint of normative legitimacy, one should take those views. They reflect very little thought and little consideration of opposing possibilities. On the other hand, if those views survive a serious deliberation unchanged, then they take on the added legitimacy of the public's considered judgements. Those views have been tested in a context of opposing arguments with good information. Hence, regardless of change, the conclusions at the end of a well constituted Deliberative Poll offer a representation of what the public would think if it were thinking about the issue under transparently good conditions. It is those judgements, change or no change, that should have a recommending force to policy makers and representatives and those concerned with the public dialogue. While some of those views may correspond with the views in conventional polls, one can never be sure, unless they have been tested by adverse arguments, unless they have been tested by serious deliberation about policy alternatives.

It is worth adding that some Deliberative Polls have occurred in contexts soon before a vote where the results were widely publicized by broadcast media partners. In those cases – the British General Election, the Australian referendum on the Republic, the Danish referendum on the euro – there were significant changes in voting intention. Hence the opinion changes are not only significant; they can also be politically consequential.

Avoiding distortions: inequality and polarization

Critics of deliberation worry that the apparent commitment to equal consideration of everyone's views on their merits will in fact mask domination of the process by the most privileged. The problem is that any microcosmic deliberation taking place in a modern developed society will be in one in which there are significant social and economic inequalities in the conduct of ordinary life in the broader society. It seems difficult or impossible to 'bracket' these inequalities – for participants to behave 'as if' they do not exist (see Fraser 1993: 1–32, especially 10–11).

How might the apparent equality of deliberative processes mask domination by the more privileged? Iris Marion Young distinguishes 'external' and 'internal' forms of exclusion. The external forms are the most obvious. Not letting someone be part of the participating group, either because their participation is barred or they are not effectively recruited, has been the focus of electoral/political reform for decades. And even in survey work, efforts to get at non-response, to reach the more difficult to reach, those with difficult schedules, those without phones, internet access or even fixed addresses[7] can rightly justify significant expenditures of time and effort.

But Young's point is that there are more subtle forms of exclusion that turn on manners of speaking and listening. Some people, even if formally included, may not have their voices, if they speak at all, taken seriously. They may give off cues that indicate they are not well informed or not worth listening to. Those who are accustomed to every advantage in the conduct of their everyday lives may be more assertive in pressing their views on others and less open to listening to those without similar advantages (Young 2000). They may also be more accustomed to orderly forms of reason giving argument that weigh with other participants. Or so the argument goes.

The empirical question for our research programme is whether or not those advantaged in actual life use the opportunity for shared deliberation to dominate the process. If all or most of the opinion changes move sharply in the direction of the more advantaged viewpoints, then that might be an indication that the advantaged are dominating. The issue is complex in that the advantaged may be more informed, at least on some issues, and if the idea of deliberation is that participants move in the direction of their more informed opinions, then participants may move in that direction because of information effects, not because of distortions, by a factor extraneous to the merits of the issues, that is, the social positions of some of the participants.

Those coming to this debate from a feminist perspective will be concerned about men dominating. Those focused on socio-economic inequalities will be concerned about domination by the rich and the more educated. The metrics for evaluating this claim could turn on the movement of policy attitudes toward or away from the supposedly dominating group, as well as on the distribution of speaking time among the participants.

In some of the Deliberative Polls, all the small group discussions were recorded, permitting study of the distribution of words used and the kinds of reasons offered. In a study of five American Deliberative Polls, Alice Siu looked at these two questions. About the distribution of talk, she concluded 'that no particular gender, race, or demographic dominates deliberations'. In one of the Deliberative Polls, on health care and education in the US, by far the most talking (measured in number of words used) was done by non-white, less educated females with non-white higher educated females close behind. The least number of words were expressed by the white higher educated males. In a separate Deliberative Poll on the 2004 primary campaign, the pattern was largely reversed. All of the Deliberative Polls used representative samples of the US adult population (Siu 2009).

Even if talk is evenly distributed, it is possible that influence is not. If we look at issue indices for each topic of discussion and analyze the movement at the small group level, the five Deliberative Polls had 354 small group issue combinations (the number of issue indices in each Deliberative Poll times the number of groups calculated for all five Deliberative Polls). Siu found no significant pattern of movement in the direction of the initial positions of the whites, the males, the high income participants, or the more educated. In each case, movements in the direction of the more advantaged groups occurred only about half the time. In other words, about half the time a group ended up moving toward the initial position of the more advantaged (the more educated, the whites, the rich or the male) but about half the time it moved away. And when the magnitudes of the movement are examined, rather than the numbers of movements in each direction, the amounts are small considered as a percentage of the total range of possible movement (Siu 2009).[8]

Regardless of socio-economic and gender inequalities, there are long-standing concerns that the process of group discussion itself may bring distortions. Cass Sunstein (2003), building on earlier work on the so-called 'risky shift', has claimed there is an inevitable 'law of group polarization'. If there is a dimension for which there is a midpoint, and the mean of a small group starts out on one side of that midpoint, he hypothesizes that it will move farther out from the midpoint in the same direction. If it starts out to the right it will move further right. If it starts out to the left it will move further left. The argument is not dependent on liberal and conservative accounts of left and right – just on there being a dimension with a midpoint. The effect is meant to apply generally to any issue dimension that is the topic of discussion.

The idea is that this distortion will occur because of two dynamics. First, if the group starts out on one side of the midpoint, then there is likely to be an imbalance in the argument pool on that side of the issue. More arguments will be offered to motivate further movement in that direction. The second dynamic is a social comparison effect. People will compare their own positions to that of the others in the small group and feel social pressure to conform to the direction of the new consensus.

The argument is a challenge to the legitimacy of deliberative democracy because if there is a reliable pattern of group psychology that predicts the movement of opinion, then it is hard to hold that the movement is based on the merits. Regardless of the merits in a particular case, the group will supposedly move in a stated direction. The issue is an empirical one and may well vary with the precise institutional design of a deliberative process. Sunstein (2003), however, holds that it will apply generally to group discussion processes.[9]

The polarization argument put forward vigorously by Cass Sunstein, represents a different kind of distortion. Sunstein argues that there is a predictable pattern: group discussions lead to extremes. If there is an issue for which there is a midpoint, his 'law of group polarization' asserts that, if the mean position of the group begins on one side of the midpoint, it would move farther out from the middle in the same direction. If the mean position begins on the other side of the midpoint it will move farther out from the middle in that direction (Sunstein 2006; Schkade et al. 2007).[10]

However, we looked at the degree of polarization in fifteen Deliberative Polls with 1,848 group/issue combinations (the number of issue indices in a given Deliberative Poll times the number of small groups in that Deliberative Poll for all fifteen Deliberative Polls). The proportion of small groups moving away from the midpoint turns out to be 50 per cent. In other words, the other 50 per cent of the time, the movement was toward the midpoint and so there was no tendency at all towards polarization in Sunstein's sense. These Deliberative Polls took place in various countries, including the US (six cases), Britain (five cases), Bulgaria, China, Greece, and Australia. All employed scientific random samples and face to face discussion (Luskin et al. 2007a).

Public spiritedness

Discussions of deliberation and political participation have long speculated that forms of public consultation that involve shared discussion and decision about public issues will foster 'public spiritedness' – a greater support for policies of broad rather than narrow public interest. J. S. Mill, building on Tocqueville's account of town meetings and juries in America, praised institutions that serve as 'schools of public spirit' – local decision-making bodies where the interests of the whole community are discussed and individual citizens have some role in decisions. More recent writers like Jane Mansbridge have continued the speculation, but have encountered difficulty finding clear empirical confirmation (Mill 1861 [1991] especially Chapters 1 and 8: 78–9, 171–3; Mansbridge 1999).

Mill argued that when the private citizen participates in public functions

> [h]e is called upon, while so engaged, to weigh interests not his own; to be guided in case of conflicting claims, by another rule than his private partialities; to apply, at every turn, principles and maxims which have for their reason of existence the general good. He is made to feel himself one of the public and whatever is in their interest to be his interest.
>
> (Mill 1861 [1991])

Mill called for more 'schools of public spirit' and experimentation with their design. In a sense the Deliberative Poll, like other microcosmic deliberations is potentially a 'school of public spirit'. But whether or not it functions that way is an empirical question (de Tocqueville 1863 [1961]; Mansbridge 1999; Fishkin et al. 2010).[11] We have already seen in China that when local citizens were gathered to deliberate about infrastructure choices, they increased their support for projects, among the thirty possible ones, that would serve a broader community, as opposed to projects that would benefit only a single village. In addition, in the eight Texas projects on energy choices, the percentage willing to pay more on their monthly utility bills in order to provide wind power to the whole community rose by about thirty points, averaged over the eight projects. And the percentage willing to pay more on their monthly bills in order to provide conservation efforts for the community (demand side management) also rose about thirty points. The notion that one would pay more on a monthly bill in order to subsidize the cost of windmills, or in order to subsidize conservation efforts, seems an indication, in at least a small way that one is willing to contribute to the broader public interest.

A similar result can be inferred from the project in New Haven about local issues facing the fifteen towns in the metropolitan region. In Connecticut, the town is the unit of government and at the beginning, there was a strong presumption that the towns would not share revenue amongst each other. But after deliberation, there was considerable movement toward revenue sharing to promote new development that might benefit the region as a whole. The experimental design of this project allowed us to attribute the movement to the process of discussing the issues together, rather than to learning at home in anticipation of the event or any of the other elements of the process (Farrar et al. 2010).

Knowledge gains

We always include information items and these routinely show statistically significant gains, as in the first Deliberative Poll in Britain (Luskin et al. 2002), the National Issues Convention in the US, and almost all others. Sometimes the changes are large. Consider the Deliberative Poll in Northern Ireland on education policy. Even though the sample was drawn from parents only (because that is what the government authorities regarded as directly and legally relevant to education policy), there were massive gains in knowledge. On average, the sample answered only 22 per cent of the information questions about Northern Ireland's education system correctly before deliberation, but answered 50 per cent correctly after deliberation. For example, the percentage knowing that schools receive more funding for older pupils increased from 21 per cent to 79 per cent, and the percentage knowing that the new entitlement curriculum requires that 'every school provide all fourteen-year-olds with a choice of at least twenty-four subjects' increased from 21 per cent to 74 per cent (Fishkin et al. 2007).[12]

We have found a consistent pattern in that those who gain information are also those who change their views (Luskin et al. 2002).[13] The information driven model, which we found in the first Deliberative Poll, has defined a pattern for others.

To what effect?

How can deliberation by a microcosm of the public in a Deliberative Poll actually change policy or politics? While at first glance one might think that only a binding deliberative process could have an effect, the Deliberative Poll has been applied in a number of cases where it played an advisory role and had demonstrable policy effects. When a credible, scientific sample deliberates in a transparent and balanced way, in dialogue with public officials, its conclusions take on a recommending force. We have found that the conclusions of deliberative sessions have been implemented in Texas decisions about energy choices, in Chinese decisions about the choice of which infrastructure to build, in the choice of candidate for a party in Greece, and in a budget crisis in Italy.

In 2006, the Regione Lazio, the state in Italy for which Rome is the capital, held Italy's first Deliberative Poll.[14] The state faced budgetary difficulties, especially from a deficit caused by health care costs incurred by the previous government. A principal issue was the cost of maintaining the large number of hospital beds in Rome. With a large number of teaching hospitals, Rome has far more hospital beds than any other part of Italy. While policy makers had long hoped to cut the number of beds and use some of the health care money more efficiently, particularly by investing in poly-ambulatory clinics that could bring health care closer to the people, they were reluctant to cut the number of hospital beds. The fact that Rome had so many more than any other part of Italy was a point of pride and very popular.

The most notable result was that the percentage believing the Regione should 'convert some of its beds into other resources that make the structures more efficient' went from 45 per cent before deliberation to 62 per cent afterwards. Support for converting some of the hospital beds specifically into 'poly-ambulatory facilities where you can go for some checks that now you can receive only through hospitalization' changed only slightly, but was very high both before and after – 87 per cent before and 85 per cent after deliberation.

After the Deliberative Poll, the state government moved to implement a plan to reorganize the hospital network, lower the number of hospital beds and redistribute resources to poly-ambulatory clinics. Luigi Nieri, the state treasurer, commented on the Deliberative Poll: 'It was an exciting experience that has shown how great is the people's desire to participate and to express their opinion … It's exactly what we want: encouraging direct participation to democratic life and promoting new transparency practices' (Buonocore 2007).

The Rome Deliberative Poll received extensive press coverage in Italy and its perceived legitimacy certainly helped to influence policy. But there is also a sense in which the results gave officials 'cover to do the right thing'. The informed and representative conclusions of the sample could be invoked as a way out of the budgetary impasse.

The Poll encapsulated in a day's deliberations a connection to policy making that played out over two years in eight projects in Texas. The transparent and representative deliberations of a sample, as it became more informed, acquired enough legitimacy to be invocable by policy makers. The involvement of stakeholders from different perspectives in the briefing document and in the question and answer sessions, combined with media coverage of both the process and its results to create a platform for amplifying the influence of the public's considered judgements. Once the microcosm was seen as a legitimate representation of the views of ordinary citizens, and once its process was seen as transparent and balanced, the conclusions acquired a recommending force. The results were well received throughout the policy community and were even treated favourably in press releases by the utility companies and the Environmental Defense Fund on the same day.

One difference between the Italian and Texas projects was that the Rome project was sponsored by the state government in conjunction with civil society. In the case of the Texas projects, the deliberations were sponsored by the utilities themselves, with supervision by stakeholder committees and the participation of the Public Utility Commission. But the basic dynamic was the same – perceived legitimacy and transparency for deliberations by a representative microcosm.

Before the Texas Deliberative Polls, the state of Texas had the lowest usage of wind power on a percentage basis of any state in the US (Sloan 2007).[15] Based on the successive Deliberative Polls, the Integrated Resource Plans, which took account of their results, and then the Renewable Energy Standard (RES) that was supported by the Deliberative Poll results, Texas surpassed California as the leading state in wind power in the US in 2007. The eight projects took place across Texas (as well as across the border in Louisiana).[16]

The Texas energy projects set an example for public consultation that led to policy impacts in other jurisdictions that did not have Integrated Resource Planning or any actual requirement that utilities consult the public. For example, in August 2003, the Nebraska Public Power District held a Deliberative Poll with local public television broadcast, to decide on its energy priorities, comparing wind power, methane generation (from animal manure), natural gas and coal. By the end of the deliberations, 96 per cent supported a large increase in wind power (200 MW) and 81 per cent an investment in methane (Guild et al. 2003). Following the Deliberative Poll, the utility's board approved the state's largest wind farm with plans for additional renewable energy investments (Nebraska Public Power District 2003).

Nova Scotia Power, the province's electric utility company, held a Deliberative Poll in November 2004 to get informed public input from the entire province about its energy choices. As with all the other Deliberative Polls about energy choices, a media partner produced a broadcast about it so that those who did not participate could be informed about the process and its results. In this case, the media partner was the CBC (the Canadian Broadcasting Corp). As in other Deliberative Polls, a highly representative sample of the province was gathered to a single place (Halifax, Nova Scotia) and the participants became far more informed as demonstrated by their answers to information questions (Guild et al. 2004). Participants were asked about factors to consider in the generation and delivery of electric power, such as providing enough electricity, contributing to the global effort to control greenhouse gases, controlling emissions locally, and economic factors such as stable cost and securing the lowest price. The importance of the economic factors was strong pre-deliberation but, after the event, dropped by half. The environmental considerations such as contributing to the control of emissions and contributing to the global effort to deal with climate change went to the top. After the Deliberative Poll the company proceeded with major new investments in renewable energy[17] and also decided not to retrofit a major coal plant.

In November 2007, the State of Vermont sponsored a Deliberative Poll to help its Department of Public Service chart the state's energy future on issues such as reliance on energy efficiency (reducing the need), investment in wind, nuclear and hydro, as well as natural gas, oil or coal.

There was strong support at the end of the day for hydro, wind, solar, wood and nuclear in that order. There was much less support for oil or coal. Respondents expressed overwhelming support (86 per cent) for the state continuing to buy electricity from Hydro Quebec and from Vermont based independent Power Producers (97 per cent) but only a slender plurality at the end of the day for continuing to buy from the Vermont Yankee nuclear plant (Luskin et al. 2008). Much of the initial opposition to wind on aesthetic grounds clearly abated in the face of broader environmental concerns.

The support for Hydro Quebec increased by twenty points after deliberation, and support for the independent Power Producers in Vermont by eight points. There were other significant increases in support for energy efficiency measures and for hydro and wood as fuel sources. Support for coal and oil decreased after deliberation. Within a few months after the project concluded, these results were explicitly incorporated into the Vermont Comprehensive Energy Plan. As of this writing, the plan is out for public comment, but it offers a good reflection of the public's views expressed in the Deliberative Poll (Vermont Department of Public Service 2009).

In the various projects on energy choices in eight different utility districts in Texas (and nearby Louisiana), in Nebraska, in Nova Scotia and in Vermont, the same basic dynamic unfolded as in Rome. A scientific sample was convened, its deliberations were transparently balanced in a dialogue involving public officials, its conclusions showed dramatic changes in comparison to the initial top of the head opinions, the participants became demonstrably more informed about the issues and media coverage amplified the public voice. Relevant officials found the results compelling and reasonable. In Texas, as in Rome, policy makers independently offered the same comment – it gave them 'cover to do the right thing'.

The dynamic of consulting representative and informed opinion and having it implemented was not much different even in China. While the local projects were not widely covered in the broadcast or print media, they were widely discussed on the internet. Most importantly, they were big events locally – public and transparent forms of consultation building on the local tradition of *Kentan* ('heart to heart' discussion meetings). In the Chinese case, local innovation provided a novel answer to the question of how citizen deliberations can be connected with elite deliberations. By the time the fourth Deliberative Poll in Zeguo occurred in February 2008, the Local People's Congress (LPC) had become less a rubber stamp and more an effective decision-making body. In this project, the entire budget of the town was opened up to scrutiny by the deliberating sample of 175 recruited again through random sampling. But this time, sixty deputies from the Local People's Congress observed the entire process. The LPC met a week later and considered both the quantitative results of the Deliberative Poll and their own observations of the process and then adjusted the budget in light of both.

The most recent Chinese case highlights the issue of how deliberations by the people might be connected, institutionally, to deliberations by actual decision makers. In the case of the Texas utility projects, the actual decisions were made by regulated utilities, but in light of plans that had to be approved by the Texas Public Utility Commission (an appointed government body). In the case of the Nebraska and Nova Scotia cases, the decisions were made by the companies themselves. In the case of the Rome Deliberative Poll, the decision was made by the elected government of the Regione Lazio, while in the case of Vermont, the Deliberative Poll played a role in the state's comprehensive energy planning process by the Department of Public Service. In China, however, we see the first glimmerings of another model, one that fuses elite deliberation with deliberative democracy by the people themselves.

A more ambitious innovation: Deliberation Day

Some of the Deliberative Polls have taken place before national elections or referendums. As noted, these have produced substantial opinion changes, including changes in voting intention, for the microcosm, as a result of deliberation. While these projects have been transparent and public events, with national broadcast, the effect on the broader public has only been through the media. The deliberators change on the basis of good information and their discussion of competing reasons, but the broader public is less informed and may not have considered all the arguments that the microcosm has. The broader public's voting is a function of the usual campaign dynamics of political campaigning, advertising and mobilization.

In order for something like deliberative public opinion to be consequential in an election or referendum, it would be most effective for voters themselves to deliberate. The Deliberation Day proposal (Ackerman and Fishkin 2004) is carefully structured to spread something like the experience of the Deliberative Poll – balanced materials and small group discussions alternating with plenary sessions with competing experts and party representatives answering questions from the small groups. This basic format has now been the subject of considerable research, and by randomly assigning people throughout the nation to sessions within their geographical area, it can be roughly duplicated on a large scale. The collective action is overcome by paying a significant incentive (we proposed US$300) for a day's work of citizenship. No opinions are gathered at the end, but we would assume exit polling would amplify the deliberative views. Political actors would have to assume that on a date certain – Deliberation Day – the vast bulk of the population would be well informed about the issues. In anticipation of such a development, the entire campaign dynamic would change and, we believe, become more substantive.

Just as an ordinary poll represents non-deliberative public opinion, the aspiration is that a Deliberative Poll represents more or less what would happen on Deliberation Day. Both proposals attempt to realize two fundamental political principles – political equality and deliberation. The first does so via a revival of the ancient Athenian idea of the deliberative microcosm chosen by lot, updated with modern social science and media for amplification. The second does so by spreading the process to a more powerful form of inclusion. Instead of everyone having the same opportunity to be part of the random sample, everyone has the same opportunity to actually participate. The latter strategy vastly amplifies the effects but, of course, at greatly increased cost. Both overcome the dilemma with which we started – the apparent forced choice between political equality and deliberation.

If Deliberation Day can successfully scale up the results of the Deliberative Poll then it would be a distinctive innovation adding the realization of mass participation to the realization of deliberative democracy. Thus far, participatory and deliberative democracy have been at odds, but the point of democratic innovation should be the redesign of institutions so that key values are mutually enhancing rather than necessarily conflicting.

Notes

1 This chapter summarizes an argument I develop more fully in *When the People Speak: Deliberative Democracy and Public Consultation* (Oxford University Press 2009).
2 See Gutmann and Thompson (2004: 5) for a 'loose' definition of 'binding': '[The participants] intend their discussion to influence a decision the government will make or a process that will affect how future decisions are made.' By this criterion, many of the televised Deliberative Polls before elections or referenda, or advisory to government bodies would fall within the 'binding' category.
3 See Lehr et al. (2003). A much lengthier process designed to resemble Deliberative Polling, the Citizens Assembly in British Columbia, led to the selection of a referendum topic for electoral reform in 2004 (Blais/Carty/Fournier 2006).
4 Essentially the same methodology was applied in California on an even larger scale in a health care deliberation called CaliforniaSpeaks. 120,000 people were initially solicited. An eventual 3,500 participated but only 60 per cent were from this process. About 40 per cent were 'indirectly recruited' (friends or family who came along to the event were 21 per cent and persons recruited by interest groups or grass roots organizations were 19 per cent) (Fung and Lee 2008). Fung and Lee note that in comparison to a separate survey of the general public from the Public Policy Institute of California, the participants are politically different (only 18 per cent self-identified as conservative as opposed to 37 per cent of the California general public), demographically different (only 13 per cent Latino compared to 36 per cent of the California public) and much more interested in politics (61 per cent very interested in politics compared to 21 per cent of the general public).
5 Luskin et al. (2007a) find that the mean absolute net change, on a 0 to 1 scale to which the indices were normed, is .096.
6 Across the nine Deliberative Polls the correlation between the time one mean knowledge score and the mean absolute net change is -.583 (Luskin et al. 2007a).
7 See Brehm (1993) for the threat of non-response to the validity of surveys. The problem has only gotten worse since he wrote, given the spread of cell phones, the disappearance of landlines, and the tumbling of response rates.
8 Siu (2009) found that the small groups moved toward the initial position of the males 51 per cent of the time, toward the initial positions of the more educated 54 per cent of the time, toward the initial positions of those with higher income 52 per cent of the time and toward the initial positions of the white participants 48 per cent of the time. This strategy for analyzing the issue of domination by the more advantaged was suggested by Robert Luskin.
9 See for example Sunstein (2003). See the discussion in our sections on polarization (Fishkin and Laslett 2003).

10 While Sunstein has treated the Deliberative Poll as a possible exception to his law, he has since been asserting that the law is general and applies to Deliberative Poll like processes (Sunstein 2006, especially Chapter two; and Schkade et al. 2007). The latter, most recent experiment uses a jury like process and a deliberation limited to only fifteen minutes. It is difficult to generalize from such an experiment either to the DD proposal (which is meant for a whole day without an agreed verdict) or the Deliberative Poll, which also involves moderated discussion, no agreed consensus and at least a whole day of deliberation.

11 We begin to examine that empirical question below. The issue has a long history (see Mansbridge 1999). Mansbridge frames the issue about participation in general but many of her cases are discursive participation. J. S. Mill was heavily influenced by de Tocqueville and the two long reviews he wrote of *Democracy in America* were a precursor to his discussions of the issue in representative government. They are reprinted as introductions to each edition in Alexis de Tocqueville's *Democracy in America*, Vols I and II (de Tocqueville 1863 [1961]). For public spiritedness in the China case see Fishkin et al. (2010).

12 These questions are taken from an index of seven questions (Fishkin et al. 2007).

13 The model put forward in Luskin et al. (2002) has been applied to many Deliberative Polls.

14 The Deliberative Poll was held by Regione Lazio – Assessorato a Bilancio, programmazione economico finanziaria e partecipazione (Department of Budgeting, Financial Planning and Participation). It was promoted and carried out by the magazine *Reset* with the support of Ispo (Istituto per gli Studi sulla Pubblica Opinione – Institute for Studies on Public Opinion) and directed by Renato Mannheimer. The survey and the final event were sponsored by the bank Dexia, Lega Coop (the Italian association of cooperative societies) and the newspaper *E-polis*. Since then the Associazione per la Democrazia Informata has been created to promote Deliberative Polling in Italy.

15 In November 1995 there were no commercially viable wind projects in Texas (Sloan 2007).

16 The first of this series was hosted by Central Power and Light (CPL) in Corpus Christi, Texas, in May, 1996; followed by West Texas Utilities (WTU) in Abilene; Southwestern Electric Power Company (SWEPCO) in Shreveport, Louisiana; El Paso Electric (EPE) in El Paso; Houston Light and Power (HLP) in Houston; Entergy in Beaumont; Southwestern Public Service Company (SPS) in Amarillo; and then Texas Utilities in Dallas.

17 See the company report at http://www.canelect.ca/en/pdf_Review_05/RA05_NScotia_P_eng.pdf

References

Achen, C. H. (1975) Mass Political Attitudes and the Survey Response, *American Political Science Review*, 69, 4: 1218–31.

—— (1983) Toward Theories of Data: The State of Political Methodology, in Finifter, A. W. (ed.), *Political Science: The State of the Discipline*, Washington, DC: APSA.

Ackerman, B. and Fishkin, J. S. (2004) *Deliberation Day,* New Haven, CT and London: Yale University Press.

Bishop, G. F. (2005) *The Illusion of Public Opinion: Fact and Artifact in American Public Opinion*, Lanham, MD: Rowman and Littlefield.

Blais, A., Carty, K. R. and Fournier, P. (2006) *Do Citizen Assemblies Make Reasonable Choices?*, Paper presented at the Princeton Conference on Deliberative Democracy: Princeton University, NJ.

Brehm, J. (1993) *The Phantom Respondents: Opinion Surveys and Political Representation*, Ann Arbor, MI: University of Michigan Press.

Buonocore, M. (2007) *The First Time in Italy*, *Reset*, 101 (May–June). (English translation provided by the author.) Available at http://cdd.stanford.edu/press/2007/reset-firstitaly-eng.pdf (accessed 10 April 2011).

Citizens' Assembly on Electoral Reform. (2004) *Making Every Vote Count: The Case for Electoral Reform in British Columbia*. Available at http://www.citizensassembly.bc.ca/resources/final_report.pdf (accessed 10 April 2011).

Converse, P. E. (1964) The Nature of Belief Systems in Mass Publics, in Apter, D. (ed.), *Ideology and Discontent*, New York: Free Press.

—— (1970) Attitudes and Non-attitudes: Continuation of a Dialogue, in Tufte, E. R. (ed.), *The Quantitative Analysis of Social Problems*, Reading, MA: Addison Wesley: 168–89.

de Tocqueville, A. (1863) [1961] *Democracy in America*, Vols I and II, New York: Schocken Books.

Delli Carpini, M. X. and Keeter, S. (1996) *What Americans Know About Politics and Why It Matters*, New Haven, CT: Yale University Press.

Farrar, C., Fishkin, J. S., Green, D. P., List, C., Luskin, R. C. and Paluck, E. L. (2010) Disaggregating Deliberation's Effects: An Experiment within a Deliberative Poll, *British Journal of Political Science*, 40: 333–47.

Fishkin, J. S. (1991) *Democracy and Deliberation: New Directions for Democratic Reform*, New Haven, CT: Yale University Press.

—— (1997) *The Voice of the People: Public Opinion and Democracy*, New Haven, CT: Yale University Press.

Fishkin, J. S. and Laslett, P. (2003) Avoiding Distortions: Polarization and Group Think, in Fishkin, J. S. and Laslett, P. (eds), *Debating Deliberative Democracy*, Oxford: Blackwell, Chapter 4.

—— (2003) Movement to Extremes?, in Fishkin, J. S. and Laslett, P. (eds), *Debating Deliberative Democracy*, Oxford: Blackwell.

Fishkin, J. S. and Luskin, R. C. (2005) Experimenting with a Democratic Ideal: Deliberative Polling and Public Opinion, *Acta Politica*, 40 (September): 284–98.

Fishkin, J. S., Gallagher, T., Luskin, R., McGrady, J., O'Flynn, I. and Russell, D. (2007) *A Deliberative Poll on Education: What Provision Do Informed Parents in Northern Ireland Want?* Available at http://cdd.stanford.edu/polls/nireland/2007/omagh-report.pdf, p. 32 (accessed October 2010).

Fishkin, J. S., Luskin, R. C., Panaretos, J., Siu, A, and Xekalaki, E. (2008) *Returning Deliberative Democracy to Athens: Deliberative Polling for Candidate Selection*, Paper presented at the annual meeting of the American Political Science Association. Available at http://cdd.stanford.edu/research/papers/2008/candidate-selection.pdf (accessed 10 April 2011).

Fishkin, J. S., He, B., Luskin, R. C. and Siu, A. (2010) Deliberative Democracy in an Unlikely Place, *British Journal of Political Science*, 40(2): 435–48.

Fraser, N. (1993) Rethinking the Public Sphere: A Contribution to the Critique of Actually Existing Democracy, in Robbins, B. (ed.) *The Phantom Public Sphere*, Minneapolis, MN: University of Minnesota Press.

Fung, A. and Lee, T. (2008) *The Difference Deliberation Makes: A Report on the CaliforniaSpeaks Statewide Conversations on Healthcare Reform*. Available at http://archonfung.net/docs/reports/CASpeaksReportFinalv3.pdf (accessed 11 April 2011).

Guild, W., Lehr, R. and Thomas, D. (2003) *Nebraska Public Power District Customer Meeting on Energy Alternatives Summary of Results*, Prepared by The Public Decision

Partnership. Available at http://cdd.stanford.edu/polls/energy/2003/nppdresults.pdf (accessed 11 April 2011).

—— (2004) *Nova Scotia Power Customer Energy Forum: Summary of Results*, 19–20 November 2004. Available at http://cdd.stanford.edu/polls/energy/2004/ns-results-summary.pdf (accessed 11 April 2011).

Gutmann, A. and Thompson, D. (2004) *Why Deliberative Democracy?*, Princeton, NJ: Princeton University Press.

Hill, J. and Kriesi, H. (2001) An Extension and Test of Converse's 'Black-and-White' Model of Response Stability, *American Political Science Review*, 95: 397–413.

Kinder, D. M. (1998) Opinion and Action in the Realm of Politics, in Gilbert, D. T., Fiske, S. T. and Gardner, L. (eds), *The Handbook of Social Psychology,* 4th ed. New York: McGraw-Hill.

Lehr, R .L., Guild, W., Thomas, D. L. and Swezey, B. G. (2003) *Listening to Customers: How Deliberative Polling Helped Build 1,000 MW of New Renewable Energy in Texas*, National Renewable Energy Laboratory.

Luskin, R. C. (1987) Measuring Political Sophistication, *American Journal of Political Science,* 31: 856–99.

Luskin, R. C., Fishkin, J. S. and Jowell, R. (2002) Considered Opinions: Deliberative Polling in the U.K., *British Journal of Political Science*. 32: 671–86.

Luskin, R. C., Fishkin, J. S. and Hahn, K. (2007a) *Consensus and Polarization in Small Group Deliberations*, Paper presented at meetings of the American Political Science Association, Chicago. Available at http://cdd.stanford.edu/research/papers/2007/consensus-polarization.pdf (accessed 11 April 2011).

—— (2007b) *Deliberation and Net Attitude Change*, Paper presented at the ECPR General Conference, Pisa, Italy.

Luskin, R. C., Crow, D. B., Fishkin, J. S., Guild, W. and Thomas, D. (2008) *Report on the Deliberative Poll® on 'Vermont's Energy Future'*, Center for Deliberative Opinion Research University of Texas at Austin. Available at http://cdd.stanford.edu/polls/energy/2008/vermont-results.pdf (accessed 11 April 2011).

Madison, J. (1787) *Federalist No. 10*. See http://en.wikisource.org/wiki/The_Federalist/10

Mansbridge, J. (1999) On the Idea that Participation Makes Better Citizens, in Elkin, S. L. and Soltan, K. E. (eds), *Citizen Competence and Democratic Institutions*, University Park, PA: Penn State University Press, 291–328.

Mill, J. S. 1861 [1991] *Considerations on Representative Government*, New York: Prometheus Books.

Nebraska Public Power District. (2003) *NPPD Board Approves State's Largest Wind Farm*. Available at http://www.nppd.com/Newsroom/NewsRelease.asp?NewsReleaseID=159 (accessed 11 April 2011).

Price, V. (2000) Political Information, in Robinson, J. P., Shaver, P. R. and Wrightsman, L. S. (eds), *Measures of Political Attitudes*, San Diego, CA: Academic Press.

Schkade, D., Sunstein, C. R. and Hastie, R. (2007) What Happened on Deliberation Day?, *California Law Review*, 95(3): 915–40.

Siu, A. (2009) *Look Who's Talking: Examining Social Influence, Opinion Change, and Argument Quality in Deliberation*, Doctoral dissertation. Available from ProQuest Dissertations and Theses database (UMI No. 3343885).

Sloan, M. (2007) *Testimony of Managing Consultant, The Wind Coalition, before the House Select Committee on Energy Independence and Global Warming*, Hearing on 'Renewable Electricity Standards: Lighting the Way', 20 September 2007. Available at http://globalwarming.house.gov/tools/assets/files/0038.doc (accessed 11 April 2011).

Sunstein, C. R. (2003) The Law of Group Polarization, in Fishkin, J. S. and Laslett, P. (eds), *Debating Deliberative Democracy*, Oxford: Blackwell: 80–101.
—— (2006) *Infotopia: How Many Minds Produce Knowledge*, Oxford: Oxford University Press.
Vermont Department of Public Service. (2009) *Vermont Comprehensive Energy Plan*. Available at http://publicservice.vermont.gov/planning/CEP%20%20WEB%20DRAFT%20FINAL%206-4-08.pdf (accessed 11 April 2011).
Young, I. M. (2000) *Inclusion and Democracy*, Oxford: Oxford University Press.

5 Deliberative democracy and mini-publics

Graham Smith

In the last three decades, we have witnessed increased experimentation with a family of democratic innovations that collectively have been termed 'mini-publics' (Goodin and Dryzek 2006): citizens' juries, planning cells, consensus conferences, deliberative polls and most recently Citizens' Assemblies. While there are some important differences, all models share significant design features: participants are selected using random sampling techniques; they are brought together for a period of between two to five days, except for Citizens' Assemblies which last much longer; facilitators aim to ensure fairness of proceedings; evidence is provided by expert witnesses, who are then cross-examined by participants; citizens are given an opportunity to deliberate amongst themselves in plenary and/or small group sessions before coming to decisions. There is a shared assumption amongst proponents of mini-publics that ordinary citizens are both 'willing and able to take important decisions in the public interest' (Coote and Mattinson 1997: 4).

Initially developed in the US in the 1970s by Ned Crosby (Crosby and Nethercut 2005), citizens' juries were widely popularized in the late 1990s, particularly amongst UK local government and health authorities (Coote and Lenaghan 1997; Smith and Wales 1999; Stewart et al. 1994). Citizens' juries typically bring together between twelve and twenty-four citizens who are required to develop recommendations in response to a 'charge' (one or more questions) set by the sponsoring organization. The process is facilitated by an independent organization. An interesting modification to jury practice is the Citizens Council established by the UK's National Institute for Clinical Excellence (NICE) in 2003. The Council has a degree of permanence, meeting twice a year for a long weekend to deliberate and provide advice on ethical and moral questions related to resource use and allocation in a health priority setting (Davies et al. 2006).

Around the same time that Crosby was developing the citizens' jury model, Peter Dienel was independently establishing the planning cell in Germany (Dienel and Renn 1995; Smith and Wales 1999; Hendriks 2005). Whilst often confused with citizens' juries, planning cells have some significant differences in design (see also Geissel in this volume). First, although each planning cell typically includes twenty-five citizens, they are usually run concurrently or in series, thus involving larger numbers of citizens. To date, the largest planning cell project involved around 500 citizens from across Germany. Second, Dienel is less concerned about the independence of facilitators, placing more emphasis on their ability to provide technical advice. Given the number of cells involved in any one project, Dienel believes that any influence on the part of particular facilitators will be marginal. Third, the larger number of cells and participants means that facilitators are responsible for collating an overall report drawn from the results of individual cells. Finally, Dienel requires commissioning organizations (typically public authorities) to enter into a contractual agreement to take into account the recommendations of the planning cell in future decisions, explaining publicly how and why recommendations were or were not followed. This practice has been adopted by many organizers of citizens' juries.

Consensus conferences have been run regularly since the 1980s by the Danish Board of Technology as a means of incorporating the perspectives of the lay public within the assessment of new scientific and technological developments that raise serious social and ethical concerns (Joss and Durant 1995; Joss 1998; Hendriks 2005). Consensus conferences differ from juries in two main respects. First, the organizers advertise for interested citizens from whom the panel is selected. Second, the participants attend two preparatory weekends where they are involved in the process of selecting the questions to be answered by the conference and relevant witnesses. As with juries, consensus conferences produce a report of their recommendations – in Denmark these are sent to members of parliament, scientists, interest groups and members of the public.

The deliberative poll is the creation of the well-known democratic theorist James Fishkin and the subject of a dedicated chapter elsewhere in this book (Fishkin and Luskin 2000; Fishkin and Farrar 2005; Fishkin 2009). Compared to the other mini-public designs, an individual deliberative poll can involve hundreds of citizens. Participants in deliberative polls hear evidence from witnesses who they are able to question in plenary sessions and have the opportunity to discuss issues and develop questions amongst themselves in facilitated small groups. The distinctive feature of deliberative polls is that citizens are not asked to craft collective recommendations, but instead to complete a questionnaire before and after the event – hence, organizers have a record of changes of opinion as citizens become more informed about the issues under consideration. For this reason, Fishkin perceives the design to be a development of the traditional polling method:

> Ordinary polls model what the public is thinking, even though the public may not be thinking very much or paying much attention. A deliberative poll attempts to model what the public *would* think, had it a better opportunity to consider the question at issue.
>
> (Fishkin 1997: 162)

Recently, Fishkin and his colleagues have begun to experiment with an online version of deliberative polling (Fishkin 2004; Iyengar et al. 2005; Luskin et al. 2006).[1]

In 2004, a step-change in the practice of mini-publics occurred when the government of British Columbia (with full support from the legislature) established the British Columbia Citizens' Assembly (BCCA) on Electoral Reform (Warren and Pearse 2008). In the wake of growing dissatisfaction with the democratic quality of recent election results, the BCCA was charged with reviewing the province's simple plurality electoral system and, if necessary, recommending an alternative system. The Assembly comprised 160 citizens: a female and male from each electoral district, plus two citizens with Aboriginal backgrounds. The BCCA can be understood as a development of previous mini-public models on two fronts. First, it met regularly over a period of eleven months during which time citizens were engaged in learning and deliberating about electoral reform. Over a series of weekends for the first four months (January to April), members learnt about electoral systems. For the next two months, members were involved in fifty hearings across the province, taking evidence from fellow citizens and interest groups. The Assembly also took 1,603 written submissions. Finally, between September and November 2004, the 160 participants discussed and debated competing electoral systems, before coming to a decision. After eleven months of work, the Assembly recommended that the current electoral system should be replaced by a version of single transferable vote (STV). In December 2004, the Assembly published its final report, *Making Every Vote Count*, which explained its activities and recommendation (Citizens' Assembly on Electoral Reform 2004).[2]

A second aspect of the design of the BCCA that takes us beyond the practice of earlier mini-publics was the government's commitment, made prior to the Assembly being established, to a binding province-wide referendum based on the Assembly's recommendation. As the Chair of the Assembly dramatically argued: 'Never before in modern history has a democratic government given to unelected, "ordinary" citizens the power to review an important public policy, and then seek from all citizens approval of any proposed changes to that policy' (Citizens' Assembly on Electoral Reform 2004: xiii).[3]

The referendum took place in May 2005, with the following question on the ballot: 'Should British Columbia change to the BC-STV electoral system as recommended by the Citizens' Assembly on Electoral Reform? Yes/No.' The government had placed two significant thresholds for the referendum to pass: at least sixty per cent of votes across the province needed to be in favour; and at least forty-eight (sixty per cent) of the seventy-nine electoral districts needed to vote in favour. The referendum passed the second threshold with seventy-seven districts in favour. However, the overall vote was 57.69 per cent, missing the first threshold by only 2.31 per cent. Given the close result, a second referendum was held in 2009. On this occasion the ballot was firmly defeated: the Yes vote was only 39 per cent of the popular vote with a majority in only eight electoral districts.[4]

Following in British Columbia's footsteps, the government of Ontario established its own Citizens' Assembly on Electoral Reform, which sat between September 2006 and April 2007. In its final report *One Ballot, Two Votes*, the Assembly recommends a mixed-member proportional (MMP) system (Ontario Citizens' Assembly on Electoral Reform 2007).[5] Again, this recommendation was put to a binding referendum in October 2007 with sixty-three per cent of voters rejecting the proposition.[6]

The Dutch Burgerforum Kiesstelsel – the Electoral System Civic Forum – which sat between March and November 2006 might be seen as a third example of the Citizens' Assembly model, although it differs in one important respect. While it was charged with reviewing and making recommendations on the electoral system of the Dutch Lower House, it was not linked to a referendum: it only had recommendatory force. The Civic Forum supported the continued use of proportional representation, but with a reform in the voting procedure (Electoral System Civic Forum 2006).

Deliberative democracy and mini-publics

Deliberative democracy remains the most influential development within contemporary democratic theory in the last couple of decades, generating a powerful theoretical critique of, and corrective to, the tendency within both democratic theory and practice to focus on the aggregation of preferences as the primary mode of legitimation. For deliberative democrats, the process of formation of preferences is fundamental to any account of democratic legitimacy. As James Bohman states, 'Deliberative democracy, broadly defined, is … any one of a family of views according to which the public deliberation of free and equal citizens is the core of legitimate political decision making and self-government' (Bohman 1998: 401). Amy Gutmann offers a similar construction: 'the legitimate exercise of political authority requires justification to those people who are bound by it, and decision-making by deliberation among free and equal citizens is the most defensible justification anyone has to offer for provisionally settling controversial issues' (Gutmann 1996: 344).

A few years ago, it was an accurate diagnosis of the deliberative democracy literature that it was strong on theoretical prescription, but had relatively little to say about institutional design (Smith 2003: 79). In a much cited review article published in the late 1990s, Bohman argues 'there is still a surprising lack of empirical case studies of democratic deliberation at the appropriate level and scale' (Bohman 1998: 419). The intervening years have witnessed a burgeoning literature that evaluates the deliberative qualities of various institutional arrangements, from the courts and legislatures of advanced industrial democracies (Gutmann and Thompson 1996), to the more informal networks and organizations of civil society (Schlosberg 1999; Dryzek 2000).

Mini-publics have been a growing focus of attention (e.g. Smith and Wales 2000; Gastil and Levine 2005; Parkinson 2006; Chambers 2007; Warren and Pearse 2008; Fishkin 2009), not least because they appear to realize a compelling combination of two democratic goods: inclusiveness and considered judgement. Inclusiveness – or political equality – is typically conceptualized by deliberative democrats in terms of both presence and voice: not only should the politically excluded be present in the political process, they should also have equal substantive opportunities to express their perspectives and influence decisions. Given our extensive knowledge of the uneven rates of political participation across social groups, achieving equality of presence is challenging enough;

responding to differentials in political skills, confidence and efficacy to ensure equality of voice raises the bar even higher. The practice of mini-publics attracts deliberative democrats because of their use of random sampling techniques that aim to ensure the presence of a diverse body of citizens, and active facilitation that encourages fairness in proceedings, in particular, support and encouragement for less confident and politically skilled participants to voice their perspectives.

Realizing considered judgement generates further pressures on institutional design in two senses. First, to counter critics of a Schumpeterian disposition, citizens need sufficient technical knowledge and understanding to make a sound decision. In all mini-publics, participants are exposed to competing expert viewpoints on the matter under consideration: witnesses offer their evidence and are cross-examined by participants. But, deliberative democrats ask even more of citizens: not only technical competence, but also an openness to and appreciation of the views of other citizens with quite different social perspectives and experiences (Offe and Preuss 1991: 168). Mini-publics are explicitly designed so that participants gain a level of technical understanding of the issue at hand *and* hear the perspectives of a diversity of fellow participants. Mini-publics create a 'safe haven' in which citizens are able to learn in both senses, away from the social and political pressures that typically shape our prejudices.

The encounter between the practice of mini-publics and deliberative democratic theory is productive on two fronts. First, it provides a theoretical perspective from which to evaluate a challenging mode of citizen engagement. To what extent do mini-publics live up to the expectations of deliberative democrats? At the same time, the actual practice of mini-publics enables us to interrogate the commitments and evaluative claims of democratic theorists and to open up areas for theoretical consideration that may have been overlooked in more abstract theoretical discourse. The analysis that follows will be ordered around a number of institutional characteristics of mini-publics that generate insights for both democratic theory and practice, namely:

- random selection
- facilitation
- decision rules
- publicity
- popular control.

Random selection

Arguably, the most striking aspect of mini-publics is the mode of selection.[7] Random selection (or sortition) has a long democratic heritage: it was the preferred method for selecting positions of political authority in the Athenian polis and continued to play a part in republican thought and practice throughout the Middle Ages and the Renaissance and into the seventeenth and eighteenth century (Manin 1997). Given this democratic heritage, it is perhaps surprising that it has played little or no role in contemporary politics, where selection by competitive elections is generally perceived to be the democratic mechanism of choice. The most prominent exception to this rule is the randomly selected jury used in a number of legal systems in advanced industrial democracies. For Athenians, lot and rotation gave full expression to the principle of democratic citizenship by providing the occasion for citizens to rule and be ruled in turn. As Barbara Goodwin notes, the 'choice of leaders by lot averted the danger that power would go to the rich or to those who desired it' (Goodwin 2005: 46). The use of random selection acts as a defence against oligarchic tendencies and realizes the democratic principle that any citizen is capable of political judgement (Barber 1984: 293).

Random selection replaces the principle of equal opportunity to participate that is the hallmark of open or popular assemblies with an equal *probability* of being selected to participate (Saward 2000: 16; Brown 2006: 212–13). Advocates argue that this is a just and acceptable restriction: where the opportunity to participate is to be limited, then random selection is a fair mechanism to distribute an ineradicable inequality (Goodwin 2005: 45). It is a mechanism that ensures that no citizen or social group from the given population is *systematically* excluded from participation.

In actual practice, mini-publics rely on 'near-random selection' (Warren and Pearse 2008: 6). There are three reasons why pure random selection is not achieved. The first two are well-known sampling problems that affect recruitment. The first relates to the incomplete nature of any database from which the sample of citizens is taken. For example, the initial sample for the BCCA was drawn from the province's voters' list. Not all residents of the province will or can be registered.

A second sampling problem relates to the element of self-selection in the recruitment process. Since none of the innovations can *require* participation, those who are invited can choose not to participate. In the case of the BCCA, citizens from a large random sample drawn from the electoral register were asked twice whether they would be willing to participate:

> The initial letter, mailed to 23,034 randomly chosen citizens, invited the recipients to decide if they wanted to participate in the Assembly process. Those who responded positively and then attended a selection meeting were again asked to confirm their willingness to commit to the project and accept the responsibilities of membership. The Assembly members were then chosen by lot from this group of attendees.
>
> (Citizens' Assembly on Electoral Reform 2004: 39)

From the initial 23,034 invitations, 1,715 citizens responded positively; 964 attended selection meetings; those who wished to participate were entered into a lottery.

There is a danger that such a low response rate will skew the sample and thus undermine the legitimacy of mini-publics. Organizers of the BCCA were confident that 'the final membership of the Assembly generally reflected the distribution of the provincial population' (Citizens' Assembly on Electoral

Reform 2004: 40). Similarly, the Ontario Assembly appeared to reflect many of the socio-demographic variations across the province, including place of birth, languages and occupations (Ontario Citizens' Assembly Secretariat 2007: 47). Experience from deliberative polls suggests that '[t]hose who decide to attend are usually somewhat more politically active and better educated than the initial sample' (Fishkin and Farrar 2005: 74). However, differences between the final sample and the wider population should not be exaggerated: the use of random selection ensures that participants are drawn from a range of social groups and are not simply the self-selecting few who typically engage in the political process.

The third reason why pure random selection is not achieved in most mini-publics is actually by design. The Citizens' Assemblies, citizens' juries and consensus conferences all use a form of stratified sampling. Quotas are assigned to particular social groups to ensure their presence and then participants from these groups are selected randomly. Pure random selection for a single mini-public (especially one small in size) is likely to lead to the absence of citizens from numerically small social groups and potential imbalances between other groups. While no systematic bias would have been in operation, the lack of presence of certain groups means that their perspectives may not be articulated or considered in deliberations, thus potentially affecting the perceived legitimacy of the body and its recommendations. The BCCA used three criteria – geographical district, gender and age – as the basis of quotas in its selection process. In comparison, citizens' juries and consensus conferences often stratify the sample to include other characteristics, for example, ethnicity, social class and – on occasion – political or social attitudes. Over-sampling of particular social characteristics ensures that the panel reflects politically salient characteristics from within the wider population. Given their larger size, deliberative polls and planning cells tend not to use quotas.

The failure of the BCCA to select on the basis of ethnicity may have had ramifications on the proceedings and the selection of a preferred electoral system. As Michael James argues: 'by stratifying for region and gender but not for race or ethnicity, citizen assemblies deliberating about electoral systems could potentially skew the agenda against the interests of racial or ethnic minorities and in favour of women and regional minorities' (James 2008: 180). There was official recognition that the selection process had failed to recruit citizens from aboriginal communities – hence the Assembly chair requested that two additional members be included in the process; a request that was granted (Citizens' Assembly on Electoral Reform 2004: 39). But there were no quotas for other potentially salient minority ethnic groups. Learning a lesson from British Columbia, the Ontario Assembly ensured that one self-defined Aboriginal citizen was selected, although, again, the presence of other minority ethnic groups was not considered significant.

If certain mini-public designs are not aiming to achieve as pure a random selection of the population as is practicable, precisely how much presence is required for different social groups? One or two participants from a particular group is unlikely to be adequate – for example, the two Aboriginal members who were recruited as an afterthought to the BCCA, or the single self-defined

Aboriginal member required in the Ontario Assembly. James argues that the presence of a 'critical mass' from minority social groups may be necessary for a number of reasons. First, to ensure that there are sufficient numbers to communicate effectively – one voice can become isolated in a large assembly. Second, to provide support and bolster the confidence of speakers who may be offering a perspective that is uncomfortable for other participants. Third, to ensure that the perspective is heard in the different locations within the body – for example, the various break-out groups in the BCCA. Finally, in recognition that there is likely to be a plurality of perspectives from within social groups – they are not homogenous and closed communities (James 2008: 120–23). Achieving critical mass may require significant over-representation of small minority social groups, something that is difficult to achieve (if not impossible if there are a number of groups) in smaller mini-publics such as citizens' juries and consensus conferences.

We are left with a series of difficult conundrums. How far should mini-publics move away from the principle of equal probability of selection (pure random selection) and towards stratified samples that ensure the presence and/or over-recruitment of particular social groups? Which social groups should be considered for quotas? And at what point do we achieve a critical mass for particular minority groups? These are highly pertinent theoretical and practical questions that demand further attention (and correspond to dilemmas faced by proponents of electoral quotas).

Once citizens agree to participate in mini-publics, evidence suggests that they typically do attend. Even the BCCA – which ran for eleven months and was thus more demanding than other designs – suffered only one withdrawal. Commenting on the recruitment process, the Assembly's final report suggests: 'This process appeared to create a sense of "buy-in" for the Assembly members that contributed significantly to their commitment to the process … the fact that only one member withdrew in the course of 11 intensive months, suggests that this process of recruitment deserves further examination' (Citizens' Assembly on Electoral Reform 2004: 39).

The use of random selection might be a significant factor in encouraging engagement, particularly amongst citizens from politically marginalized social groups. The formal invitation to participate in a selective forum, combined with a modest honorarium, appears to play a crucial role in motivating citizens' participation and support for the process. Citizens who typically do not participate in other forms of political activity are willing to engage in what are more intensive forms of political engagement. Citizens perceive they are being offered a rare opportunity to participate in a politically significant process. This was certainly the perception of participants in the NICE Citizen Council, where citizens reported that their motivation to participate was based on a variety of factors: on the belief that institutions should be more open to the public voice; that it is a public duty to make a contribution; and for reasons of personal growth and fulfilment. Citizens 'also frequently referred to a sense of being "privileged" to have been selected' (Davies et al. 2006: 80–1).

Random selection generates a variety of claims about the representativeness of mini-publics, although there are relatively few studies dedicated to exploring this issue in much theoretical depth (Brown 2006; Warren 2008). It is not uncommon to find practitioners and theorists claiming that mini-publics achieve statistical, descriptive or microcosm representation. This claim needs to be tempered on several accounts. First, the effect of the sampling problems involved in recruitment and the use of stratified sampling in many designs render such representative claims problematic (Parkinson 2006: 76). Second, descriptive representation is an unhelpful categorization because it often assumes that participants are somehow representing 'people like them' in a strong sense (Smith 2003: 91). There is a danger here of creating false essentialisms that fails to recognize that there are multiple perspectives within social groups. Jeffrey Abramson draws out the potential tension between representing a social group and achieving inclusive deliberation in relation to legal juries:

> We do not want to encourage jurors to see themselves as irreconcilably divided by race, selected only to fill a particular racial or gender slot on the jury. Yet we do want to encourage jurors to draw upon and combine their individual experiences and group backgrounds in the joint search for the most reliable and accurate verdict. The difference is subtle but real.
>
> (Abramson 1994: 11)

Abramson is pointing towards a different way in which mini-publics can be said to represent the broader public. Here, we can return to Fishkin's much repeated comment: 'A deliberative poll attempts to model what the public *would* think, had it a better opportunity to consider the question at issue' (Fishkin 1997: 162). Arguably this is a different sort of claim: a claim that mini-publics offer a representation of the public's considered judgement (Brown 2006: 216).

The use of random selection challenges our prejudices of what legitimate representation entails, but it does ensure that mini-publics engage a broad cross section of citizens with a diversity of social perspectives. The recruitment process generates a panel of highly motivated citizens who differ markedly from the highly skewed characteristics of citizens who routinely engage in consultation processes. For this reason alone, random selection deserves much more attention within theoretical work on institutional design (see also Geissel in this volume).

Facilitation

Random selection – with or without stratification of the sample – generates the diversity amongst participants that is a precondition for realizing the goods of inclusiveness and considered judgement. However, even a basic knowledge of group dynamics suggests that most participants will feel uncomfortable speaking in front of strangers and it is likely to be the more skilled and charismatic who will dominate proceedings. This is a long way removed from the respectful and reflective deliberation envisioned by theorists. Arguably, the most critical factor that enables the realization of equality of voice and considered judgement amongst participants is active facilitation. Given the significance of the facilitator, it is surprising that there has been little theorizing of this intermediary role.[8] For some, the reliance on such an intermediary has anti-democratic overtones – there is a danger that they will unduly influence or even manipulate the deliberations of participants. But it is difficult to conceive of free and fair deliberation within a diverse group of strangers without a degree of intervention from a third party. Sensitive facilitation is one way in which significant virtues, such as reciprocity, can be grounded and realized in practice (Thompson and Hoggett 2001: 359). The pertinent question would seem to be: what is and is not legitimate facilitation? An initial, but partial, response is that facilitators should be independent from the sponsoring organization: a degree of separation and freedom of operation for the facilitator is necessary as an initial step in avoiding the charge of elite manipulation.

Mini-publics are an unusual environment for citizens to find themselves in and many will feel incapable or unwilling to speak. Facilitators use a number of techniques to encourage and enable voice and considered judgement and ensure a degree of fairness. Typically, ground rules are established early in the proceedings, which remind citizens of the need to respect the views of others and to encourage participation by all those present (Smith and Wales 1999: 303; Citizens' Assembly on Electoral Reform 2004: 68). Such procedural values and rules set important parameters for acceptable behaviour amongst participants and provide an important reference point for facilitation. Where participants are involved in their drafting, they help citizens to develop a sense of ownership and control over the process (Davies and Sang 1998: 48; Thompson and Hoggett 2001: 359).

The larger mini-publics – Citizens' Assemblies and deliberative polls – hold plenary sessions where witnesses make presentations and are questioned. These can be particularly intimidating environments for the less confident, so the role of the facilitator in encouraging contributions is significant. In reviewing the plenary sessions of the BCCA, Dennis Thompson observes:

> equal respect does require that some positive steps be taken to ensure that the opportunities to speak are as equal as possible, and that the occasions for speech are as supportive as possible. The chair of the Assembly made creditable efforts to create an environment that encouraged extensive participation. He informally solicited members' views and encouraged them to speak in the public forums. In most of the sessions, before recognizing the more active members, he made sure that first-time speakers had the chance to participate.
>
> (Thompson 2008: 45)

Facilitators also break participants into smaller groups as a way of encouraging more reluctant citizens to contribute. The 160-strong BCCA often broke up into twelve facilitated discussion groups of between ten to fifteen citizens. Citizens were assigned randomly to these groups and the membership changed each weekend 'which helped members to get to know one another better while exposing them to a variety of perspectives' (Citizens' Assembly on Electoral Reform 2004: 66). In evaluating the work of the BCCA, participants noted that 'these small group discussions were crucial opportunities for learning, asking questions of clarification, sharing ideas, testing theories, building consensus, generating solutions, and so on' (Citizens' Assembly on Electoral Reform 2004: 240).

Deliberative polls also use small discussion groups, but the time in groups is limited and membership appears not to be rotated. Participants are therefore less likely to confront as many of the relevant differences in their group discussions and the limited time they spend together may not be enough 'to go through all the stages of breaking down barriers, expressing emotions freely, and searching for mutual understanding' (Parkinson 2006: 78). Here, the longer Citizens' Assembly model and smaller citizens' juries, consensus conferences and planning cells have a distinct advantage: in these smaller mini-publics facilitators also have the luxury of being able to break up participants even further into smaller groups of three or four, to provide more opportunities for individuals to speak and to understand the views of others.

Simon Thompson and Paul Hoggett are alert to the way in which different facilitation styles can affect the emotional dynamics of mini-publics: a non-interventionist 'hands-off' style can lead to domination by more vocal and confident citizens; a more interventionist, 'hands-on' approach that equalizes opportunities for voice may be too domineering. Both extremes undermine deliberation. As they note: 'There is an inherent tension in the role of the moderator that cannot easily be resolved' (Thompson and Hoggett 2001: 361; for an example, see Davies et al. 2006: 92). Similarly, facilitators make judgements about the extent to which different forms of discourse are valued: some facilitators may well value anecdotes and stories from participants; others may promote more reasoned and principled forms of debate. As difference theorists have been quick to point out, emphasis on more dispassionate forms of reasoning can itself silence the already marginalized, reinforcing illegitimate relations of power (Young 1990; Sanders 1996).

The operation of mini-publics suggests that the achievement of inclusiveness in the interactions between citizens requires a fairly structured environment, with clear rules and processes that orientate citizens towards mutual respect and reciprocity. Such virtues will not necessarily emerge naturally. The facilitator becomes a critical figure in the promotion of free and fair exchanges between citizens and orientating citizens towards public-spirited judgements. As such, the legitimacy of facilitation per se and the different facilitation techniques and styles of these democratic intermediaries are clearly worthy of further theoretical elaboration and reflection.

Decision rules

Mini-publics express a variety of different decision rules. At one end of the spectrum are citizens' juries and consensus conferences, where participants collectively craft recommendations in response to a charge; at the other end, deliberative polling, where participants offer individual responses to a survey instrument that is delivered pre- and post-deliberation. Somewhere in-between is the Citizens' Assembly model where participants develop solutions in response to a charge, but vote in private at the end of the process to decide the final recommendation. The relative impact of these decision rules on the preceding deliberation lacks systematic attention within the theoretical literature.

The structure of deliberative polling limits the potential for creativity amongst participants. While participants hear evidence from and are able to question competing experts, they are not in a position to develop alternative policy solutions: the preset questionnaire structures the output of the design. This entails the unlikely assumption that the survey instrument is able to capture the various potential directions that deliberations might take between participants and the different understandings of a policy issue that might emerge during the process. This is indicative of a significant difference in scope between deliberative polls and other designs: the function of the former is to provide a more informed sense of public opinion based on preordained questions; other mini-publics provide more freedom for citizens to develop recommendations for how to solve a current policy problem.

But the more open structure of other mini-publics may have its own unintended effects. First, there may be an implicit (or even explicit) pressure to achieve consensus between participants that suppresses conflict. The very name 'consensus conference' implies a search for areas of consensus on controversial issues of scientific and technology policy. As a project manager from the Danish Board of Technology stresses: 'every effort is made to attain the greatest consensus between the lay-panel members on the actions to be recommended. Minority opinions should be allowed only when the process reveals very wide differences of opinion' (Grundahl 1995: 37). There is a fine line between the search for consensus and the suppression of disagreement and much rests on the skills and approach of the facilitator – another reason why that particular role requires more theoretical attention.

We find growing concerns that the judgements of citizens in mini-publics may be shaped by irrational group dynamics, rather than reasoned argument (Merkle 1996: 607). Cass Sunstein offers an overview of relevant social psychology literature, arguing that deliberation in small groups may lead to group polarization – movement towards and adoption of more extreme positions (Sunstein 2000). He argues that there are two broad mechanisms at work: a reputational effect where participants aim to maintain their self-conception in relation to the group; and the effect of limited argument pools where participants tend to hear only arguments that reinforce their own point of view. However, his findings suggest that these tend to be properties of socially homogenous groups with a shared identity, rather than the more diverse groups that constitute mini-publics. Sunstein contrasts his findings with evidence from deliberative polls, which indicates that the nature of opinion change within the small discussion groups is not consistent with polarization (Sunstein 2000: 116; Luskin et al. 2002: 477–8; Ackerman and

Fishkin 2004: 61–5). The design of deliberative polls is a crucial factor in enabling depolarization: participants are highly diverse in their social perspectives; the process is facilitated to ensure openness; balanced information is provided; and citizens are not required to make decisions as a group – their opinions are sought in private. As Sunstein notes: 'Fishkin's experiments suggest that group polarization can be heightened, diminished, or possibly even eliminated by seemingly small alterations in institutional arrangements' (Sunstein 2000: 117; see also Fishkin in this volume).

But, as we have already noted, one of the characteristics isolated by Sunstein – citizens are polled individually – is not common to all mini-publics. The design of the BCCA shares this characteristic: while citizens worked together to evaluate different electoral systems, their final decisions were made through secret ballot. The extent to which the freedom to craft recommendations in citizens' juries and consensus conferences heightens the possibility of group polarization is a topic that deserves more attention and, again, arguably relates to the style of facilitation.

Publicity

Theories of deliberative democracy tend to emphasize publicity as a critical element of democratic practice. This is a pertinent consideration for mini-publics because whilst participants go through a process of mutual learning and reflection, the general public are rarely aware of the existence of these institutions. Rafe Mair, one of British Columbia's best-known political voices, suggests why publicity is important in discussing the BCCA:

> We should start with the thought that 160 of our fellow citizens, in an overwhelming favourable vote, and after the most careful of examination of plenty of evidence, have made a recommendation. While that doesn't mean we must agree with them – it does tell us that since none of us have gone through that exercise, we should give considerable weight to the recommendation made.
>
> (quoted in Cutler et al. 2008: 174)

Polling evidence from the 2005 referendum in British Columbia indicates the significance that publicity can have in the development of broader public opinion: those citizens who were aware of the BCCA were more likely to support the proposition in the referendum. Citizens tended to be influenced by the Assembly's expertise or the knowledge that a 'representative' group of ordinary citizens had come to a near consensus opinion (Cutler et al. 2008). However, publicity was far from fully realized: significant numbers of British Columbia voters remained oblivious to the existence and recommendations of the BCCA, as Amy Lang notes:

> With advance polls indicating that only one-third of the population had heard of the Citizens' Assembly or the referendum on electoral reform, one can

> imagine the surprise of many voters arriving at the ballot booth expecting to vote in a provincial election and being asked to approve or reject the voting system itself!
>
> (Lang 2007: 36)

Critics contend that the lacklustre and poorly funded referendum debate failed to raise the Assembly's profile. On this reading, the failure to fully realize publicity is the main reason why the proposition was rejected in 2005. This was reinforced in the 2009 rerun of the referendum, by which time the role and function of the Citizens' Assembly was arguably long-forgotten in the minds of most citizens.

If most citizens were unaware of the BCCA – a mini-public that ran its own consultation process, where all households received a summary of the final report and where many participants acted as ambassadors, undertaking media interviews and giving talks – we should not be surprised about the low level of public awareness of most other mini-publics that lack such outreach activities. One significant reason is the difficult relationship between mini-publics and the media. First, in most mini-publics, much of the deliberation takes place behind closed doors in small-group sessions: typically only the plenary sessions are open to the public and the media. While plenary sessions of the BCCA and a number of deliberative polls have been broadcast on television (usually on public broadcast channels) and on the internet, small-group sessions are generally held in private (although they have been filmed in the coverage of some deliberative polls). Removing the glare of the media is seen as important for creating an environment free from the pressures that can undermine open deliberation between citizens (Elster 1998; Chambers 2004).

Second, media interest depends on the salience of the issue under consideration (Parkinson 2006). The BCCA had an advantage compared to many other mini-publics. It was a high profile institution – the design had not been used before and it was considering a politically charged issue, one which had caused public conflict and disagreement. There was a general recognition that the existing electoral system was unsatisfactory, but little agreement amongst political elites about the necessary shape of reforms. But even then, the proceedings and recommendations of the Assemblies in British Columbia and Ontario did not receive as much media attention as might be expected, particularly given that they framed province-wide referendums.

In many ways, deliberative polling was designed with the media (in particular, television) in mind (Fishkin 1997: 175) and it has been reasonably successful in achieving television coverage: two National Issues Conventions were broadcast by PBS in the US before elections in 1996 and 2003 and deliberative polls have been broadcast in the UK by Channel 4 on subjects including the future of the monarchy and the National Health Service (NHS) and on ABC and Channel 9 in Australia as part of the run-up to the referendum on the republic. John Parkinson's analysis of the NHS poll in the UK raises concerns about the way in which public deliberation is, or even can be, captured on television. He argues that the dramatic structure imposed on the three-part broadcast tended to highlight areas of conflict and polarization – for example, between the competing health spokespersons for the three main political parties – and the strong personality of the celebrity chair of the plenary sessions (Parkinson 2006: 108–13). What makes good television does not necessarily reflect the virtues of deliberation:

> The issue here is not that the television crew failed to capture the vast majority of the actual deliberating; it is that they could not do so using the medium of television in an environment where the needs of the audience are a significant factor … media dramatisation limits the access viewers have to any reason-giving that went on between participants over the three days, which gives viewers little basis on which to judge the quality of conclusions to which the participants come.
>
> (Parkinson 2006: 112)

Rachel Gibson and Sarah Miskin offer a complementary analysis of the way that the Australian deliberative poll was televised, arguing that the crucial decisions about the structure and scheduling of the event 'were clearly made in deference to media concerns rather than for the optimal knowledge gathering and deliberation on the part of poll participants' (Gibson and Miskin 2002: 169). The current affairs program *60 Minutes* was, like Channel 4 in the UK, highly selective in what it considered newsworthy (ibid.: 173). Gibson and Miskin highlight a paradox inherent in deliberative polling (and arguably in the practice of mini-publics more generally): Fishkin has long been a critic of the manner in which media coverage (especially the focus on ever-shorter sound bites) undermines the possibility of democratic deliberation (Fishkin 1991: 62–3), and yet he must rely on the self same media to publicize the poll's existence and findings (Gibson and Miskin 2002: 172).

Popular control

Arguably, popular control is a neglected democratic good within theories of deliberative democracy. Although the familiar definitions of Bohman and Gutmann that we offered earlier in this chapter explicitly link deliberation among free and equal citizens with the legitimacy of decision making, much of the theoretical work on deliberative democracy separates these two considerations. For example, Jurgen Habermas locates will-formation in the informal public sphere, while decision making takes place elsewhere in the institutions of government (Habermas 1996; Squires 2002). John Dryzek's reinterpretation of deliberative democracy explicitly warns against the co-option and absorption of authentic deliberation by the state. As such, his theory of discursive democracy completely avoids questions of institutional decision making by locating deliberation within networks of civil society, in particular within new social movements (Dryzek 2000). In both accounts, deliberation is considered an ongoing process of mutual understanding and a direct relationship with formal decision making is liable to undermine the dynamics of deliberation: rather than focus on achieving mutual understanding, instrumental calculations will come to the fore and public authorities and other actors are likely to engage in agenda-setting strategies. There is a tension between the goods of mutual understanding and efficiency (Chambers, 1995: 241; Mansbridge 1996: 47).

This tension between deliberation and decision in theoretical debates is to a certain degree mirrored in the practice of mini-publics, where the record of impact on political decision making is patchy at best. As Robert Goodin and John Dryzek admit, cases of mini-publics 'actually making policy … when a forum is formally empowered as part of a decision-making process' are rare (Goodin and Dryzek 2006: 7). In this sense, mini-publics appear to be nothing more than a fairly sophisticated method of public consultation. Even writers such as Fishkin – amongst the most vociferous promoters of mini-publics – recognize that the lack of formal accountability mechanisms would likely lead to a legitimacy problem and, therefore, argue that mini-publics (in his case deliberative polls) can have at best only recommendatory force:

> A deliberative poll is not meant to describe or predict public opinion. Rather it prescribes. It has recommendatory force: these are the conclusions people would come to, were they better informed on the issues and had the opportunity and motivation to examine those issues seriously.
>
> (Fishkin 1997: 162)

But this generates problems. How much effect do mini-publics actually have on the political process (see also Geissel in this volume)? Is there any meaningful relationship between the outputs of mini-publics and political decision making? Even in Denmark, where consensus conferences are organized by the Board of Technology, evidence is mixed (Joss 1998). While there is evidence that the recommendations of specific conferences have had some impact – for example, the exclusion of transgenic animals from the first governmental biotechnology research and development program following a consensus conference on genetic engineering in industry and agriculture (Klüver 1995: 44) – others had no recognizable material effect. Planning cells appear to have had fairly significant effects at the local and regional level in Germany, although 'independent evaluations are scarce' (Hendriks 2005: 92). Fishkin makes strong claims that the results of deliberative polls run for Texas utilities 'led to further investments in natural gas (which was regarded as relatively clean) and in renewable energy. In fact, the decisions resulting from the Deliberative Polls made Texas a national leader in renewable energy' (Ackerman and Fishkin 2004: 46). However, a more cautious assessment states that 'it would be disingenuous to suggest that the results of the deliberative polling process alone were responsible for the regulatory and legislative changes that followed' (Lehr et al. 2003 quoted in Goodin and Dryzek 2006: 9). We need to recognize that it is generally difficult to ascertain the impacts of mini-publics on substantive policy outcomes. As Carolyn Hendriks argues:

> Citizens' reports are conceived as advisory, and their recommendations invariably compete with other forms of advice from political parties, expert

> committees, and interest groups, for example. Moreover, when some of these other sources of policy advice happen to recommend the same policies and celebrate the same values articulated in the citizens' reports, it can be difficult to determine which recommendation held more sway.
>
> (Hendriks 2005: 91)

There is reasonable concern that commissioning bodies will simply 'cherry-pick' those recommendations or trends in opinions that support their perspective, while ignoring those that are uncomfortable. In recognition of this potential problem, Dienel developed the practice of drawing up a contract between the commissioning body, the organizers and the participants of planning cells, requiring the former to explain within a certain time frame how it has responded to the recommendations of the citizens' report. This practice has been picked up by other mini-publics, in particular citizens' juries, although in reality it still leaves a great deal of room for manoeuvre on the part of sponsors.

The BCCA (and its Ontario cousin) can be seen as the exception to the rule in that its recommendation on electoral reform formed the basis of a province-wide referendum that the government had committed itself to implement if the proposition passed. The mini-public's deliberations and decision were explicitly tied to a public ratification process. This is a significant development in the practice of mini-publics and responds directly to those theorists who are troubled by the way that mini-publics lack traditional mechanisms of accountability. It also points to the potential for creative integration of different democratic innovations, such that more compelling combinations of democratic goods are realized. Mini-publics are celebrated for the manner in which they realize inclusiveness and considered judgement, but there is normally a failure to realize popular control in any strong sense. Direct legislation on the other hand receives a hostile reception amongst theorists of deliberative democracy because it embeds a form of majoritarianism that hinders the cultivation of mutuality and reciprocity (Chambers 2001; Dalton et al. 2001; Parkinson 2001; Uhr 2002). However, it is a rare institutional form that realizes popular control. By integrating mini-publics and direct legislation, we can begin to construct creative combinations of innovations that realize more compelling combinations of democratic goods. Using the language of democratic principles, rather than goods, Michael Saward suggests: 'the single most important question when thinking through the new possibilities for democracy is this: *which devices, singly and in combination, enact desired interpretations of democratic principles within and across the different stages of the decision-making process?*' (Saward 2003: 168).

Such combinations of innovations may also open up new ways of thinking about democratic theory – for example, a reappraisal of the potential connections between deliberative and direct theories of democracy. These two theories are often seen as highly antagonistic: the BCCA sequence (and other possible combinations) may indicate areas of productive mutual engagement (Saward 2001). As Saward has argued, 'devices favoured by advocates of particular "models" of democracy may be combined in new ways to enact new styles of democracy' (Saward 2003: 169).

Concluding remarks

This chapter hopefully demonstrates that there is practical and theoretical value in evaluating mini-publics in light of developments in democratic theory. This is not to claim that mini-publics are a complete expression of deliberative democracy; that they are the only democratic innovation that has deliberative qualities; or that deliberative democracy is the only significant theoretical development. Rather, it is a more limited assertion that by studying the actual practice of institutions, we are in a better position to interrogate the evaluative claims of democratic theory and to open up areas of theoretical inquiry that may have been overlooked at a more abstract level of analysis. So, for example, our analysis of mini-publics suggests that the realization of the goods of inclusiveness and considered judgement can come at the cost of the effective realization of publicity and popular control. While the innovative design of the BCCA offers one way in which the deliberations of a mini-public can be tied to a public ratification process, it still proved difficult to achieve effective levels of public awareness and its very existence relied on a (rare) willingness of the executive to experiment with a new form of public participation. No single design can realize all the democratic goods we value; any design is a compromise. At more abstract theoretical levels, democratic theorists can ignore such compromises: analyzing the actual practice of institutions forces us to reassess our theoretical claims and commitments.

We did not have to focus on mini-publics: there are plenty of other democratic innovations worthy of investigation (Smith 2005). The relatively small, but growing literature that attempts to bridge the disciplinary gap between normative theory and empirical political analysis through the evaluation of democratic innovations, includes not only studies of mini-publics, but also other institutional designs such as participatory budgeting, community policing and schooling, direct legislation, and so on (Fung 2003; Fung and Wright 2003; Smith 2009). A number of these designs are discussed elsewhere in this collection. The promise is two-fold: the emergence of democratic theory that better reflects practical design choices; and a better understanding of what democratic participation might mean and become.

Notes

1 For up-to-date information on deliberative polls, see http://cdd.stanford.edu/.
2 The Citizens' Assembly's dedicated website provides reports, videos and other information: http://www.citizensassembly.bc.ca/.
3 There is a striking similarity between the design of the BCCA and the randomly selected advisory councils or 'mini-populus' that Robert Dahl has on occasion promoted (Dahl 1970: 149–53; 1989: 340). One significant difference, however, is that Dahl envisioned these as advisory bodies, not connected to a binding referendum (Smith 2009).

4 See http://www.elections.bc.ca/index.php/referenda-recall-initiative/referenda/ for details of the referendum results.
5 See the Assembly's dedicated website for reports, videos and other information http://www.citizensassembly.bc.ca/public.
6 Available at http://www3.elections.on.ca/internetapp/realtimereferendum.aspx?lang=en-ca&gf73=0&contestid=2&channel_id={923146e7-4d81-42a8-99f0-e61f5ab50387}&lang=enm.
7 A rare example of the use of random selection beyond mini-publics is the appointment process for Community Fund regional boards in England (Smith 2005: 61–2). The irony is that this public body uses a form of lottery to select citizens to sit on boards that make decisions about the distribution of national lottery funds!
8 John Forester (1999) is a rare theorist who has focused attention on the role of democratic facilitation, but predominantly within the planning process – a context very different from mini-publics.

References

Abramson, J. (1994) *We, The Jury*, New York: Basic Books.

Ackerman, B. and Fishkin, J. S. (2004) *Deliberation Day*, New Haven, CT: Yale University Press.

Barber, B. (1984) *Strong Democracy: Participatory Politics for a New Age*, Berkeley, CA: California University Press.

Bohman, J. (1998) The Coming of Age of Deliberative Democracy, *Journal of Political Philosophy* 6: 400–25.

Brown, M. B. (2006) Survey Article: Citizens Panels and the Concept of Representation, *Journal of Political Philosophy* 14: 203–25.

Chambers, S. (1995) Discourse and Democratic Practices, in White, Stephen K. (ed.) *The Cambridge Companion to Habermas*, Cambridge: Cambridge University Press.

Chambers, Simone (2001) Constitutional Referendums and Democratic Deliberation, in Mendelsohn, M. and Parkin, A. (eds) *Referendum Democracy: Citizens, Elites, and Deliberation in Referendum Campaigns*, Basingstoke: Palgrave.

Chambers, S. (2004) Behind Closed Doors: Publicity, Secrecy, and the Quality of Deliberation, *The Journal of Political Philosophy* 12: 289–410.

—— (2007) Quantity Versus Quality: Dilemmas of Mass Democracy, *Centre for the Study of Democratic Institutions Working Paper: Citizen Engagement No. 3.* Available at http://democracy.ubc.ca/fileadmin/template/main/images/departments/CSDI/working_papers/ChambersCSDIWorkingPaper2007CE3.pdf (accessed 11 April 2011).

Citizens' Assembly on Electoral Reform (2004) *Making Every Vote Count: The Case for Electoral Reform in British Columbia (Technical Report)*. Vancouver: Citizens' Assembly on Electoral Reform.

Coote, A. and Lenaghan, J. (1997) *Citizens' Juries: Theory into Practice*, London: IPPR.

Coote, A. and Mattinson, D. (1997) *Twelve Good Neighbours*, London: Fabian Society.

Crosby, N. and Nethercut, D. (2005) Citizens Juries: Creating a Trustworthy Voice of the People, in Gastil, J. and Levine, P. (eds) *The Deliberative Democracy Handbook: Strategies for Effective Civic Engagement in the 21st Century*, San Francisco, CA: Jossey-Bass.

Cutler, F., Johnston, R., Carty, K., Blais, A. and Fournier, P. (2008) Deliberation, Information and Trust: The BC Citizens' Assembly as Agenda-Setter, in Warren, M. E. and Pearse, H. (eds) *Designing Deliberative Democracy: The British Columbia Citizens' Assembly*, Cambridge: Cambridge University Press.

Dahl, R. (1970) *After the Revolution*, New Haven, CT: Yale University Press.
—— (1989) *Democracy and its Critics*, New Haven, CT: Yale University Press.
Dalton, R. J., Burklin, W. and Drummond, A. (2001) Public Opinion and Direct Democracy, *Journal of Democracy* 12: 141–53.
Davies, C., Wetherell, M. and Barnett, E. (2006) *Citizens at the Centre: Deliberative Participation in Healthcare Decisions*, Bristol: Polity Press.
Davies, S. and Sang, B. (1998) Facilitating a Citizens' Jury, in Davies, S., Elizabeth, S., Hanley, B., New, B. and Sang B. (eds) *Ordinary Wisdom; Reflections on an Experiment in Citizenship and Health Care*, London: King's Fund.
Dienel, P. and Renn, O. (1995) Planning Cells: A Gate to 'Fractal' Mediation, in Renn, O., Webler, T. and Wiedemann P. (eds) *Fairness and Competence in Citizen Participation: Evaluating Models for Environmental Discourse*, Dordrecht: Kluwer.
Dryzek, J. (2000) *Deliberative Democracy and Beyond*, Oxford: Oxford University Press.
Electoral System Civic Forum (2006) *Recommendations*, Electoral System Civic Forum, The Netherlands.
Elster, J. (1998) Deliberation and Constitution Making, in Elster, J. (ed.) *Deliberative Democracy*, Cambridge: Cambridge University Press.
Fishkin, J. S. (1991) *Democracy and Deliberation*, New Haven, CT: Yale University Press.
—— (1997) *The Voice of the People*, Durham: Duke University Press.
—— (2004) *Online 'Deliberative Poll' Gives Picture of Informed Public Opinion in Election*, San Francisco, CA: Center for Deliberative Democracy, Stanford University.
—— (2009) *When the People Speak: Deliberative Democracy and Public Consultation*, Oxford: Oxford University Press.
Fishkin, J. S. and Farrar, C. (2005) Deliberative Polling, in Gastil, J. and Levine, P. (eds) *The Deliberative Democracy Handbook: Strategies for Effective Civic Engagement in the 21st Century*, San Francisco, CA: Jossey Bass.
Fishkin, J. S. and Luskin, R. C. (2000) The Quest for Deliberative Democracy, in Saward, M. (ed.) *Democratic Innovation: Deliberation, Representation and Association*, London: Routledge.
Forester, J. (1999) *The Deliberative Practitioner: Encouraging Participatory Planning Processes*, Cambridge, MA: MIT Press.
Fung, A. (2003) Survey Article: Recipes for Public Spheres: Eight Institutional Design Choices and Their Consequences, *Journal of Political Philosophy* 11: 338–67.
Fung, A. and Wright, E. O. (eds) (2003) *Deepening Democracy: Institutional Innovations in Empowering Participatory Governance*, London and New York: Verso.
Gastil, J. and Levine, P. (eds) (2005) *The Deliberative Democracy Handbook: Strategies for Effective Civic Engagement in the 21st Century*, San Francisco, CA: Jossey-Bass.
Gibson, R. K and Miskin, S. (2002) Australia Decides? The Role of the Media in Deliberative Polling, in Warhurst, J. and Mackerras, M. (eds) *Constitutional Politics*, St. Lucia: Queensland Press.
Goodin, R. E. and Dryzek, J. S. (2006) Deliberative Impact: The Macro-political Uptake of Mini-Publics, *Politics and Society* 34: 1–26.
Goodwin, B. (2005) *Justice by Lottery*, Exeter: Imprint Academic.
Grundahl, J. (1995) The Danish Consensus Conference Model, in Joss, S. and Durant, J. (eds) *Public Participation in Science: The Role of Consensus Conferences in Europe*, London: Science Museum.
Gutmann, A. (1996) Democracy, Philosophy, and Justification, in Benhabib, S. (ed.) *Democracy and Difference*, Princeton, NJ: Princeton University Press.

Gutmann, A. and Thompson, D. (1996) *Democracy and Disagreement*, Harvard, MA: Harvard University Press.

Habermas, J. (1996) *Between Facts and Norms*, Cambridge: Polity.

Hendriks, C. M. (2005) *Consensus Conferences and Planning Cells*, San Francisco, CA: Jossey-Bass.

Iyengar, S., Luskin, R. C., and Fishkin, J. S. (2005) *Deliberative Preferences in the Presidential Nomination Campaign: Evidence from an Online Deliberative Poll*, Paper available from The Center for Deliberative Democracy, Stanford University. Available at http://cdd.stanford.edu/research/index.html (accessed 11 April 2011).

James, M. R. (2008) Descriptive Representation in Citizen Assemblies, in M. E. Warren and H. Pearse (eds) Designing Deliberative Democracy: The British Columbia Citizens' Assembly, Cambridge: Cambridge University Press.

Joss, S. (1998) Danish Consensus Conferences as a Model in Participatory Technology Assessment: An Impact Study of Consensus Conferences on Danish Parliament and Danish Public Debate, *Science and Public Policy, 25*(1), 2–22.

Joss S. and Durant J. (eds) (1995) *Public Participation in Science: The Role of Consensus Conferences in Europe*, London: Science Museum.

Klüver, L. (1995) Consensus conferences at the Danish Board of Technology, in Simon, J. and Durant J. (eds) *Public Participation in Science: The Role of Consensus Conferences in Europe*, London: Science Museum.

Lang, A. (2007) But is it for Real? The British Columbia Citizens' Assembly as a Model of State-sponsored Citizen Empowerment, *Politics and Society* 35: 35–69.

Luskin, R. C., Fishkin, J. S. and Jowell, R. (2002) Considered Opinions: Deliberative Polling in Britain, *British Journal of Political Science* 32: 455–87.

Luskin, R. C., Fishkin, J. S. and Iyengar, S. (2006) *Considered Opinions on U.S. Foreign Policy: Face-to-Face versus Online Deliberative Polling*, Paper available from The Center for Deliberative Democracy, Stanford University. Available at http://cdd.stanford.edu/research/index.html (accessed 11 April 2011).

Manin, B. (1997) *The Principles of Representative Government*, Cambridge: Cambridge University Press.

Mansbridge, J. (1996) Using Power/Fighting Power, in Benhabib, S. (ed.) *Democracy and Difference*, Princeton, NJ: Princeton University Press.

Merkle, D. M. (1996) The National Issues Convention Deliberative Poll, *Public Opinion Quarterly* 60: 588–619.

Offe, C. and Preuss, U. K. (1991) Democratic Institutions and Moral Resources, in Held, D. (ed.) *Political Theory Today*, Cambridge: Polity.

Ontario Citizens' Assembly on Electoral Reform (2007) *One Ballot, Two Votes: A New Way to Vote in Ontario*, Ontario Citizens' Assembly on Electoral Reform.

Ontario Citizens' Assembly Secretariat (2007) *Democracy at Work: The Ontario Citizens' Assembly on Electoral Reform*, Ontario Citizens' Assembly on Electoral Reform.

Parkinson, J. (2001) Deliberative Democracy and Referendums, in Dowding, K., Hughes, J. and Margetts, H. (eds) *Challenges to Democracy*, Basingstoke: Palgrave.

—— (2006) *Deliberating in the Real World: Problems of Legitimacy in Deliberative Democracy*, Oxford: Oxford University Press.

Sanders, L. (1996) Against Deliberation, *Political Theory* 25: 347–76.

Saward, M. (2000) *Direct and Deliberative Democracy*, Paper presented at the Copenhagen ECPR Joint Sessions.

—— (2001) Making Democratic Connections: Political Equality, Deliberation and Direct Democracy, *Acta Politica* 36: 361–79.

—— (2003) Enacting Democracy, *Political Studies* 51: 161–79.

Schlosberg, D. (1999) *Environmental Justice and the New Pluralism: The Challenge of Diversity for Environmentalism*, Oxford: Oxford University Press.

Smith, G. (2003) *Deliberative Democracy and the Environment*, London: Routledge.

—— (2005) *Beyond the Ballot: 57 Democratic Innovations from Around the World*, London: Power Inquiry. Available at http://www.powerinquiry.org/publications/documents/BeyondtheBallot_000.pdf (accessed 11 April 2011).

—— (2009) *Democratic Innovations: Designing Institutions for Citizen Participation*, Cambridge: Cambridge University Press.

Smith, Graham and Wales, C. (1999) The Theory and Practice of Citizens' Juries, *Policy and Politics* 27: 295–308.

—— (2000) Citizens' Juries and Deliberative Democracy, *Political Studies* 48: 51–65.

Squires, J. (2002) Deliberation and Decision-Making: Discontinuity in the Two-Track Model, in Passarin D'Entreves, M. (ed.) *Democracy as Public Deliberation: New Perspectives*, Manchester: Manchester University Press.

Stewart, J., Kendall, E. and Coote, A. (1994) *Citizens' Juries*, London: IPPR.

Sunstein, C. R. (2000) Deliberative Trouble? Why Groups go to Extremes, *Yale Law Journal* 110: 71–119.

Thompson, D. (2008) Who Should Govern Who Governs? The Role of Citizens in Reforming the Electoral System, in Warren, M. E. and Pearse, H. (eds) *Designing Deliberative Democracy: The British Columbia Citizens' Assembly*, Cambridge: Cambridge University Press.

Thompson, S. and Hoggett, P. (2001) The Emotional Dynamics of Deliberative Democracy, *Policy and Politics* 29: 351–64.

Uhr, J. (2002) Rewriting the Referendum Rules, in Warhurst, J. and Mackerras, M. (eds) *Constitutional Politics*, St Lucia: University of Queensland Press.

Warren, M. E. (2008) Citizen Representatives, in Warren, M. E. and Pearse, H. (eds) *Designing Deliberative Democracy: The British Columbia Citizens' Assembly*, Cambridge: Cambridge University Press.

Warren, M. E. and Pearse, H. (2008) Introduction, in Warren, M. E. and Pearse, H. (eds) *Designing Deliberative Democracy: The British Columbia Citizens' Assembly*, Cambridge: Cambridge University Press.

Young, I. M. (1990) *Justice and the Politics of Difference*, Princeton, NJ: Princeton University Press.

6 Deliberation as an ideal and practice in progressive social movements

Dieter Rucht

Power, defined by Max Weber as the capacity to impose one's will against the will of one or several others, appears to be ubiquitous. It can be found not only in clear-cut hierarchical settings such as the military and bureaucracies but also, though often in more subtle forms, in voluntary associations, families, partnerships and youth gangs. This, however, does not mean that every concrete interaction is dominated by power relations. Just consider a decision of close friends where and when to meet next, a casual chat among neighbours about gardening, or two scholars debating the validity of an argument. However, the establishment of some sort of power as a structural feature is probably inevitable when it comes to groups or organizations that develop a certain degree of division of labour and repeatedly, or even routinely, have to solve internal conflicts and take decisions. Therefore, power is often considered to be 'natural' or 'necessary'.

But what is the role of power in social groups that, based on their political ideology, promote equality, solidarity and self-determination within their own ranks at least? Such groups are especially frequent among various social and political movements that locate themselves in a leftist, liberal or emancipatory tradition and, for the lack of a better term, might be called 'progressive'. As a rule, they invest considerable energy in minimizing or even abolishing internal power structures. Instead of embracing strong leadership or taking decisions based on the majority rule, they seek to reach, in a process of deliberation, a consensus in which, ideally, every participant full-heartedly agrees.

Whatever the ambitions and self-descriptions of such groups, as social scientists we cannot take them at face value. First, promoting an idealized self-image may be part of a deliberate tactic to strengthen internal cohesion and/or to attract newcomers. Second, a group's positive self-image may also result from blind spots that become visible only from the perspective of a scientifically trained and emotionally detached observer. Third, power, because of its negative image in some groups, may occur in subtle or more disguised forms so that it is difficult to identify for both activists and scientific observers.

In the following, I will present and discuss both the ideals and practices regarding power and deliberation in several progressive movements from the labour movement in the 20th century to the contemporary Global Justice Movements. Given the enormous breadth of this field, the limited space of a book chapter and, last but not least, the lack of systematic data, I can only draw a rough picture. Whenever available and appropriate, I try to provide empirical illustrations for more general phenomena. Quantitative data on communicative practices are available only for Global Justice Movements. However, before moving to the empirical sections of this chapter, first some conceptual clarifications and theoretical assumptions will be offered. This is especially needed because key terms such as power, deliberation and democracy have multiple meanings and their relationship is far from clear.

Conceptual clarifications and theoretical reflections[1]

Deliberation is not a term of everyday language. Rather, it belongs to the domains of political philosophy and social sciences. In its broadest sense, deliberation refers to an individual operation or interactive process in which claims and/or arguments are submitted to scrutiny and reflection. In a more narrow understanding that is adopted here, deliberation is a specific way of interaction resulting from a conflict or disagreement. This interaction is characterized by a respectful articulation of claims, viewpoints, arguments and experiences among the participants who ultimately seek a grounded judgement on the validity and legitimacy of their positions. At any rate, all concepts of deliberation set it apart from the use of power based on coercion, hierarchy, threat, manipulation and the like.

Deliberation, translated into the language of movement activists, roughly equals what they term 'democratic debate', 'democratic decision making' and/or 'consensus-building'. When applying notions of 'democracy' or 'democratic' with respect to their own structure and internal ways of solving conflicts and making decisions, these activists usually imply a specific meaning of democracy. It is not democracy as an institutionalized framework based on the election of representatives, the rival interplay between government and opposition, and the reliance on the majority rule. Rather, the activists refer to communication among equals who, preferably under conditions of absent or minimized internal power structures, actively participate in regulating their own affairs without repressing or marginalizing dissenters.

Scholarly literature has provided different conceptualizations of deliberation and how it is linked to democracy. Probably the most prominent and influential approach has been presented by Jürgen Habermas who, in his early writings, used the term *discourse* instead of deliberation. According to him, discourse (or deliberation) is a specific form of communication. It presupposes a conflict or disagreement that it aims to settle by means of specific requirements and rules that, taken together, produce an 'ideal speech situation'. These requirements are: free access to deliberation, identity of meaning and saying (*Wahrhaftigkeit*), comprehensibility (*Verständlichkeit*) of speech acts, and elimination of all forms of power except the '*forceless force of the better argument*' (Habermas 1971: 137, my translation).[2]

Habermas' concept of deliberation received mixed reactions. Some praised it as key for rational conflict-solving and a model for public debates in democracies. Others criticized the concept for its normative baggage, its alleged unreal assumptions[3] and/or its cognitive bias.[4] However, most scholars tend to agree that coercion, hierarchy, inequality and other forms of power violate the very idea of deliberation. In line with this idea, several social scientists have suggested various essentials for deliberation. Burkhalter et al. (2002: 398) define public deliberation as 'a combination of careful problem analysis and an egalitarian process in which participants have adequate speaking opportunities and engage in attentive listening or dialogue that bridges divergent ways of speaking and knowing'. Della Porta (2005: 74), drawing on various strands of the literature, lists preference transformation, orientation to the public good, rational argument, consensus, equality, inclusiveness and transparency. Overlapping with such proposals, I characterize deliberation as an interaction of speakers who (1) do not exclude other people willing to speak, (2) consider themselves as equal in their potential to reason, (3) present experiences, facts and arguments, and (4) are open to modify their original views, attitudes and opinions in reaction to the perceptions and reasons of others. In short, deliberation is a non-exclusive discursive interaction in a spirit of mutual recognition, understanding and search for a consensus instead of playing power games.

Deliberation and democracy

Deliberation, understood in this way, is by no means a trivial matter. If it occurs at all, it will be in small and homogenous groups rather than in large settings with highly different actors promoting strong and vested interests. But it may even fail in small groups when the participants are willing to act in good faith but, for whatever reasons, are unable to reach a consensus. Still, some political philosophers and social scientists are propagating the idea of deliberation at a large scale: the idea of a deliberative democracy (Cohen 1989; Bohman 2000; Dryzek 2000; for an overview: Chambers 2003; Thompson 2008; see also Fishkin and Smith in this volume). And, of course, there are also political groups who not only wish to practise deliberation among their own ranks but strive, though not necessarily using this term, for a deliberative democracy.

Even when we have a reasonably clear idea what deliberation means, what deliberative *democracy* is still remains open. This uncertainty does not only result from the different definitions and empirical variations of democracy, but also from the different weight of deliberation in various forms of democracy. In most conceptions of democracy, deliberation is not mentioned or plays only a marginal role. In others, it is a constitutive element and, in the words of a non-governmental group Tomorrow's Europe, 'the lifeblood of democracy'.[5] A similar view is expressed by Cohen (1989: 144) who states: 'When properly conducted, democratic politics involves public deliberation focused on the common good, requires some form of manifest equality among citizens, and shapes the identity and interest of citizens in ways that contribute to the formation of a public conception of common good.'

Some authors, for example Gerhards (1997), broadly distinguish between a representative-liberal and a deliberative (or discursive) concept of democracy, often implying that the latter is based, or even identical with, broad and extensive citizen participation. Habermas (1996) identifies three models of democracy. He argues that the deliberative model can overcome some of the deficiencies of the liberal and the republican models. Ferree at al. (2002), focusing on the role assigned to the public sphere in different conceptions of democracy, identify a representative liberal, a participatory liberal, a constructionist and a discursive (or deliberative) strand.

On a closer look, however, it is not so easy to distinguish a deliberative type of democracy from other types. Even in an elitist concept of democracy, deliberation may play an important role, even though deliberation is restricted to small circles of highly educated, well-informed and allegedly competent people. Second, a participatory concept of democracy does not necessarily imply extensive deliberation. Hence participatory and deliberative democracy should not be equated (Mutz 2006). Granting people a say in the form of voting for representatives or participating in a referendum does not require a preceding deliberation. And even when deliberation is considered to be crucial in a democratic system, one needs to specify its role relative to non-deliberative forms of interaction.

In response to these considerations, it might be useful to distinguish between a strong and a weak version of deliberative democracy. In the former case, all fundamental and controversial political matters are a subject of extensive and intensive deliberation that, ideally, includes all interested and/or concerned citizens. In this perspective, political decision making is not just preceded but ultimately guided and enlightened by an open and participatory process in which the better arguments prevail, as opposed to other criteria such as status, threat or sanction. Consensus almost naturally flows from such a process. However, I would argue that such a democratic system is a utopian ideal that can serve as an orienting principle but which will never be met in large political communities such as nation-states. Whatever form and no matter how much time deliberation takes, there will always remain conflicts of interests and values that cannot be settled by exchanging views and arguments.[6] No wonder that some mechanisms beyond the 'forceless force of the better argument' are applied in order to reach, usually by a majority vote, a decision that is binding even though not everybody has agreed (see also Flynn 2004).

More likely is the possibility of establishing a *weak version* of deliberative democracy. Even in large political settings, a political community may move towards a modest version of deliberative democracy, that is a representative political system (with more or less participatory elements) in which the final act of decision taking is preceded by a phase of deliberation over conflicting matters. This may occur in various arenas, for example a parliamentary assembly, a public hearing or an extended discourse in mass media where facts on the issue are presented, guiding interests and norms are spelled out, and, above all, a free exchange of arguments is secured (Bohman 2000). It is assumed that this exercise is not performed as an act of window dressing. Rather it is an open process in which the original views are not set in stone but can be modified. So some initial assumptions and affirmations may turn out to be definitely wrong, some interests as purely idiosyncratic and selfish, and some arguments as evidently weak so that the initial differences gradually shrink and common ground grows. While some conflicts may be settled by such a deliberative process so that the final act of decision making is not only unanimous[7] but full-heartedly agreed upon, there remains the probability that deliberation is simply impossible with regard to other matters.[8] Nevertheless, as long as there is at least the habit or an even an institutionalized attempt to deliberate within a democratic system, we may characterize such a system as a weak version of deliberative democracy.

Deliberation in context

Most definitions and concepts of deliberation remain at the general level without considering the structural and situational factors that enhance or reduce the possibility of deliberation. However, when studying attempts to deliberate, it is important to reflect about the potential impact of the conditions under which such endeavours take place.[9]

First, in terms of the *setting* and the context, various aspects should be taken into consideration. Deliberation may be direct or indirect (West and Gastil 2004: 2). The participants can either meet in small encounters and interact face to face, or they are separated in time and place so that their debate requires some kind of media that connect the participants. This occurs, for example, when speaker B responds in newspaper Y to what speaker A said the other day in the television channel X. Speaker A may be verified or falsified before B replies. It is also likely that B responds in a more controlled way than he would in a direct encounter where an immediate response is expected. In addition, discussion in a situation of time pressure may look differently than in a relaxed atmosphere in the absence of a long agenda. It is very likely that under time pressure latent or manifest power structures and tensions come into play. Finally, the presence or absence of an audience, the audience's knowledge about the background of and facts pertaining to the debate, and its assumed stances and stakes in the conflict may have an impact in what the actors say, how they frame it, and whether or not they take other views seriously.

Second, the kind of *issue* may also influence the course and outcome of deliberation. Some issues, for example the legitimacy of the death penalty, are perceived in terms of either/or. In these kinds of questions the speakers typically refer to fundamental and sometimes incompatible values so that deliberation goes on and on. Under these conditions, compromise, let alone consensus, is unlikely. Other issues can be framed in terms of more or less. This applies, for example, to wage negotiations or the question of appropriate speed limit on highways. In these discussions, the moral and emotional load tends to be lower and an agreement seems easier to reach. Still, both kinds of issues refer to a normative debate on the question of what is appropriate and what should be done, as opposed to the empirical question on whether or not a statement about 'reality' is true or false. While in real life situations both kinds of discourse tend to be intertwined, it still makes sense to keep them analytically separate.[10] Consider again the debate on the death penalty. Deliberation on whether this penalty has a deterring effect on potential perpetrators is one thing; whether or not the death penalty is compatible with human values is another thing. While the first question can be answered, in principle, by empirical research and, more concretely, by means of statistical analysis, such data are of little help to answer the second question, at least as long as legitimacy is not reduced to supportive public opinion.

Third, the kind and composition of *participants* influences the possibility and process of deliberation (see also Geissel in this volume). In part, this is related to the kind of issue. Some issues affect masses of people if not the world population, while others are directly relevant to small groups only. In the former case, attempts to deliberate are mainly undertaken by representatives or advocates of large groups. In the latter case there is a higher chance of the affected people directly participating so that authenticity, personal experience and (probably) emotions play a greater role. Further, participants can be more or less experienced with deliberation, putting different emphasis on symmetric and rational communication so that deliberation is more or less likely. Finally, it matters whether the deliberating actors are more or less homogeneous in terms of their social composition and ideological background. It may be assumed that homogeneous groups can deliberate more easily than heterogeneous groups.

To sum up, though it is necessary to develop a general definition and concept of deliberation, this should be differentiated when applied to different situations. By the same token, it is advisable to avoid sweeping generalizations on the basis of narrow empirical evidence when it comes to deliberation. Much of the literature on deliberation and deliberative democracy carries a high normative load. Sometimes, it is merely wishful thinking, particularly with regard to the strong version of deliberative democracy in contemporary nation-states. Sceptics even doubt that weak versions of a deliberative democracy have ever been put into practice. A different matter, however, may be the possibility of deliberation in more specific settings such as associations, religious congregations, social movements and informal citizen groups. Are there at least some pockets of civil society where deliberation actually takes place? Let us first have an overview of communication practices in a number of progressive movements before moving to an empirically grounded study of controversies in Global Justice Movements' groups.

Communication practices in selected progressive movements

As indicated above, progressive movements tend to embrace the concept of democracy, and especially a participatory democracy, at both the level of political regimes and their own ranks. They vary in their emphasis of this ambition as well as how it is specified and actually put into practice. Considering only the internal side of movements, my emphasis is not on the structure of the hardware, e.g. the form of networks and organizations and the distribution of resources. Instead, I focus on their software, especially their ways of communicating in face-to-face settings when controversies arise. Even when upholding democratic, participatory and egalitarian values in principle, it remains an open empirical question to what extent and in what historical and situational contexts deliberative practices can take place. After all, social movements, and probably all (public) interest groups with a voluntary membership, tend to be torn between two demands that often are in conflict with each other. At a more general level, this has been described as a zero-sum game between democracy and efficacy (Dahl 1994).[11] At the level of interest groups, it has been interpreted as a conflict between the logics of membership and the logics of influence (Schmitter and Streeck 1981). On the one hand, social movement organizers, especially because they have almost no material incentives to offer, seek to be highly responsive to the beliefs and wishes of their adherents in order to sustain the latter's motivation. This would lead the organizers to maximize democratic participation even when this implies time-consuming and cumbersome procedures. On the other hand, social movement organizers aim to act strategically, effectively and quickly, especially when they are under pressure from outside. This drives them towards decision making in small circles or the establishment of strong leaders. Beyond this fundamental conflict, even progressive movements, or rather strands within them, differ in their conceptions of democratic practices. Some accept informal or formal leadership, the election of delegates and the majority rule. Others strictly adhere to the principle of equality and consensus. Still others take a more pragmatic stance in trying to avoid a decision by majority vote but not excluding it under all circumstances. In the following, I will illustrate, mainly referring to the German context with which I am most familiar, how different kinds or generations of progressive movements deal with internal controversies.

a The practices of the *labour movement* are extremely difficult to overview for various reasons: the movement has undergone significant changes in time, differs from region to region, and is composed of quite diverse ideological strands that range from loose anarchist circles to centralized communist organizations. In the main, there has not been much emphasis on truly internal democracy throughout the 20th century in the core capitalist countries of central and northern Europe. To be sure, formal procedures such as a system of delegates and majority votes were in place in socialist or Social Democratic parties, trade unions and ideologically akin organizational bodies. Yet the overall approach was one of top down. Quite often, the existing leadership preselected candidates for office, channelled discussions and resolutions in the direction they deemed to be appropriate, and tried to avoid what they perceived to be longish and fruitless debates. Discipline was meant to guarantee organizational unity and strength. Although harsh political conflict was relatively rare within the mainstream, it engaged in bitter struggles with rival tendencies on the political left, whether non-dogmatic Marxist, orthodox Stalinist, Leninist, syndicalist or anarchist. The idea of deliberation, however worded, certainly did not figure as prominent in the socialist and Social Democratic mainstream. If at all, deliberation was a matter for small circles of left intellectuals but not for the rank and file.

b The *New Left* of the 1960s, including the *student movement* in the second half of this decade, deliberately distanced itself from the Old Left's emphasis on discipline, unity and formal leadership (Breines 1982). Debates and discussions were seen as constitutive elements of raising political awareness, identifying the right course and choosing the appropriate strategies. At least in Germany, it became a common habit to discuss something until it was resolved (*ausdiskutieren*). This could involve discussing the same issue for sessions lasting many hours (sometimes until early morning) and occasionally over a series of gatherings (Verheyen 2010). There was also a strong emphasis on collecting information, as epitomized by the teach-in that presumably would lead to the right conclusions. In addition, there was an emphasis on reading and correctly interpreting the left classics, especially Karl Marx. This, in turn, was a matter of long meetings that tended to be dominated by those who combined theoretical knowledge with rhetorical skills. At a first glance, this might appear as a widespread practice of deliberation. At a closer look, however, the space for deliberation, as defined above, was limited for two main reasons. First, besides its reflective and partly deliberative traits, especially the student movement of the second half of the 1960s included an anti-authoritarian strand that was oriented towards spontaneous and provocative action, including the expression of emotions, irony and fun, as exemplified in the strategy of the *Spassguerilla* (fun guerrilla). Second, the idea of equality that is so central to the concept of deliberation was violated in various respects, for example by accepting movement leaders (partly as a product of prominence in mass media) and marginalizing female activists who, as a consequence, began to establish their own groups and networks. Not accidentally, these feminist groups put much weight on non-hierarchical forms of interaction.

c One remarkable outgrowth of the student movements were the so-called *K-Gruppen* (K-groups, with K as the acronym for *kommunistisch* = communist). These groups were relatively small but ideologically highly loaded. Though they embraced the general idea of communism, they engaged in bitter rivalry over the one and only politically correct line – a struggle that made them appear as political sects, each considering itself as the true avant-garde of a forthcoming proletarian revolution (Koenen 2001). As a rule, these groups were marked by strong but mostly informal hierarchy. Debates, to the extent that they occurred at all, were led and controlled by the leaders. In public appearances, for example in large gatherings of the student body, the leaders engaged in long authoritative speeches resembling a teacher in front of pupils. When leaders of different K-groups happened to be in the same gathering, there was a tendency to grab and never give back the microphone so that rival opinions were silenced. Not surprisingly, such situations could end in a wrestling match in front of an audience of competing tribes.

d A quite different outgrowth of the New Left and the student movement are the so-called *new social movements* (NSMs). These are anchored in the well-educated middle classes, especially those in the human service sector. They cover a broad spectrum of issues such as peace and disarmament, human, civic and social rights, environmental protection, urban planning, and Third World development. Like the student movement, the NSMs share an emphasis on participatory democracy and scepticism about hierarchical organization. Yet they refrain from the revolutionary zeal of the student movement that implied an idealization of liberation movements in Third World countries and the marginalized groups in core capitalist countries. Even more so, they distanced themselves from the sectarianism of the K-Gruppen and their repressive patterns of internal communication. Instead, the NSMs promoted a strategy that one might call 'radical reformism'. This allowed them to engage, mainly via alternative or green parties, in the electoral arena and, after a few years, even to cooperate with state administrations, especially at the local level. Unlike parts of the student movement and most clearly the K-Gruppen, the NSMs have a more pragmatic and pluralistic ideological stance. This is reflected in their emphasis on egalitarian, internal communication, best exemplified in the consciousness-raising groups of radical feminists and many other groups adhering to the idea of a grass roots democracy (Epstein 1991). These groups fully embraced the principle of consensus, whereas others, notably those with larger and more formal organizations, did not shy away from delegation and majority voting. As a whole, however, the trend towards informality and authenticity prevailed. This movement probably peaked in the late 1970s and early 1980s when a so-called 'second culture' or 'alternative culture' flourished (Reichardt and Siegfried 2010), triggering fears that major parts of the younger generation would drift away from bourgeois values such as discipline and the ethics of achievement.

The egalitarian communication practices of the NSMs also left their mark in various waves of student protests after the late 1980s. When observing the patterns of interaction in large and self-organized assemblies of the student body, one is struck by their forms of communication that, in several respects, are exactly the opposite of those of the K-Gruppen: speech acts rarely last longer than two or three minutes; there is careful attention to the inclusion of female speakers and avoiding gendered (male) language; the audience uses gestures to signal consent or dissent; leaders are suspiciously absent, though it is clear that some individuals, mainly based on their investment in time and experience, are more influential than others.

Unfortunately, apart from occasional observations and scattered accounts of activists, we have very little information on the internal structures and communication patterns of the movements mentioned thus far. There exist, however, systematic data for the communication practices of the most recent wave of progressive movements: the Global Justice Movements. This allows us to go into more detail about them, though direct comparison with earlier movements is not possible because we lack corresponding data.

Studying communicative practices in Global Justice Movements

The Global Justice Movements (GJMs) can be interpreted as a new generation of the NSMs. As the label indicates, they emphasize the global dimension of the problems they tackle. They also tend to be oriented globally, or at least transnationally, in their organizational forms and scope of mobilization (della Porta 2007). Compared to the NSMs, the range of issues and problems addressed has not fundamentally changed. However, more than before these problems are seen as interrelated and, to a large degree, interpreted as negative consequences of an economic and political regime of a globalized neoliberalism (Rucht 2003). GJMs, like the NSMs, favour a decentralized structure based on the full autonomy of groups and networks. In their communicative practices, they promote equality, empathy and respect for the other. This becomes obvious in their large meetings, most prominently the World Social Forums, where no group is entitled to speak on behalf of other groups (Sen et al. 2004). Accordingly, no decisions or list of priorities and no strategic choices are made on the level of the so-called 'movement of movements', apart from the recognition of a (very general) mission statement such as that of Charter of Porto Alegre. Also, there is a widespread reluctance to create 'stars' that can be viewed as speakers or representatives of the ensemble of groups, networks and alliances that subscribe to the slogan of 'Another World is Possible!'.

These movements are composed of variegated and mostly loosely coupled organizations and networks centred around specific ideological tendencies and/or thematic foci. They are connected by major campaigns, overlapping memberships, newsletters and other means of communication including the internet. Only on rare occasions, for example an outstanding international congress or protest event, do component parts of the GJM come together. For example, the World Social Forum may attract up to 200,000 participants in hundreds of meetings and workshops (Rucht 2011). While it would be difficult to study one of these huge meetings closely, covering the total of the communicative practices of these movements would be impossible.

Therefore, one can focus on a more modest selection of small and mostly locally based groups belonging to the wider networks of GJMs. Usually, these groups are composed of ideologically similar-minded people and also socially homogeneous individuals who know each other from more or less regular meetings. In addition, we can also study selected groups located at the intermediary level between the micro and macro-cosmos of movements. In these meso-mobilization groups, members or delegates of various local and issue-specific groups come together to share experiences, to discuss priorities, strategies and tactics, and coordinate and mobilize for specific campaigns. With regard to these different kinds of groups, it is interesting to know whether, and under what conditions, deliberation takes place.

However, it might be useful to take a broader perspective by looking at different communication practices among which deliberation is just one variant. This has been done, both in conceptual and empirical terms, in the context of an international research project (see note 17). Let us first take a look at the conceptual considerations before presenting and discussing empirical findings.

A conceptual framework for analysing controversies[12]

As already stated, deliberation may occur in the context of controversies. A controversy starts when people disagree about a statement, a judgement or a decision. The ways in which controversies are handled can vary considerably. Some scientists rely on a dual conception of coercion vs persuasion (Mansbridge 1996). Others distinguish between coercion, bargaining and persuasion or, as Rummel (1976, Chapter 20) does, between coercive, bargaining, intellectual, authoritative and manipulative forms of power. Physical coercion and the use of words or, more particularly, the use of convincing arguments, can be a source of power.[13] However, when it comes to categorizing forms of power other than physical force, it might be useful not just to come up with a list of forms but to develop a more systematic categorization of controversies that is based on two analytical dimensions.

By the dimension of *symmetry* of a controversy, we refer to the way the speakers relate to each other. Symmetric (or reciprocal) relations exist when the speakers respect/recognize each other as being equal and act accordingly. In an asymmetric constellation one side is considered/treated as inferior or less important than the other side. The dimension of *power-type* refers to the source of influence on each other. In this regard, one can distinguish between 'soft' power (power based on words, arguments and/or symbols) and 'hard' power (non-communicative power[14] ultimately based on material, physical or similar kinds of sanctions, e.g. expressing a veto, threat of exit, application of the majority rule). From these two dimensions, we wish to keep separate the quantitative distribution of participation.[15]

By combining the dimension of symmetry/asymmetry of the speakers with the kind of power they exercise, one can create a four-fold table representing different types of interaction in a controversy. Each type represents a distinct way of handling conflicts and its logically corresponding outcome (Table 6.1).

Pressure is a process in which one actor (or conflict party) exerts 'hard' power on another actor or conflict party in a fundamentally asymmetric relation. Because hard power ultimately rests on non-verbal sanctions, the actor using it can impose his/her will on others. Thus dominance is both the background situation and the likely outcome in a situation of sustained pressure. The typical speech act of this type of discourse is a directive. In a radicalized version, pressure is exerted by an order to which the inferior actor obeys to avoid hard sanctions.

Bargaining is a process in which all conflict partners are interested in a common solution while, at the same time, having the potential power to negatively affect the other side. Bargaining usually results in a compromise that, by definition, is accepted by all partners although it does not fully correspond to their genuine interests and preferences. A typical act of bargaining is to make offers and counter offers. In its purest version, there is a balance of power between the actors so that the compromise is fixed halfway between their original positions.

Agitatory persuasion (in German: *überreden*) is the process in which one actor, without really putting the superiority of his or her views or arguments into question, influences the others by means of assertion and/or agitation. If successful, the others accept the view of the persuader by acclamation without having thoroughly

Table 6.1 Types of interaction in a controversy

	Relationship of speakers	
Type of power	*Asymmetric*	*Symmetric*
'Hard'	pressure/coercion (dominance)	bargaining (compromise)
'Soft'	agitatory persuasion (acclamation)	deliberation (consensus)

scrutinized his or her position. A typical act of agitatory persuasion is the use of rhetorical tricks and the manipulation of emotions.

Deliberation is a process in which actors consider each other as equals and rely on reasonable arguments to identify legitimate claims and make decisions. Ideally, deliberation results in a consensus, i.e. a decision or proposition of which every participant is fully convinced. In its radical version, deliberation neutralizes all other factors that might restrict the power of arguments. In other words, in deliberation, views or opinions diverge but a solution (finding common ground, the truth, developing a proposal, etc.) is sought by non-coercive and non-manipulative means.

These are four ideal types. In the real world, they tend to exist in more diluted forms.[16] Also, they may occur in combination or sequentially in a given setting. For example, bargaining may be increasingly flanked or supplanted by pressure. Moreover, it is important to stress that the outcome attributed to each type is not inevitable. As long as we refer to controversies in democratic settings or controversies in which, for instance, hard power is limited, the actors have an exit option that, under certain conditions, will result in a situation of stalemate, non-decision and the like.

Besides these key factors, a number of additional features are supposedly relevant for group communication in general and controversies in particular. For example, a group may have a strong preference for certain modes of decision making, such as applying majority rule or aiming at a consensus. Also, controversies can focus on different thematic levels (substantive discourse or meta-discourse), or thematic concerns (organizational matters, value conflicts, personal relations, etc.). Finally, as argued above, group communication can vary with regard to the number of participants, a more or less competitive spirit, a more or less relaxed atmosphere, and more or less time pressure. As hypothesized above, these factors are likely to have an impact on whether or not deliberation does occur.

The framework of empirical investigation

In an ambitious research project involving various subprojects and lasting for several years, seven teams have conducted participant observation of groups in six European countries.[17] In each of these countries, one or two researchers observed most or all meetings of local groups belonging to the GJMs for a period ranging from several months to almost two years.

Local GJMs groups usually meet one to four times per month. For the most part, their meetings are filled with reports, information exchange, preparation and assessments of activities, brainstorming, chatting, joking, etc. We observed these activities and provided three different kinds of documentation: first, a general portrait of the group under investigation with information on its history, structure, cleavages, personnel, etc.; second, a record of each group session including the agenda items, the patterns of participation and decision making, and the occurrence of controversies; finally, a rather detailed protocol of the controversies.

Controversies, defined as 'an explicit and extended verbal disagreement in the group',[18] were at the centre of our empirical interest. For each controversy, participant observers filled a codesheet during the interaction or, based on their notes, immediately after the group session. In pilot exercises, we found that the coding of every speech act during the controversies was impossible. Too much had to be registered in a short time. Almost all groups disliked tape recording. This was also a reason not to apply some sort of a 'discourse quality index' as proposed by Steenbergen et al. (2003). Instead, after a series of tests, we aimed at a more holistic or comprehensive coding of sequences of speech acts, relying on the intelligence and emphatic judgement of a trained coder who, for most of the time, was able to distinguish, for example, between an interaction in which the speakers treat each other as equal or unequal, between an intervention based on hard or soft power, and between a relaxed, a tense and a mixed atmosphere during a controversy. For each of these categories, we provided a number of examples. Admittedly, boundaries are sometimes difficult to draw when it comes, for example, to discerning degrees of hard power ('rather hard power' vs 'hard power clearly prevailing').[19] While some particular coder decisions remained arbitrary, we still are confident that generally the coders' decisions were both valid and reliable. However, apart from the training phase in which we reached satisfying levels of inter-coder reliability, no further reliability tests have been conducted.

Selected quantitative findings

The data presented in the following are based on the observation of 97 group sessions with 510 agenda items.[20] Among the latter, informational inputs or proposals on activities are most frequent (36.1 percent). Controversies are often part of a discussion, which is the second largest category (35.9. percent).

When looking at the modes of decision making and ignoring those cases in which no decision was taken, we find that nodding/tacit agreement is by far the most frequent form (43.5 percent of all decisions; all decisions: N = 111). Unanimity comes next (17.7 percent), while majority votes overruling a minority as well as straw polls are very rare (2.8 percent). The first two categories roughly correspond to the idea of a consensus and, taken together, account for about 60 percent of all decisions.

Interestingly, *controversies* are far from being rare. We registered a total of 143 controversies, which corresponds to roughly 1.5 per group session. Hence, controversies are considered a 'normal' part of the group life. Although there were some instances of incivility and direct clashes, most of the time the groups communicated in a relaxed manner. This is particularly true for smaller and homogeneous groups. A clear exception from this rule was Attac France whose national steering committee engaged in bitter fights (including later substantiated accusations of 'electoral fraud'). It was also in this group that the question was repeatedly raised whether only elected members are entitled to speak in the group (as opposed to those who were no longer delegates).

Controversies vary considerably in their duration. They may last from a few minutes to significantly more than one hour. The average number of group members present at a controversy is close to 14 (median = 10). The number of people actively involved by providing one or more speech acts is 6.9 (median = 5). In other words, half of those who are present during a controversy actively take part. On average, men are clearly overrepresented in the groups but, relative to their proportional presence, are only slightly more engaged in controversies. While the average percentage of women in group sessions is 32.1 percent, the proportion of women among the attendants actively taking part in controversies is 33.0 percent. However, we did not measure the frequency and length of speech acts. The general impression we got is that men tend to speak more frequently and longer than women. The duration of controversies averages at 16.8 minutes but varies greatly with a maximum value of 150 minutes.

Among the themes of controversies, the relationship of the groups with reference groups, both within and outside the movement, prevails (external group action: 37.8 percent; strategic decision: 23.1 percent) over internal aspects such as organizational questions, the groups' structure, and debates over principal values (see Table 6.2).

Coming back to the four types of controversies based on the dimensions of power and symmetry, we can look at the distribution of these types. In order to reduce complexity, the four-point scale for each of the two dimensions has been transformed into a dummy variable (hard or soft power; asymmetry or symmetry). Contrary to our expectation, deliberation was by far the most common form of interaction in controversies (83 out of 143 valid cases; see Table 6.3).

Table 6.2 Themes of controversies

	Percent of responses	*Percent of cases*
External group action	28.6	37.8
Strategic decision	17.5	23.1
Organization (technical)	14.8	19.6
Internal structure (basic)	11.6	15.4
Principal values	11.6	15.4
Meta-discourse	10.1	13.3
External delegation	2.1	2.8
Other	3.7	4.9
Total (percent)	100.0	132.3
n (cases/responses)	143	189

Table 6.3 Distribution of types of controversies (absolute numbers)

	Relationship of speakers	
Type of power	*Asymmetric*	*Symmetric*
'Hard'	20	20
	pressure	bargaining
'Soft'	20	83
	agitatory persuasion	deliberation

n = 143

One might suspect that the high number of cases of deliberation results from the crude categorization of combining only one value on each of the two dimensions (soft power and symmetric relationship). By using a two-point scale for each half of the measures ('rather soft power' and 'soft power clearly prevailing'; 'fairly symmetric' and 'very symmetric'), we can subdivide the generic category of deliberation (83 cases) into four cells. However, the value combination of 'clearly soft' and 'very symmetric' still accounts for 36 (44.6 percent) of all forms of deliberation, whereas only 14 deliberations fall into the weakest deliberation category ('rather soft power' and 'fairly symmetric'). In other words, the most 'pure' cases of deliberation were far from being rare in the observed controversies. One should, however, remember that controversies are only one of the elements of group sessions. Not every session includes a controversy.

How are the four types of communication related to other characteristics of the group and its controversies? Only a few aspects can be considered here. It is plausible that a number of factors have an impact on the kinds of controversies that prevail. Drawing on the sparse literature on this aspect (Gastil 1993a; Bächtiger and Steenbergen 2004; Bächtiger and Steiner 2005; Mansbridge at al. 2006) as well as common sense reasoning, one can hypothesize that deliberation is more likely when:

- the number of participants is small
- the issue debated is organizational rather than substantial
- the style of interaction is cooperative rather than competitive
- uncivil speech acts are rare or even absent
- the atmosphere is relaxed
- no or little time pressure exists.

Table 6.4 gives a rough idea of the extent to which these assumptions hold. Surprisingly, the percentage of deliberation is lowest in the category of the smallest group in the sample. Yet, unsurprisingly, deliberation usually goes along with a cooperative attitude, civil forms of interaction and a relaxed atmosphere. But it is also worth noting that deliberation is not impossible in a tense atmosphere. As expected, deliberation occurs more frequently in the absence of time pressure.

As stated earlier, not every controversy has a clear result, nor does deliberation always lead to unanimity, let alone consensus. If a decision was reached at all,

Table 6.4 Types of controversy by group characteristics

	Pressure	*Bargaining*	*Agitation*	*Deliberation*	*Total (%)*
Number of participants					
3–7	20.5	20.5	15.4	43.6	100
8–14	11.8	15.7	7.8	64.7	100
15+	11.3	7.5	18.9	62.3	100
All cases	14.0	14.0	14.0	58.0	100
Mode of interaction					
Cooperative	2.4	13.1	8.3	76.2	100
Competitive	31.0	15.5	22.4	31.0	100
All cases	14.1	14.1	14.1	57.7	100
Incivility					
No incivility	6.8	13.6	9.7	69.9	100
Rare incivility	35.5	16.1	19.4	29.0	100
Some incivility	25.0	0.0	50.0	25.0	100
Frequent incivility	20.0	20.0	40.0	20.0	100
All cases	14.0	14.0	14.0	58.0	100
Atmosphere					
Relaxed	2.8	8.3	5.6	83.3	100
Mixed	22.4	20.4	20.4	36.7	100
Tense	31.8	18.2	27.3	22.7	100
All cases	14.0	14.0	14.0	58.0	100
Time pressure					
None	7.0	14.0	15.0	64.0	100
Somewhat	26.1	21.7	8.7	43.5	100
High	36.8	5.3	15.8	42.1	100
All cases	14.1	14.1	14.1	57.7	100

n = 142 or 143 for all variables

deliberation mostly ended with nodding/tacit agreement (54 cases) or unanimity (27 cases).[21] Interestingly, there were also instances of straw polls and even majority votes concluding a phase of deliberation. It may well have been that the gaps between conflicting views were on their way to coming closer but due to other factors, for example the need to take a decision before people have to leave, the discussion could not continue.

The kind of decision has to be distinguished from the outcome of the controversy. For example, the group may decide by nodding that no decision is to be taken or that the decision is delegated to a subgroup. As can be seen from the second part of Table 6.5, frequently no decision was taken at the end of a controversy

Table 6.5 Types of controversies by types of decision and outcome (absolute values)

	Pressure	*Bargaining*	*Agitation*	*Deliberation*	*All forms*
Mode of decision in controversy					
Straw poll	0	3	1	5	9
Nodding, tacit agreement	16	9	13	54	92
Majority vote	3	2	0	7	12
Unanimity	1	3	1	27	32
Not applicable/unclear	5	6	5	11	27
n (sum column)	25	23	20	104	172
Outcome of controversy					
No decision was taken	7	6	9	25	47
Postponing	2	2	1	7	12
Delegation of decision	0	1	0	3	4
Rather decree	4	1	3	2	10
Rather acclamation	0	0	1	3	4
Rather compromise	6	5	4	12	27
Allowed consensus	1	0	1	8	10
Rather consensus	0	5	0	23	28
n (sum column)	20	20	19	83	142

(47 cases). Consensus (allowed consensus[22] and rather consensus[23]) was second most frequent, followed by 'rather compromise'. A delegation of the decision and 'rather acclamation' each occurred in four instances only.

It is important to stress that, in the eyes of most activists, the ability to reach consensus is not based on a naive assumption of the absence of power. This is illustrated by the interpretation of consensus provided by Christophe Aguiton, a French social scientist who is also involved in trade union campaigns and is an experienced activist in networks of the GJMs. With regard to the latter, he affirmed that decisions are mostly taken by consensus. When asked what consensus means, he answered:

> The consensus is one of the characteristics of this new network. It's a way to decide. The consensus is not unanimity. The consensus is a very powerful tool. And it is not a tool without a correlation of forces. In the consensus, some groups are stronger than others, because if there is an issue they don't accept voluntarily, they leave. (…)
>
> Question: 'So consensus means everybody has to agree to the decision?'
>
> 'No, that means that no one has to refuse, which is not the same.'[24]

Conclusion

Scattered information suggests that not all progressive movements within the large spectrum of the political left try to reduce inequality among their own ranks and seriously aim to deliberate when it comes to handling internal controversies. Some groups following a Leninist principle rely on strong leadership to which the rank and file is supposed to submit. Examples for such a pattern can be found in some strands of the labour movement and, in the German context, the so-called K-groups that emerged in the wake of the student movement in the early 1970s. The socialist and Social Democratic branch within the labour movement took a middle position between the elitist Leninist pole on the one hand and the anarchist–egalitarian pole on the other. More recent progressive movements, including the new social movements emerging in the 1970s and the contemporary GJMs, generally put much emphasis on reducing what they perceive as illegitimate forms of power within their own ranks. They try to deliberate as much as possible. Nevertheless, they exhibit aberrations from this ideal. Probably as in any social group, one can identify informal hierarchies, struggles over and misuse of power, hidden agendas, forms of incivility and so forth.[25] Some observers may be tempted to become cynical in view of such examples, particularly when these groups have explicit and high moral standards regarding their own structures, forms of communication, and decision making. However, the findings of our large, multinational research project, as well as my observations during the last few years in these and other kinds of groups, do not lend support to such a cynical perspective.

It is obvious that the majority of new social movements, especially the GJMs, are extremely sensitive to issues of power and democracy in their internal communication (Young 2001; Haug 2010). They show an open and accessible style of communication, a willingness to listen to different viewpoints, a readiness to rotate leadership roles or to accept moderators or facilitators, a preference for participatory discussions and avoidance of long speech acts. These characteristics are also found in earlier 'progressive' social movements, but, I would argue, to a lesser extent. Taken together, these elements are not a democratic innovation in the strict sense, but at least a move towards deliberative practices that previously have been largely perceived as ineffective, if not impracticable.

The research findings presented here suggest that deliberation, at least at the level of small-scale groups, is not just a dream but actually occurs. And it occurs to a greater extent than we expected at the outset of our research. Again, sceptics may argue that the researchers were biased in being too sympathetic to their research objects, that categories used for the research were not defined rigidly enough, or inter-coder reliability was unclear. Perhaps there is some truth in such doubts. Nevertheless, I would contend that the majority of these groups are more successful in reducing 'hard' power and enabling deliberation than most trade unions, political parties and big non-governmental organizations. Most highly institutionalized groups tend to equate the idea of democracy and participation with formal procedures such as majority vote and delegation. They also give much greater weight to 'strong' leadership and to experts as the proper agents in processes that they still consider to be democratic and rational. However, if applied to the GJMs, these practices very likely would put an end to the GJMs in the long run.

Notes

1 The first and third sections of this chapter draw upon a chapter in another book (Rucht, forthcoming).
2 In his later work, when referring to political contexts, Habermas also emphasized the role of a political–ethical (instead of an abstract moral) and a pragmatic foundation of political action (Habermas 1992: 297ff.).
3 Habermas was often misinterpreted as a dreamer who denied the factual restrictions of empirical communication. His point, however, was that the ideal speech situation is a counterfactual assumption of speakers to which they adhere as soon as they honestly start, and not just pretend, to argue. In this sense, the exchange of arguments is resting on 'ideal' presuppositions as if these were in place. In other words, the interlocutors, in the act of arguing, bracket the restrictions of an empirical discourse, for instance, time constraints or the different status of the speakers.
4 For an extension of Habermas' model of discourse see, for example, Young (1996). Like some of her colleagues, she thinks that Habermas gives too much weight to the cognitive and rational aspects of the discourse. Therefore, she pleas for the inclusion of greeting, rhetoric and storytelling. For the role of the latter aspect in deliberation, see also Poletta 2006, Chapter 4.
5 See http://www.tomorrowseurope.eu/spip.php?article30. The full citation also includes criteria for defining deliberation: 'The lifeblood of democracy is healthy deliberation – not mere conversations and one-sided debates, but discussions which require exposure to conflicting views and a willingness to be challenged and to listen.'
6 For sceptical views, see, for example, Dahl 1997; Sanders 1997; Shapiro 1999; and Kohn 2000.
7 Unanimity based on exhaustion of the dissenters or respect of an overwhelming majority view is not the same as a consensus to which everybody agrees by strong conviction.
8 Deliberation is very unlikely to occur when the participants perceive each other as enemies or are 'true believers' in fundamentally different values, when the stakes are extremely high or when the rules of the game, though privileging clearly one conflict party, cannot be altered. In cases of insurmountable disagreement, Ackerman (1989) suggests bracketing the issue. This, however, is only possible in some situations.
9 For a discussion of such factors, see Steiner et al. 2004; and Ryfe 2005.
10 Habermas (1973) distinguishes between a theoretical discourse (on a factual question) and a practical discourse (on a normative question). While the former searches for 'truth', the latter is oriented towards the 'rightness' or 'adequacy' (*Richtigkeit/Angemessenheit*) of norms.
11 Poletta (2002: 148), in her analysis of the US New Left in the sixties, does not see a trade-off between these aims: the participatory democratic dilemma that new leftists faced lay neither in the tension between democracy and efficacy nor in that between unity and difference. Rather, it was in the intrinsic limits of pedagogy and friendship as models for democratic principles.
12 Most of the ideas of this section as well as the three methodological tools are the result of a close collaboration in which, apart from the author, Christoph Haug, Simon Teune and Mundo Yang participated.
13 On the strategic use of arguments in a process of bargaining, see Elster 1992.

14 We use the term non-communicative power with regard to the underlying source of power that is ultimately not based on words but on acts, for instance coercion. Obviously, in group discussion, the threat to act in such a way has to be communicated to other group members.

15 In our research, participation means taking part in communication and/or decision making regardless of the content of speech acts. Participation, in its minimal form, can be nodding or uttering yes or no. On the other hand, it can also be a lengthy contribution within or beyond a phase of controversy. Because the quantitative distribution of participation in controversies is independent from the qualitative type of controversies, the dimension of participation is not part of our four-fold analytical scheme.

16 Various attempts have been made to empirically measure the quality of discourse or the degree of deliberation. See, for example, the edition by Bächtiger and Steiner 2005. It also includes comments by Habermas (2005) on empirical studies on deliberation.

17 The project 'Democracy in Europe and the Mobilization of Society' was coordinated by Donatella della Porta and funded by the European Union (see http://demos.iue.it/). I wish to thank all researchers who have done the participatory observation and coding work on which the empirical analysis of this chapter is based.
The groups investigated are: Italy: National campaign on water; Attac-Florence; Britain: Thanet Friends of the Earth; University of Kent Conscious Consumers' Group; Germany: Attac Berlin Financial Markets Group; Berlin Social Forum; France: No-Vox Network; Attac France; Spain: Córdoba Solidaria; Ecologistas en Acción Córdoba; Switzerland: Attac Geneva; Forum Social Lemanique. In addition, meetings of the transnational network Reclaim our UN Campaign have been observed. In these meetings, however, the standardized methods of observation have not been applied. Accordingly, this part of research is not included in the data presented here. For more details on the methodology, see della Porta and Rucht 2008. On methodological aspects of studying deliberation in social movement settings, see also Haug and Teune 2008.

18 A controversy was identified at the basis of the following rule: 'It starts as soon as a dissenting voice is followed by a reaction (e.g. a justification) of at least three speech acts or of a reaction that lasts more than three minutes. If two or more controversies can be connected to one and the same issue, they are considered as a single controversy.' (See also the methodological notes and the codebook in della Porta and Rucht 2008).

19 'The scale measures the degree to which hard power was present in the controversy. A high degree of hard power exists when either many speakers rely on some kind of hard power or when one or a few speakers use hard power to such a degree that the whole discussion is dominated by this' (della Porta and Rucht 2008). Typical speech acts addressing hard power refer to negative or positive sanctions. One way to assess the importance of hard power is a thought experiment: whenever it makes an important difference *who* (or how many) put forward a certain argument or position, there is relevant hard power. Note that hard power can be used in a symmetric as well as an asymmetric manner. So asymmetry should not be confused with power.

20 'An agenda item typically comprises a discussion or a cluster of contributions related to a specific topic. Excurses or subordinated discussions are considered part of the related agenda item. Of course, moderation and/or an agenda distributed in advance are helpful to identify separate agenda items. Aberrations and blending with other issues, however, are likely to appear in reality and make the distinction of agenda items difficult. Changes in the type of communication and/or transitional phrases ('so much for this issue', 'any further questions?') will help to identify a new agenda item. To identify an agenda item one could imagine what somebody would report as the main points of the meeting to somebody who missed it' (della Porta and Rucht 2008).

21 Up to three modes of decision taking have been coded for each controversy.

22 'The decision is not a consensus in the literal sense because dissent has been made explicit, but all participants agreed to a decision in order to reach a common goal' (della Porta and Rucht 2008).

23 'All or most participants are fully convinced by the decision taken' (della Porta and Rucht 2008). This implies that no dissent is made explicit in the immediate context of taking the decision and no signs of frustration or apathy are observable (for example, nobody signals through body language that he/she is unwilling to repeat dissent).

24 Extract from an interview conducted by the author at the 4th European Social Forum 2006 in Athens.

25 For a discussion of obstacles to democracy and deliberation in small groups, see Gastil (1993a, 1993b) and Young (2001).

References

Ackerman, B. A. (1989) Why Dialogue?, *Journal of Philosophy*, 86: 5–22.

Bächtiger, A. and Steenbergen, M. M. (2004) *The Real World of Deliberation. A Comparative Study of its Favorable Conditions in Legislatures* (EUI Working Paper SPS No. 2004/17), Florence: European University Institute.

Bächtiger, A. and Steiner, J. (eds) (2005) Empirical Approaches to Deliberative Democracy (Second of the Two Special Issues), *Acta Politica*, 40(3): 153–68.

Bohman, J. (2000) *Public Deliberation. Pluralism, Complexity, and Democracy*, Cambridge, London: MIT Press.

Breines, W. (1982) *The Great Refusal: Community and Organization in the New Left, 1962–1968*, New York: Praeger.

Burkhalter, S., Gastil, J. and Kelshaw, T. (2002) A Conceptual Definition and Theoretical Model of Public Deliberation in Small Face-to-Face Groups, *Communication Theory*, 12(4): 398–422.

Chambers, S. (2003) Deliberative Democratic Theory, *Annual Review of Political Science*, 6: 307–26.

Cohen, J. (1989) Deliberation and Democratic Legitimacy, in Goodin, R. E. and Pettit, P. (eds) *Contemporary Political Philosophy*, Oxford: Blackwell: 143–155.

Dahl, R. (1994) A Democratic Dilemma: System Effectiveness versus Citizen Participation, *Political Science Quarterly*, 109(1): 23–34.

—— (1997) On Deliberative Democracy, *Dissent*, 44: 54–8.

della Porta, D. (2005) Making the Polis: Social Forums and Democracy in the Global Justice Movement, *Mobilization*, 10(1): 73–94.

—— (ed.) (2007) *The Global Justice Movement: Crossnational and Transnational Perspectives*, Boulder, CO: Paradigm.

della Porta, D. and Rucht, D. (eds) (2008) *Microanalysis of Practices of Deliberative Democracy* (WP6 – Integrated Report), Florence: European University Institute (unpublished report).

Dryzek, J. S. (2000) *Deliberative Democracy and Beyond. Liberals, Critics, Contestations*, Oxford, New York: Oxford University Press.

Elster, J. (1992) *Strategic Uses of Argument*, Toronto: University of Toronto Press.

Epstein, B. (1991) *Political Protest and Cultural Revolution: Nonviolent Direct Action in the 1970s and 1980s*, Berkeley, CA: University of California Press.

Ferree, M. M., Gamson, W. A., Gerhards, J. and Rucht, D. (2002) Four Models of the Public Sphere in Modern Democracies, *Theory and Society*, 31(3): 289–324.

Flynn, J. (2004) Communicative Power in Habermas's Theory of Democracy, *European Journal of Political Theory*, 3(4): 433–54.

Gastil, J. (1993a) *Democracy in Small Groups: Participation, Decision Making, and Communication,* Philadelphia, PA: New Society Publishers.

—— (1993b) Identifying Obstacles in Small Group Democracy, *Small Group Research,* 24(1): 5–27.

Gerhards, J. (1997) Diskursive versus liberale Öffentlichkeit. Eine empirische Auseinandersetzung mit Jürgen Habermas, *Kölner Zeitschrift für Soziologie und Sozialpsychologie* 49: 1–39.

Habermas, J. (1971) Vorbereitende Bemerkungen zu einer Theorie der kommunikativen Kompetenz, in Habermas, J. and Luhmann, N. (eds) *Theorie der Gesellschaft oder Sozialtechnologie. Was leistet die Systemforschung?,* Frankfurt/M.: Suhrkamp: 101–41.

—— (1973) Wahrheitstheorien, in Fahrenbach, H. (ed.) *Wirklichkeit und Reflexion,* Pfullingen: Neske: 211–65.

—— (1992) *Faktizität und Geltung. Beiträge zur Diskurstheorie des Rechts und des demokratischen Rechtsstaates*, Frankfurt/M.: Suhrkamp.

—— (1996) Drei normative Modelle der Demokratie, in Habermas, J. (ed.) *Die Einbeziehung des Anderen. Studien zur politischen Theorie*, Frankfurt/M.: Suhrkamp: 277–92.

—— (2005) Concluding Comments on Empirical Approaches to Deliberative Politics, *Acta Politica*, 40(3): 384–92.

Haug, C. (2010) *Discursive Decision-making in Meetings of the Global Justice Movements. Cultures and Practices* (Unpublished PhD dissertation), Freie Universität Berlin.

Haug, C. and Teune, S. (2008) Identifying Deliberation in Social Movement Assemblies: Challenges of Comparative Participant Observation, *Journal of Public Deliberation*, 3(1): 1–37.

Koenen, G. (2001) *Das Rote Jahrzehnt. Unsere kleine Kulturrevolution 1967–1977,* Köln: Kiepenheuer & Witsch.

Kohn, M. (2000) Language, Power and Persuasion: Towards a Critique of Deliberative Democracy, *Constellations*, 7(3): 408–29.

Mansbridge, J. (1996) Using Power/Fighting Power: The Polity, in Benhabib, S. (ed.) *Democracy and Difference*, Princeton, NJ: Princeton University Press: 46–66.

Mansbridge, J., Hartz-Karp, J., Amengual, M. and Gastil, J. (2006) Norms of Deliberation: An Inductive Study, *Journal of Public Deliberation*, 2(1), Article 7. Available http://services.bepress.com/jpd/vol2/iss1/art7 (accessed: 26 July 2007).

Mutz, D. (2006) *Hearing the Other Side: Deliberative Versus Participatory Democracy*, Cambridge: Cambridge University Press.

Poletta, F. (2001) Activist Challenges to Deliberative Democracy, *Political Theory*, 29(5): 670–90.

—— (2002) *Freedom Is an Endless Meeting: Democracy in American Social Movements*, Chicago, IL and London: The University of Chicago Press.

—— (2006) *It Was Like a Fever: Storytelling in Protest and Politics*, Chicago, IL and London: The University of Chicago Press.

Reichardt, S. and Siegfried, D. (2010) *Das alternative Milieu. Antibürgerlicher Lebensstil und linke Politik in der Bundesrepublik Deutschland und Europa 1968–1983*, Göttingen: Wallstein.

Rucht, D. (2003) Social Movements Challenging Neo-liberal Globalization, in Ibarra, P. (ed.) *Social Movements and Democracy*, New York: Palgrave Macmillan: 211–28.

—— (2011) Social Forums as Public Stage and Infrastructure of Global Justice Movements, in Smith, J. et al. (eds.) *Handbook on World Social Forum Activism*, New York: Paradigm.

—— (forthcoming) Deliberation and Power in Global Justice Movements, in della Porta, D. and Rucht, D. (eds) *Meeting Democracy: Power and Decision-Making in Global Justice Movements*.

Rummel, R. G. (1976) *Understanding Conflict and War. Vol 2: The Conflict Helix*, Beverly Hills, CA: Sage.

Ryfe, D. M. (2005) Does Deliberative Democracy Work?, *Annual Review of Political Science*, 8: 49–71.

Sanders, L. M. (1997) Against Deliberation, *Political Theory*, 25(3): 347–76.

Schmitter, P. C. and Streeck, W. (1981) The Organization of Business Interests. A Research Design to Study the Associative Action of Business in the Advanced Industrial Societies of Western Europe, Discussion Paper, Wissenschaftszentrum Berlin.

Sen, J., Anand, A., Escobar, A. and Waterman, P. (eds) (2004) *World Social Forum: Challenging Empires*, New Delhi: The Viveka Foundation.

Shapiro, I. (1999) Enough of Deliberation: Politics is about Interests and Power, in Macedo, S. (ed.) *Deliberative Politics: Essays on Democracy and Disagreement*, Oxford: Oxford University Press, 28–38.

Steenbergen, M. R., Bächtiger, A., Spörndli, M. and Steiner, J. (2003) Measuring Political Deliberation: A Discourse Quality Index, *Comparative European Politics*, 1: 21–48.

Steiner, J., Bächtiger, A. and Spörndli, M. (2004) *The Real World of Deliberation: Favourable Conditions and Substantive Outcomes* (EUI Working Paper SPS No. 2004/17, Florence: European University Institute. Available http://cadmus.iue.it/dspace/bitstream/1814/2634/1/sps2004-17.pdf (accessed: 26 July 2007).

Thompson, D. F. (2008) Deliberative Democratic Theory and Empirical Political Science, *Annual Review of Political Science*, 11: 497–520.

Verheyen, N. (2010) *Diskussionslust. Eine Kulturgeschichte des „besseren Arguments" in Westdeutschland*, Göttingen: Vandenhoeck & Ruprecht.

West, M. and Gastil, J. (2004) Deliberation at the Margins: Participant Accounts of Face-to-Face Public Deliberation at the 1999–2000 World Trade Protests in Seattle and Prague, *Qualitative Research Reports in Communication*, 5: 1–7.

Young, I. M. (1996) Communication and the Other: Beyond Deliberative Democracy, in Benhabib, S. (ed.) *Democracy and Difference: Contesting the Boundaries of the Political*, Princeton, NJ: Princeton University Press, 120–35.

Part III

Comparing innovations

7 Making better citizens?

Ken Newton

Three general problems stand in the way of democratic innovations designed to give citizens greater power and influence over public policy. First, democratic innovations are covered by shadows of the past. They are most usually created by the political and administrative elites of the existing system, they are inevitably embedded in the structures of representative democracy and their operations are inevitably conditioned by the accepted routines and practices of the established system of government. Their effectiveness as innovations designed to change and improve political life is inevitably reduced, to the extent that they are sponsored and guided by the very individuals, institutions and routines they seek to modify.

Second, there is a long-standing doubt about the capacity of ordinary people, or at least a large proportion of them, to carry out their citizenship duties. This requires a degree of intelligence, knowledge and understanding, as well as a readiness to give the time and effort necessary for effective participation in public affairs. Many writers from Plato onwards doubt that many citizens are able or willing to do this. The merit of representative democracy, it is argued, is that it places power in the hands of elites who are qualified to rule. Experiments with democratic innovations, particularly those of a direct democratic nature, are bound to fail because they simply do not recognize the limits of mass political capacities.

Third, there is the closely related problem of the extent to which democratic innovations are able to combat the powerful social, economic and political forces that induce political ignorance and inactivity. One study after another has demonstrated how difficult it is to increase the levels of political awareness and participation of those who are not already informed and engaged. Many attempts to overcome this problem report, at best, modest and partial success – even when time, money and effort are invested in them. The effects also have a nasty habit of fading over time as the patterns of normal life reassert themselves.

This chapter will examine these three questions in the light of the growing literature on democratic innovations and the attempts to evaluate their impact.

Representative and direct democracy

One of the major conclusions reached by both Budge and Kriesi in earlier chapters in this book is that the instruments of direct and participatory democracy operate in close partnership in practice, and should do so in theory if direct democracy is to avoid the problems that seem to beset it in a pure form. This line of argument raises an important question about democratic innovations, especially those intended to introduce direct democracy: to what extent are the workings of democratic innovations limited and conditioned by the fact that they are created by and embedded in the institutions of established forms of government, and to the extent that their operations are guided by, or even controlled by, traditional political elites?

This chapter will examine the question by looking closely at the main forms of direct citizen involvement in the government and politics of established democracies. The forms in question are town meetings, citizen initiatives, election recalls, referendums, and experiments with co-governance. Some of these can no longer claim to be innovatory because they date back to the nineteenth century. Nevertheless, they are found in only a few rather restricted areas of the world and continue to be held up as models of direct democracy in practice that should be replicated in other parts of the globe. Another advantage is that we can judge their effectiveness from their long history.

Town meetings

Town meetings have largely fallen into disuse although they are still held in some small communities and communes in New England and Switzerland. These are probably the simplest form of direct democracy, and one that stands as good a chance of success as any other form of direct democracy, because they involve small, local communities of people in the local issues that are close to them. In spite of de Tocqueville's admiration of them in the US, they seem to provide a poor example of direct democracy in action. Small is not necessarily beautiful where politics and participation are concerned. The participation of minorities often requires a sizeable critical mass, and the participation of majorities also requires populations large enough to develop a competitive party system, competitive elections, a media market large enough to provide regular local news, and a set of voluntary organizations and pressure groups large and varied enough to represent popular opinion (Newton 1982; Mansbridge 1983). In an increasingly large-scale, centralized and globalized world, small communities also lack the resources and capacity to deal with the most important problems of the modern world. The unavoidable limits set on their capacity sets limits on their powers, which, in turn, limits citizen involvement with them. This, as Dahl (1994) argues, creates a dilemma of system effectiveness versus participation.

Consequently, the decision-making powers of local and community government are limited to a few local matters and, even then, some town meetings are purely consultative, with no legislative authority of their own. Attendance is generally low (especially among the young and politically uninvolved) and two thirds of those who attend do not speak (Zimmerman 1999). None of this is surprising, given that one classic study of a New England township shows it to be closed, conservative, hierarchical, elitist and hard on minorities (Vidich and Bensman 1958). This does not make town meetings irrelevant or without influence, but it suggests caution in drawing too many optimistic conclusions about giving power to the people, even in small communities where they might, in theory, have substantial influence over local affairs.

Initiatives

In this volume Kriesi distinguishes carefully between popular or citizen initiatives and referendums, arguing that they follow different political logics (see also Geissel in this volume). Referendums are top-down instruments that give the electorate power to accept or reject a proposal of the political elite. They are reactive in nature. Citizen initiatives give citizens the power to propose legislation or a constitutional change and thus constitute an agenda-setting device for launching a public debate on a particular issue. They are proactive in nature. Initiatives are, therefore, a stronger form of direct democracy than referendums.

Citizen initiatives are found mainly in Switzerland (Kriesi 2005: 20–1), and in some states and local jurisdictions of the USA (where they are sometimes called 'ballot measures' or 'propositions'), most famously in California in 1978 where Proposition 13 altered the state constitution to permit the capping of property taxes. Initiatives are increasingly used in Italy (see also Geissel in this volume).

It would seem that the initiative is a perfect vehicle for direct democracy, yet they are often hedged about by a variety of restrictions that limit their impact. The higher the level in the political system, the less likely it is, in general, to make provisions for recalls. In the USA, initiative provisions are most common at the city level (61 per cent), rather less common at the state level (48 per cent), and not allowed at all in the higher reaches of the federal government. Where they are allowed, they often require conditions that can be difficult to meet without an efficient, effective and well-funded political organization. They often require the collection of a large number of signatures of registered electors within a specified time period and within a specified geographical area, and it is not uncommon for them to fail this first hurdle. Some local and state authorities in the USA place limits on the number of initiatives that may be considered in any one election.

In California, a state where initiatives are used more frequently than any other in the USA except Oregon, 1,187 initiatives were launched between 1912 and 2002. Of these, 824 (69.4 per cent) failed to qualify for a ballot, and of the remaining that did qualify, 99 were approved by the voters. In other words, of the original 1,187 initiatives that were launched, 8.3 per cent were successful (http://www.sos.ca.gov/elections/init_history.pdf). At around 10 per cent, the success rate of initiatives in Switzerland (LeDuc 2003: 160) is the same as in the USA. In New Zealand, only three citizen initiatives since 1993 have managed to reach the stage of being presented to the House of Representatives: the government rejected one, and no agreement could be reached on another (Morris 2007). In Switzerland, the Federal Assembly and Council can delay the vote on a proposed initiative for up to four years, by which time the issue may raise little interest (Kobach 1994: 106). In some places, initiative outcomes must be referred to supreme or constitutional courts that can reject them, and in Italy there are constitutional checks before a referendum can be held.

Although many initiatives do not succeed in being put to a general ballot, and most of these do not succeed in being passed, they can still have an impact on citizens and governments. In New Zealand, they have achieved their intended purpose in unexpected ways, because legislators have anticipated their effects (Morris 2007). In the USA, initiatives and other forms of direct democracy have been found to encourage a sense of subject efficacy on the part of citizens and a belief that government is more responsive (Bowler and Donovan 2002). In Switzerland, direct democracy fosters engagement, participation and an interest in politics (Baglioni 2007) and in both Switzerland and the USA, the evidence suggests a wide range of political benefits, including political efficacy, interest and discussion, government responsiveness, greater legitimacy and integration (Lupia and Matsusaka 2004; Kriesi 2005: 12–14; Moeckli 2007: 121–2). In short, initiatives may have a bigger impact than is suggested by the low number of initiatives that actually go to a ballot and are then passed by popular vote (see also Kriesi in this volume).

Initiatives also have their dangers. While the political power and success of wealthy economic interests is often overestimated where popular initiatives are concerned (Gerber 1999; Broder 2000; Bowler and Donovan 2002; Kriesi in this volume) some interest groups have been able to exploit initiatives for commercial reasons (Cronin 1989). The tobacco industry in the USA has promoted initiative action against itself because the outcome would have been less damaging than judicial proceedings. Supermarket and shopping mall owners have tried to use them to prevent competition. Some initiatives have used commercial organizations to collect signatures for their petition, which gives a great advantage to wealthy interests. Bill Sizemore ('Opposition Bill') has made extensive use of initiatives in Oregon to try to limit property taxes and block public expenditure programmes, although without much success. In California, it is not unusual to have up to twenty items on the same ballot, which makes it difficult for electors to make decisions and increases the chances of random or manipulated results (Magleby 1984). It is more usual in Switzerland to have two or three items on the same ballot.

The record of initiatives, therefore, is mixed. Many are hedged about by restrictions that limit their direct democratic impact, but in spite of this they can have both good and bad consequences from the point of view of direct democracy (see also Geissel in this volume).

Recalls

The recall allows citizens to remove elected representatives from office, provided enough signatures are on the recall petition, in which case it is put to a general vote. A great many fail for technical and legal reasons, and many fail to meet the minimum threshold of votes required. The recall is used primarily in the USA where it is quite widely spread at the local government level (61 per cent of cities) and has had a degree of success. Between 1996 and 2001, recalls were filed against 4 per cent of mayors and 5 per cent of council members in the USA, with success rates of 18 per cent and 29 per cent, respectively in the subsequent votes (http://www.iandrinstitute.org/Recall.htm). Like initiatives, recalls are less common at the state level, where only eighteen provide for them, and where their use is exceptional and examples of their success even rarer. There have only been two successful examples of state governor recalls, the victory of Arnold Schwarzenegger in California in 2003 being the most notable. Recalls are not allowed at all in federal government. In other words, the more important the political level and the more there is at political stake, the less the instruments of direct democracy are likely to be put into place and the less successful they are likely to be.

Although it is possible that the danger of recall might cause politicians to be more responsive to popular wishes, it seems more likely that their ineffectiveness is well known to the political class, which is more likely to discount than fear them. Experience of the recall as an instrument of direct democracy, therefore, suggests that it does not have a great potential so far as this may be judged from the American experience.

Referendums

Referendums are regularly used in a few countries – notably in Switzerland and the USA – but they are increasingly used on occasion in other countries. A referendum (or plebiscite), in contrast to the bottom-up initiative and recall, is a general vote on a specific proposal originating from the political authorities and as such, as Kriesi points out in this volume, it is a way of concluding debates among political elites. In contrast, initiatives and recalls start discussion and help to set agendas.

Although some believe that referendums are one of the most important forms of direct democracy (e.g. Barber 1984), especially if electronic means make voting much easier (Budge 1996), their powers are often constrained in various ways. Most require a minimum turnout and some require a large majority, especially if they deal with constitutional matters. Some are consultative or advisory, not binding. Courts, legislatures or independent electoral boards often decide referendum wording and set rules and procedures for them. Those called at the discretion of governments are a form of plebiscitary democracy rather than the purer form of direct democracy found in initiatives and recalls. As a result, referendums can be used by governments in ways that blunt the cutting edge of direct democracy: they may call them when they have a good chance of winning; they can organize them in a way that prompts a cascade of preferred results; and they can repeat the referendum till they get the result they want. The European Union (EU) membership referendums held successively in Austria, Finland, Sweden and Norway in 1994 were organized in this order because the first result might influence later results in the desired way. Governments have called a second referendum when the first did not produce the 'correct' result (the

Danish EU referendum and the British Columbia referendum on a new voting system – see below).

A common criticism is that referendums usually limit voters to an over-simple Yes/No, Accept/Reject choice on complex issues. This, however, can be remedied by using preferendums or multiple choice ballots. There is some evidence of voter fatigue and random results where ballots are held frequently and when ballot papers contain a large number of propositions (Magleby 1984; Moeckli 2007: 110–12). Turnout can be high, however, in particularly controversial ballots, or where they create a buzz of political interest because they are rarely used.

Some of the more common objections to referendums (and initiatives) are not convincing. The argument that direct democracy is likely to provoke populism, authoritarianism and discriminatory measures has been rejected in research on national referendums in the USA, although there is some evidence to support it in studies of local referendums (Kobach 1994; Svensson 1996; Mendelsohn and Cutler 2000; Bowler and Donovan 2002). Since parties are often very weakly organized at the local level in the USA, or even barred from the non-partisan elections of reformed cities, this is consistent with Budge's claim in this volume that referendums work best where they are linked with party programmes and organizations. It is said that money talks in referendum campaigns, but then money talks in many political battles, including general elections. Kriesi (in this volume) finds little evidence that elites in Switzerland can buy success at the polls, a conclusion repeated in studies of initiatives in the USA (Gerber 1999; Givel 2008).

In sum, although some criticisms of referendums do not seem to be supported by the evidence, they rarely work in the way required by the advocates of the purer forms of direct democracy. The evidence strongly suggests that referendums are limited, constrained and mediated by the institutions and elites of older and more conventional forms of government. There are, according to Budge and Kriesi in this volume, good theoretical and empirical reasons for believing that this may be both inevitable and to the benefit of democracy.

Co-governance

In this volume, Julien Talpin concludes that most forms of co-governance around the world remain consultative. This is because governments prefer them that way. While some have a decisive impact at the local level, they are not, in general, numerous enough to have much effect at the national level and it remains an open question whether, collectively, they have much effect on public policy and decision making at present. When promoted by political leaders, their role tends to be vague and their powers elusive. Moreover, there is the danger that small groups of people initially recruited as a cross section of the population to take part in co-governance institutions will, themselves, come to form a sub-elite of their own over time. Worse still, self-selected participants will most probably show all the special characteristics of the usual small in-group of active and involved citizens.

The three most widely discussed, admired and imitated examples of co-governance in the world are the Citizens' Assembly on Electoral Reform of British Columbia, Participatory Budgeting in Porto Alegre, Brazil, and the community schools and police experiments in Chicago. All three cases seem to be examples to greater or lesser extent of what Fung and Wright (2003) term 'empowered deliberative governance'. They give power to the people – at least the power to influence agendas, bring about some change, and affect decisions (Fung 2003a; Lang 2007; http://www.citizensassembly.bc.ca). In this respect, they seem to be clear cases of co-governance in action, with real power and influence.

At the same time, all three were strongly influenced by political elites and the formal institutions and procedures of representative democracy. The British Columbia Assembly was, like its successor the Ontario Citizens' Assembly, the initiative and the creation of government, which was motivated to set it up in order to gain a partisan advantage over its competitors for power (Carty et al. 2006: 1; Ferejohn 2008). It may well be that most democratic reforms are introduced for reasons of narrow self-interest, rather than a deep concern for the public good, but, nevertheless, such motives may help to explain why the government of the day gave the Assembly a rather narrow mandate, decided its structure, appointed its Chair and kept control of all its resources. Though the Assembly was formally completely independent of the government once it was set up (Lang 2007: 50), some suspect it was consciously or unconsciously steered by the government officials who served it (Fagotto and Fung 2006a: 11; Lang 2007: 51).[1] In accordance with its founding brief, its decision was put to a general referendum, and when this narrowly failed to reach its 60 per cent threshold of votes in favour (referendums often come down on the side of the status quo), the government decided to give its citizens the opportunity to reverse the wrong decision of the first ballot. This also failed, but both British Columbian and EU voters, it seems, are given a second chance to make the right decision when political elites do not like the outcome of the first referendum. In sum, the British Columbia Assembly was dependent upon the officials of representative government for its creation and was structured, guided and influenced, to some degree, by elected and appointed officials who, in spite of their best efforts, failed to get its recommendations adopted.

The Porto Alegre experiment was also set up for electoral gain by a newly elected mayor, who used it to advance his national political ambitions. The mayor and his office planned and implemented its structure, and then drove the process through, coordinated its meetings, set agendas and presented information to the main central budgetary forum. The mayor's office was closely linked to every stage of the Porto Alegre process, providing guidance, support, information and coordination (Bures 2002; Minos 2002). The result was, according to a World Bank report, substantial changes, including: improved facilities for the city; more accessible, higher quality public welfare amenities; and higher levels of participation.[2]

However, beneficial outcomes do not necessarily reflect co-governance processes and, like the British Columbia Assembly, the Porto Alegre programme was initiated and guided by the elected and appointed officials of representative government. According to close observers, it was 'an impressive example of *state-fostered civic organization*' born of a need to gain public support (Abbers 1998: 511, 534; Abbers' emphasis). Another close analysis of the experiment concludes that it was a case of state-sponsored neighbourhood assemblies and institutions (Baiocchi 2003), and a third describes it as a form of 'reformist state tutelage' (Baiocchi et al. 2005: 27).

The Chicago community experiments are similarly heavily dependent upon the formal authorities and institutions of representative government. Their 'accountable autonomy' gives them significant independence, but their efforts are supported by central departments of city government that provide guidance, training, money, advertising and expertise. The local schemes are dependent upon departments of the mayor's office that monitor their performance, hold them accountable, intervene directly when things go wrong, and set a general policy framework within the city's overall programme (Fung 2001). This degree of central control and coordination has sometimes caused substantial conflict between localities and the centre, with the result that the role of civic organizations has been weakened (Fung 2003c).

When government direction and support for co-governance arrangements is weak or absent, as seems to be the case with the generously funded (US$400 million over 20 years) Minneapolis Neighborhood Revitalization Program, then devolved schemes are in danger of under-achieving (Fagotto and Fung 2006b). Equally, when coordination takes the form of centralized technocratic management, as it has in South Africa's attempts to build local democracy, then participation and deliberation suffer (Millstein 2010). There is, as Heller (2001: 133) puts it, 'a delicate and workable balance to be struck'. Co-governance schemes can work where they are supported by parties and nurtured by state resources and encouragement, but are likely to fail or underachieve without them.

The danger, of course, is that over-strong 'mediation' of direct democracy becomes neither direct nor even especially democratic – it turns into just another form of top-down, elite directed, representative government. Another danger is that political leaders create vague and weak forms of empowerment, as Talpin observes in this volume, or they may hijack direct democratic institutions and use them for their own purposes. They can also 'cherry-pick' the policies and decisions they like and ignore the rest (Smith in this volume).

This review of the workings of town meetings, citizen initiatives, election recalls, referendums and experiments with co-governance suggests several conclusions. They are often hedged about with restrictions that limit their power and effectiveness. They are often limited to lower and less powerful levels of government, leaving the matters of high politics firmly located in established democratic institutions. There is the danger that the instruments of direct democracy may be hijacked by special interests groups, especially well organized and well financed ones, although some empirical studies question this fear, finding that referendums and initiatives in Switzerland and the USA are not especially prone to plutocratic manipulation. Nevertheless, democratic innovations are usually the creations of the elites of representative democracy and are typically directed and controlled by them. They work hand in hand with the institutions and practices of representative government, and are moulded in their image. There is the danger that elected elites will pick and choose what they want from the outcomes of direct democratic practices, leaving the rest aside.

Although they rarely work as they are supposed to in theory, or according to the textbook accounts of how they should operate, there is also evidence that direct democratic forms can have indirect effects. Generally speaking, initiatives and recalls are not powerful weapons in the armoury of direct democracy but, nevertheless, the fact that they might work in any given instance may help to keep elected politicians on a tighter rein of accountability. There is also evidence that the instruments of direct democracy employed in some states in the USA and in Switzerland have the effect of encouraging more positive attitudes towards government, higher levels of political engagement, and more effective and efficient forms of public service delivery. It would be ironic, however, if direct democracy was to be judged mainly in terms of its indirect effects.

Citizen competence

For the majority of citizens, family, work, leisure and sport are the most important things in life. For most, politics come low down the list of priorities. The mass critique of democracy claims this is because the majority of people are uneducated, unintelligent and lazy, anxious to claim their citizen rights but unable or unwilling to perform their citizen duties. Schumpeter (1942: 283) wrote that the masses are 'incapable of action other than a stampede' and in a similar vein Sartori (1987: 241) claims that direct democracy will quickly and disastrously founder on the reefs of mass cognitive incompetence. For elite theorists, however, the incompetence of the masses is better explained by the failure of political elites to encourage mass political participation or to actively discourage it.

Democratic innovations have tried to address the criticisms of the mass and elite theorists in two main ways. First, they have tested the claim that the masses are incapable of intelligent and informed judgements about the complexities and subtleties of politics. Second, they have tried to activate the inactive, mainly by way of electoral reforms, exploring new ways of informing and mobilizing citizens (especially by means of e-democracy) and by creating community groups to participate in civic affairs. The next section of this chapter turns to these two forms of democratic innovation and assesses their results (see also Geissel in this volume).

The reefs of mass cognitive incompetence

For John Dewey 'Democracy begins in conversation', but for Thomas Hobbes democracy was 'The aristocracy of orators'. Social scientists have experimented with different kinds of discussion forums to test the strength of the Hobbesian view, and to see how the Deweyan ideal might best be achieved. They have created citizen panels, juries and assemblies, focus groups and forums, community councils, planning cells and consensus conferences, and the series of deliberative polls devised by James Fishkin and his colleagues. For once, the outcome of the various experiments is comparatively clear-cut and unanimous. Given the right circumstances, ordinary citizens are capable of proper deliberation, of changing their minds as a result of discussion and information, and making judicious decisions that take account of the public interest. This point is made loudly and clearly in the chapters by Kriesi, Fishkin, Rucht, Talpin and Geissel in this volume (see also Cronin 1989; Lowndes et al. 2001; Fung 2003a; Fagotto and Fung 2006a: 11; Ferejohn 2008). Moreover, the conclusion is the same whether it is based on experiments with citizen assemblies and deliberative polls, which try to create the conditions for high quality citizen deliberation, or on observations drawn from Californian initiatives and direct democracy in Switzerland, which are real-world events. If the real world is the best test of Sartori's assertion, then Kriesi's conclusion in this volume is the most telling where he states that 'the Swiss experience amounts to a powerful empirical rebuttal of the arguments raised by sceptics like Sartori'.

Citizen assemblies and forums

Some qualifications and caveats need to be aired about experimental forums, however, before drawing the conclusion that they provide an unambiguous model of direct democracy in action. Rather than reflecting the everyday discussions of bar rooms or sitting rooms, forums are conducted according to rules of debate that cover equal voice, inclusiveness and respect for the views of others. They are often handled by skilled and trained facilitators or moderators who try to ensure that proceedings meet the standards of genuine deliberation. Consequently, some feel that forums can take an elitist and perhaps even an anti-democratic turn. Saward (2000: 7, 66, 75) Budge (2000: 199–200) and Rattila (2000) claim that Cohen's account (1989) of deliberative democracy is based on a model of 'university seminar' run by a benevolent professor, preferably a philosopher, or along the lines of 'a well conducted political debate among elites'.[3] This, it is claimed, imposes codes of discussion, reason and logic that might well exclude citizens who are, for whatever reason, incapable of following the high standards of deliberation as it is defined by philosophers and political scientists. For example, as Smith states (2000: 34), it is important that deliberating citizens do not see themselves as representing 'people like them'. They should transform self-regarding preferences into generalizable, other-regarding positions (Rattila 2000). Should we exclude from the deliberative process those who fail this test of disinterest and virtue? Offe (1997: 98) doubts it, but Dryzek (2000) believes that certain forms of deliberative democracy and deliberative polls can manage it. Perhaps the acid test of deliberative forums is to see how far participants get deliberating the rules of deliberation, rather than having these decided for them by those organizing the forums. But there is something of an infinite regress or catch-22 about this, since an ability to deliberate on the rules of deliberation presupposes agreement about the rules of deliberation.

For the deliberative democracy purist, talk of rules and facilitation may smack of elite manipulation and control that damages their direct democratic credentials. For realists, however, such things are necessary and inevitable if discussion is to meet even the minimal requirements of free debate, much less the strict conditions of pure deliberation. The tension between purists and realists, in this respect, is a different version of that between direct and representative democracy, discussed earlier in this chapter.

Citizen assemblies and forums involve face-to-face meetings of relatively small numbers of people, ranging from discussion groups of 10–20 people, to a maximum of a few hundred people meeting in the same space. Other things being equal, the smaller the numbers involved, the better able they are to achieve equal voice and inclusiveness, and the easier it is for them to meet over the period of time necessary for a full exchange of views and understandings. The smaller the group, the stronger its effects on participants are likely to be and, conversely, the larger the group, the weaker its effects are likely to be. There is a trade-off between size and effects. Therefore, electronic chat rooms and Twitter with their drop-in, drop-out culture and lack of intensive, face-to-face contact, are likely to produce weak effects, although they may involve very large numbers.

One solution is to open discussion forums to all those who wish to attend, rather than restricting them to a small and carefully selected sample. The double problem with this strategy is that increasing the numbers is likely to reduce the impact, and open forums are likely to attract those who are already aware, involved and committed. Another solution is to create target forums for marginal and politically inactive people, but it can be an uphill struggle to maintain the interest of such groups (Smith 2005: 33).

The third problem with small groups that meet regularly over a period of time is, as Talpin points out in this volume, that those who participate may come to form their own world view, so creating a set of new sub-elites that becomes distanced from the groups whose opinions they were supposed to reflect in the first place (see also Pratchett 1999: 623). The paradox is that small groups are supposed to inform and influence each other by deliberating, but may in the process cease to reflect the opinions of the population they were drawn from in the first place.

Activating the inactive

Many democratic innovations of the citizen-centred variety try to broaden and deepen citizen engagement in political life. They aim to improve knowledge, awareness and understanding of politics and thereby increase the number and variety of individuals and groups involved. Have they succeeded in making citizens more informed, aware and active? For evidence, we turn first to electoral reforms designed to increase voter turnout, then to a large and assorted set of measures that encourage citizen interest and knowledge of public issues, especially those focused on the potential power of e-democracy, and, last, to the co-governance projects that have tried to involve the inactive in public decision making and policy making.

Electoral reform

Voter registration reforms try to make it easier for citizens to get their names on the electoral register and to end discriminatory practices. They include same day registration as the poll itself, the elimination of corrupt and discriminatory practices that try to prevent some social groups from registering, public registration campaigns and continuous updating of the register. Many of these are fairly simple technical and bureaucratic matters that can be accomplished with relatively little difficulty, given the political will. However, increasing the percentage registered does not necessarily increase voter turnout significantly, at least in the short term. Newly registered voters often take some time to exercise their political rights, and those who do not vote are not inclined to change, even if their name appears easily or automatically on the register (International Institute for Democracy and Electoral Assistance 2002: 63). Those who do not vote early in their adult life tend to persist with the habit (Electoral Commission 2006a). However, experience suggests that voting turnout of the newly registered may begin to rise towards national levels after a time, as generations are replaced. Voter registration innovations are important, because they help to implement the fundamental right to vote, but they remove technical barriers to voting rather than actively encouraging turnout and, to this extent, their impact is likely to be limited. The real obstacle to voting participation is in the dead weight of social forces that causes lack of political interest and involvement, and voting reforms are more likely to tackle this problem than registration measures.

Innovations that encourage voting mainly take the forms of compulsory voting, early voting, postal voting and electronic voting. Compulsory voting has always been fairly rare in established democracies (Austria, Belgium, Greece, Italy, Luxembourg, Switzerland and Australia) and, even here, the sanctions are sometimes weak, not enforced, or full of loopholes (International Institute for Democracy and Electoral Assistance 2002: 109). Nevertheless, the evidence that turnout is higher in compulsory voting systems (International Institute for Democracy and Electoral Assistance 2002: 110) has aroused some interest in other countries (Hill 2002; Ballinger 2006; Electoral Commission 2006b; Keaney and Rogers 2006; Engelen 2007), although it has also been argued that it should be accompanied by positive abstention (the none-of-the-above option on ballot papers). Others argue against compulsory voting on the grounds that it would make rather little difference to 'real' (that is, voluntary self-motivated) voter turnout, and that it is contrary to the very ethos of democratic elections (see Electoral Commission, 2006b). Compulsory voting, they argue, is to voting what compulsory religion is to religion – no religion at all.

Early voting, that is in advance of election day, is used in Texas (which also has a 'curbside' voting option) and Florida (Gronke 2004: Gronke et al. 2004) and a pilot study was run by the UK's Electoral Commission (2006a), all with no more than a very limited effect on turnout. Postal voting has been widely tried with some success in increasing turnout at relatively low cost. Against this, it has been said that postal voting simply reinforces the gap between the politically active and inactive, is subject to fraud, has problems with the secrecy of the ballot, and relies heavily on the reliability of the postal system (Slater and James 2007). The fraud problem might be cured with the appropriate checks and controls (as in any form of ballot), but the other problems are less easily solved.

In trying to assess the effect of electoral innovations, it is difficult to know whether they have little effect or whether, perhaps, turnout would have declined even faster without them. In general, it seems that most attempts to increase citizen participation in elections have not been notably successful and the effects, if any, have generally been small. According to Smith (2005: 20) the most promising device for increasing turnout seems to be the technically old-fashioned postal vote, although its impact seems to be more marginal than major. Caution is necessary before dismissing them, however, because it is always possible that it takes a time for reforms to have an impact.

E-democracy

Electronic voting is seen by some as the best option for increasing voting turnout (see, for example, Budge 1996; Stoker 2006: 190–92). Electronic voting machines in polling stations do not count in this respect, because they merely replace paper or card with electronic signals. What has potential significance for voter turnout are the electronic options that allow remote and time-displaced voting using the web at home, or specially provided computers in easily accessible public places. Although electronic voting has been tried, often experimentally, in many places, there is still rather little systematic, long-term research to evaluate its effects. What there is suggests that the effects are not strong, because the digital divide means that the new technology tends to be used by those who made heaviest use of the old technology and because what counts is not the technology so much as the motivation to use it in order to vote. As Norris (2002b) states, 'E-voting is unlikely to prove a "magic ballot"' (see also Gibson et al. 2004: 195–6).

The real importance of electronics for politics lies less in their technical uses for registration and voting systems than in their potential for informing and mobilizing citizens. One argument is that new methods of interactive electronic communication (Web 2.0) have far more potential than Web 1.0 for stimulating political interest. Whereas Web 1.0 operates as an electronic notice board, Web 2.0 makes dialogue possible between governments and citizens, and between citizens and citizens. Maybe so, though it is too early to know, partly because governments have been slow to adopt the new technology (Zittel 2004; Mahrer and Krimmer 2005), partly because in many instances, Web 2.0 dialogue, at its best, has fallen far short of the standards of deliberation (Chadwick 2009) and, at its worst, has been described as amateur 'electronic narcissism', based upon mediocrity, ignorance and opinionated misunderstanding (Flintoff 2007; Keen 2007).

Another argument is that the new electronic communication could have a significant effect on political life by reaching parts of the electorate that the old forms did not reach. In particular, it is claimed, it could inform and activate the youngest age groups in the electorate. On the one hand, they are the least interested and involved in conventional politics. On the other, they also make the greatest use of the new electronic communications, so their political interests and engagement might be raised by chat rooms, forums, blogs, Twitter, Facebook, MySpace and any one of a growing number of websites that promote the creation of networks and groups with an active interest in civic affairs and public policy. Once again, all of this is possible, but so also is the counter-argument that the electronic technology might help people to avoid politics by providing a huge number of specialist media outlets that allow people to concentrate exclusively on what they want and to avoid political reporting. According to Sunstein (2002, 8), the most striking power of the new communications technologies is the ability of viewers to filter what they see. The result might be small ghettoes of like-minded political activists engrossed in their own specialist echo chambers of opinion, and large majorities who tune in to nothing but sport, soap operas, nature programmes, cartoons, Hollywood blockbusters or sitcoms (see, among others Davis 1999; Pratchett 2002; Sunstein 2002; Bimber 2003; Norris 2004; Buchsbaum 2005; Brandenburg 2006; Oates, et al. 2006; Stevens and O'Hara 2006).

The impact of electronic notice boards, electronic consultation, various forms of e-democracy and online government also seems to be fairly slight. Although Schmitter and Trechsel (2004: 91) suggest the creation of 'democracy kiosks' in public places to make it easier to acquire political information, the sheer amount available already makes information overload a problem. And the more there is, the greater the need for centralized and hierarchically organized search engines and portals to help us find, sift and sort the facts, figures and opinion. And the greater the likelihood that editorial control (Wikipedia calls it 'flagged revisions') of web material will become more common. This defeats one of the main virtues claimed for the net in its early days – its open and democratic nature, and the direct and unmediated entry into the web of those who produce and consume its material.

Co-governance

It can be exceedingly difficult to overcome the powerful social forces and institutional inertia that result in political inactivity, and community forums, citizens' panels and consultative groups set up to attract marginal and minority groups have not been particularly successful in activating the inactive (Pratchett 1999; Smith 2005: 33; Smith and Stephenson 2005). They are more likely to involve the unrepresentative and self-selected part of the general population that is already involved. If they do attract members of the inactive target group, there is the danger that they are different in some important respects from the minority group they are supposed to represent (Pratchett 1999: 623), or will become less representative of that group after a period of intensive meetings (Talpin in this volume).

Nevertheless, some innovations have succeeded in reversing the normal pattern of political withdrawal. To their considerable credit, all three prime examples of co-governance – Porto Alegre, the Chicago community projects, and the Citizens' Assembly of British Columbia – have successfully generated the participation of the poor and unorganized. According to Lang (2007: 65), the British Columbia Assembly 'circumvented the influence of narrow interests, money and organization and re-focussed decision making around the search for common ground'. The Porto Alegre experiment succeeded in organizing and mobilizing the poor and inactive, serving as a model for successful schemes in many other Brazilian cities and slums (Baiocchi 2003; Baiocchi et al. 2005). Though patchy and inadequate, participation in the Chicago schemes 'undoubtedly increase the scope for citizen participation and deliberation' (Fung 2001: 80). The police scheme has actually reversed the normal pattern of low engagement in poorer areas, and has produced higher rates of participation among the wealthier and better educated individuals within these poor areas (Fung 2001: 92).

Not all co-governance experiments are this successful, as we have seen (Fagotto and Fung 2006b; Millstein 2010). Those in Porto Alegre, Chicago and British Columbia were expensive, all three concentrated on relatively small numbers of participants and made it possible for them to meet regularly over a long period of time, and all three were provided with the organizational support of political authorities. They were intensively proactive forms of innovation, rather than the more permissive or enabling forms such as registration and electoral change and the electronic provision of information and discussion forums. The three prime examples of co-governance success also concentrated on a relatively small population within relatively small geographical areas. Whether they can be transplanted with similar success to a higher regional or national level of government is questionable (see also Geissel in this volume).

The conclusion to be drawn from this brief assessment of attempts to activate the inactive is that general, diffuse and untargeted attempts have not been notably successful. Experiments that focus on small areas and specific target groups seem to have more success in including those parts of the population that are normally outside the political arena, provided that they are carefully set up and resourced by political authorities that really want them to succeed.

Quotas

There is one way of reforming electoral arrangements that shows remarkable success at a relatively low cost to the authorities that introduce them. This is by using electoral quotas and reserved seats to ensure greater representation of social groups on elected bodies that would otherwise be under-represented. Quotas specify a target percentage of seats to be filled by a given section of the population by election. Reserved seats set aside a specific number of places to be filled by the target population either by election or appointment (Reynolds 2005). Maoris have had reserved seats in the New Zealand parliament since 1867 (Archer 2003), but at least ten other countries reserve seats for specific ethnic, religious or linguistic groups (Meier 2007). Quotas for women are found in one form or another in more than 100 countries, some introduced as early as 1954 (Pakistan) but most in the 1990s or later (Dahlerup 2007b).

If quota rules are clear, adapted to the electoral rules of the country, and backed by sanctions, they can result in a rapid and large increase in women sitting in national and local parliaments – as they have in such diverse places as Costa Rica, South Africa and Rwanda (Matland 2007: 278–80). Fourteen of the seventeen countries with more than 30 per cent of parliamentary seats held by women in 2005 had either legal or party quotas (Dahlerup 2007b: 18). Moreover, the evidence shows that they can have a substantial effect on increasing women's representation in a short time, sometimes in the first election to which the quotas rules are applied. While most quota systems do not manage to meet their target figures, they still manage to increase the representation of the target group substantially and quickly.

The message is clear: quotas work. So it is worthwhile spelling out briefly the reasons for their efficacy, if they are correctly applied in the first place. First, although some are voluntary, some are backed by the legislative force of the state and enforced with sanctions. They are mandatory obligations: not the kind of voluntary options that can be ignored. Second, they are targeted on a specific portion of the population, rather than the general electorate. Third, female quotas are defined and demarcated in a precise way. This is not possible for many other social groups in society that might try to claim a quota, such as ethnic, religious, class or age groups. In their case, quotas would provoke huge difficulties about who exactly is covered by the legislation and who is not. Fourth, they are relatively costless for governments to introduce, if not for the organizations obliged to respond to them. Governments simply have to pass an act, which is just part of their daily routine. They do not have to set up special budgets and departments to organize complex activities or experiments and they do not have to create special agencies to monitor and control the application of policy or the spending of money. Fifth, female quotas in most countries seem to arouse little controversy. And sixth, unlike the technology of the new electronic communications that is not easily transplanted to developing countries (Heeks 2003), quotas are easily understood and, in principle, relatively easily applied.

Like any other political practice, quotas may also have unanticipated consequences. For example, if a national legislature is to represent the voting preferences of a large part of the electorate, there may be room for only one quota. To discriminate in favour of one group, however, is necessarily to exclude others from this preferential treatment and this may cause political problems and resentment on the part of the excluded.

The impact of innovations

Evidence about the long-term impacts of democratic innovations on a broad cross section of the population is hard to come by (Rowe and Frewer 2004; Abelson and Gauvin 2006: 33; see also Geissel in this volume), partly because there is little impact research, partly because the investigation is often a minefield of problems, and partly because it can be exceedingly hard to measure effects with any precision or certainty. Before-and-after research designs are not common. Governments that introduce innovations tend to be shy about monitoring effects, especially if this is costly and there is a danger of revealing failure. Some innovations also require long-term follow-up studies, which can add to expense, and government attention span is often notoriously short. Some reforms have little or no impact, because governments set them up this way. On the other side of the coin, Smith (in this volume) gives examples of mini-publics that have had an effect on public policy, though he also points out that it can be difficult to establish these among the welter of other possible influences on policy issues.

There is also the natural enthusiasm for reforms on the part of those who strongly favour them and want them to succeed. As Geissel points out in this volume, the potential and actual impact of democratic innovations has often been overstated. A good deal of the evidence about innovations, however, suggests that their successes are often relatively modest. We have already seen how little effect many electoral reforms and many of the e-government innovations have had, especially when it comes to combating the powerful forces that promote political ignorance and indifference. Few of the many and varied electoral changes that have been tried across the western world in the last two or three decades have had their intended effect of significantly lifting voting turnout or of stirring the political interest of apolitical social groups. The American Democrats made comparatively heavy use of electronic campaigning in 2008 and the election had a much higher turnout than normal, estimated at almost 57 per cent compared with 37 per cent and 55 per cent in 2004 and 2000, respectively. But this may have more to do with Obama as a candidate and the special nature of the election.

Electronic democracy has been the subject of much hope and expectation, but it too has not delivered large or lasting improvements. One comprehensive survey of the field (Margolis 2007: 765–6) observes that many cyber-democracy visionaries in the 1990s claimed that the web would bring about radical changes in government and politics by increasing citizen involvement and influence over public affairs. The predictions of the techno-utopians have not been fulfilled. Instead, there has been a normalization of political cyber-space and the replication of old patterns. Margolis (2007: 767) concludes that the limitations of e-government and e-democracy should cause us to scale down our expectations. The most they can do is encourage citizens to react to government policies, rather than encourage them to participate directly and proactively in forming those policies.

It is also necessary to allow for the possibility that some innovations may have unfortunate side effects. One may crowd out others by attracting the lion's share of money and attention. The effects of one may counteract those of another. Innovations may be used for purposes not originally intended. It is not unknown, as we have seen, for initiatives to be used against the public interest by special groups and commercial organizations.

In other cases, the side effects have proved to be positive and welcome. Referendums are intended to produce a popular decision on a specific issue, but there is evidence that they also have a general effect on public attitudes towards government, confidence in political institutions and subjective political competence. In this volume, Kriesi shows that direct democracy in Switzerland helps to improve macro-economic performance, brings public expenditure more closely into line with citizen preferences, helps to legitimate and integrate the political system, heightens the sense that it is fair and democratic, and has a direct effect on life satisfaction (see also Kriesi 2005: 12–14; Baglioni 2007; Moeckli 2007: 121–2). The same conclusions emerge from research in the USA (Bowler and Donovan 2002).

Conclusions

Democratic innovations are as old as the hills, but systematic research on them is relatively new and underdeveloped. Much of it is fragmented and piecemeal, often organized around case studies that cannot yield clear cause and effect conclusions, and often concerned with innovations and experiments set in particular places and circumstances that make their likely effects in other places and circumstances difficult to judge. Impact research is difficult and relatively rare, particularly research over time that allows for the possibility that it may take many years before an innovation produces fruit. At the same time, the longer it takes for an innovation to have an effect, the more difficult it is to sort this out from other effects. Meanwhile, it is not unusual to come across passionate and dogmatic claims about new political practices. Some are optimistic and exaggerate their potential benefits, other are sceptical and borne out of the 'nothing-works' frame of mind.

In spite of all the mist and murkiness that surrounds research, it does suggest some conclusions. First, we should set aside the idea that instruments and practices of direct democracy can supplant the old institutions and operating modes of representative democracy. Democratic innovations are inevitably bolted on to and, therefore, inevitably shaped and influenced by the machinery of representative government and its political elites. Evidence about direct democracy in Switzerland and about the best examples of co-governance in other parts of the world clearly supports this conclusion. Indeed, evidence and theory suggest that the best examples of direct democracy in practice work well precisely because they are complemented by the activities of representative democracy – that is, when they are mediated by the parties, governments and leaders of representative democracy.

Similarly, if deliberative democracy means anything, it means political discussion conducted according to certain principles and according to certain rules of the organizers of forums. Purists who aspire to free and unconstrained debate according to the rules and preferences of only those who participate may not like this idea, but we cannot ignore the empirical evidence that it is how the world works, nor the theoretical case that it works best that way.

The second conclusion is that the evidence shows that citizens can, in the right circumstances, fulfil the requirements of democratic citizenship. They can, given the right circumstances, discuss with respect for the view of others, change their minds in the light of evidence and argument, and reach judicious conclusions that take account of the public interest. At present at least, the accumulation of evidence suggests that the sceptics who doubt the civic competence of the masses are wrong. This conclusion is based not only on the evidence derived from carefully constructed experiments with mini-publics, which create very special and ideal circumstances, but also on the real-world operation of direct democratic practices in Switzerland over a long period of time. It is also the evidence of the real-world discussions of the new social movements studied by Rucht in this volume. Rarely have the social sciences produced such a clear-cut answer to an age-old controversy, in this case dating back to Plato's defence of philosopher-kings. It seems to be a case where empirical evidence is heavily on one side of the argument.

The third conclusion is that it is exceedingly difficult to overcome the powerful social, economic and political forces that induce political indifference and inactivity. Most democratic innovations, whether they are consultative arrangements, electronic communications and e-government, electoral reforms, or direct democratic instruments like New England town meetings, initiatives and recalls, have failed to make more than a small dent in the problem. Diffuse measures such as electronic notice boards aimed at large and general populations seem to preach to the converted. These are what one might term permissive innovations that ask citizens to react. In contrast, the Porto Alegre, Chicago, and British Columbian experiments with co-governance have been much more successful in activating the inactive. These are intensive, well resourced, well organized and highly focused innovations that provide citizens with the means of being proactive. They have in common a will on the part of political authorities for them to succeed, backed up by the necessary financial, organizational and professional resources.

One major exception to the generally disappointing impact of many democratic innovations involves the use of quotas for the inclusion of excluded and marginal groups on representative bodies. Women's quotas, properly implemented, have succeeded in a short space of time and at very little cost to governments. However, there are trade-offs here as well. It is not possible to implement quotas for all minority groups in society when it comes to representation on legislative assemblies. Quotas (positive discrimination) for one section of the population reduce the chances of quotas for others, which may leave them with a sense of grievance and exclusion. This is not an argument against democratic innovations any more than it is an argument against quotas, which stand or fall on completely different sorts of arguments. All forms of government and all forms of political organization contain within themselves a mobilization of bias that makes certain things more possible and other things less possible. The argument here is that we should be aware of the possible knock-on effects and try to take account of them in our calculations.

The final message is most certainly not that 'nothing works'. A few things work and some of them work very well (see also Geissel in this volume). It will be rewarding to study them more closely to see how and why.

Notes

1 In the same way, Smith (2005: 45) raises questions about citizen control over agendas and the direction of the America Speaks 21st Century Town Meetings, and about the role of officials who have to collate and synthesise at speed the simultaneous discussions of small groups.

2 See http://siteresources.worldbank.org/INTEMPOWERMENT/Resources/14657_Partic-Budg-Brazil-web.pdf.

3 Cohen argues that those engaged in deliberation should not take a narrow or group interest standpoint, but should arrive at a rationally motivated consensus focused on the common good. They should engage in free deliberation between formally and substantively equal participants who are accorded equal voice.

Bibliography

Abbers, R. (1998) From clientalism to cooperation: Local government, participatory policy and civic organization in Porto Alegre, Brazil, *Politics and Society*, Vol. 26, No. 4: 511–37.

Abelson, J. and Gauvin, F.-P. (2006) *Assessing the Impacts of Public Participation: Concepts, Evidence and Policy Implications*, Ottawa, Canadian Policy Research Networks.

Ackerman, B. and Fishkin, J. S. (2003) Deliberation Day, in Fishkin, J. S. and Laslett, P. (eds) *Debating Deliberative Democracy*, Oxford: Blackwell.

—— (2004) *Deliberation Day*, New Haven, CT: Yale University Press.

Andersen, I.-E. and Jaeger, B. (1999) Danish participatory models, *Science and Public Policy*, Vol. 26, No. 5: 331–40.

Archer, K. (2003) Representing Aboriginal interests: Experiences of New Zealand and Australia, *Electoral Insight,* Vol. 5, No. 3: 39–45.

Avritzer, L. (2002) *Democracy and the Public Space in Latin America*, Princeton, NJ: Princeton University Press: 135–65.

Baglioni, S. (2007) The effects of direct democracy and city size on political participation: The Swiss case, in Zittel, T. and Fuchs, D. (2007) *Participatory Democracy and Political Participation*, London: Routledge: 91–106.

Baiocchi, G. (2001) Participation, activism, and politics: The Porto Alegre experiment and deliberative democratic theory, *Politics and Society*, Vol. 29, No. 1: 43–72.

—— (2003) Emergent public spheres: Talking politics in participatory governance, *American Sociological Review*, Vol. 68, No. 1: 52–74.

Baiocchi, G., Heller, P, and Silva, M. K. S. (2005) Making space for civil society. Evidence from government reforms in 10 Brazilian Municipalities. Available at http://participatorybudgeting.blogs.com/MakingSpaces.pdf (accessed 11 April 2011).

Ballinger, C. (2006) *Democracy and Voting*, London: Hansard Society.

Barber, B. (1984) *Strong Democracy: Participatory Politics for a New Age*, Berkeley, CA: California University Press.

Barnes, S, and Kaase, M. et al. (1979) Political Action: Mass Participation in Five Western Democracies, Beverly Hills, CA: Sage.

Bimber, B. A. (2003) Information and American Democracy: Technology in the Evolution of Political Power, Cambridge: Cambridge University Press.
Bowler, S. and Donovan, T. (2002) Democracy, institutions and attitudes about citizen influence on government, *British Journal of Political Science*, Vol. 32: 371–90.
Bowler, S., Brockington, D. and Donovan, T. (2001) Electoral systems and voter turnout: Experiments in the United States, *Journal of Politics*, Vol. 63: 902–15.
Bowler, S., Donovan, T. and Happ, T. (2002) Ballot propositions and information costs: Direct democracy and the fatigued voter, *Western Political Quarterly*, Vol. 45: 559–69.
Brandenburg, H. (2006) Pathologies of the Virtual Public Sphere, in Oates, S., Owen, D. and Gibson, K. (eds) The Internet and Politics: Citizens, Voters, and Activists, New York: Routledge: 207–22.
Broder, D. S. (2000) *Democracy Derailed: The Initiative Movement and the Power of Money*, San Diego, CA: Harcourt.
Buchsbaum, T. M. (2005) *E-voting: Lessons learnt from recent pilots*. Paper to the Conference on E-voting and Electronic Democracy: Present and the Future, Seoul: March 2005.
Budge, I. (1996) *The New Challenge of Direct Democracy*, Cambridge, Polity Press.
—— (2000) Deliberative Democracy Versus Direct Democracy – Plus Political Parties! in Saward, M. (ed.) *Democratic Innovation*, London: Routledge: 195–212.
Buhlmann, M., Merkel, W. and Wessels, B. (2008) *The quality of democracy: democracy barometer for established democracies*, Working paper 10a, Zurich: University of Zurich, National Centre of Competence in Research.
Bures, L. (2002) Tools and practices 6: Participatory budgeting, in *Empowerment and Poverty Reduction: A Sourcebook*, New York: World Bank: 128–9.
Campbell, A., Converse, P., Miller, W. and Stokes, D. (1960) *The American Voter*, New York: John Wiley.
Caplan, B. (2007) *The Myth of the Rational Voter: Why Democracies Choose Bad Policies*, Princeton, NJ: Princeton University Press.
Carty, R. K., Blais, A. and Fournier, P. (2006) *Citizens' choice to reform SMP: The British Columbia Citizens' Assembly on Electoral Reform*, Paper presented to the 2006 meeting of Election, Public Opinion and Parties Conference, September 2006, Nottingham, England.
Catt, H. and Murphy, M. (2003) What voice for the people? Categorising methods of public consultation, *Australian Journal of Political Science* Vol. 38, No. 3: 407–21.
Chadwick, A. (2003) Bringing e-democracy back in: Why it matters for future research on e-governance, *Social Science Computer Review*, Vol. 21, No. 4: 443–55.
Chadwick, A. (2009) Web 2.0: New challenges for the study of e-democracy in an era of informational exuberance, *I/S: A Journal of Law and Policy for the Information Society* Vol. 5, No. 1: 9–41.
Cohen, J. (1989) Deliberation and Democratic Legitimacy, in Hamlin, A. and Pettit, P. (eds) *The Good Polity*, Oxford: Blackwell: 17–34.
Converse, P. (1964) The nature of Belief Systems in Mass Publics, in Apter, D. (ed.) *Ideology and Discontent*, New York: Free Press.
Cronin, T. E. (1989) *Direct Democracy: The Politics of Initiative, Referendum and Recall*, Cambridge: Cambridge University Press.
Dahl, R. (1994) A democratic dilemma: System effectiveness versus citizen participation, *Political Science Quarterly*, Vol. 109, No. 1: 23–34.

Dahlerup, D. (2007a) Equality of opportunity and equality of result, *Representation*, Vol. 43, No. 2: 73–92. Available at http://www.informaworld.com/smpp/1218702728-51275503/title~content=t741771152~db=all~tab=issueslist~branches=43 – v43 (accessed 11 April 2011).

—— (2007b) Introduction, in Dahlerup, D. (ed.) *Women, Quotas and Politics*, London: Routledge: 1–29.

Dalton, R. J. (1996) *Citizen Politics*, Chatham, NJ: Chatham House.

—— (2004) *Democratic Challenges, Democratic Choices: The Erosion in Political Support in Advanced Industrial Democracies*, Oxford: Oxford University Press.

Davis, R. (1999) *The Web of Politics: The Internet's Impact on the American Political System*, New York: Oxford University Press.

Delli Carpini, M. X., Cook, F. L. and Jacobs, L. R. (2004) Public deliberation, discursive participation, and citizen engagement: A review of the empirical literature, *Annual Review of Political Science*, Vol. 7, 315–44.

Diamond, L. J. and Morlino, L. (2004) An overview, *Journal of Democracy*, Vol. 15, No. 4: 20–31.

Donovan, T. and Bowler, S. (2004) *Reforming the Republic: Democratic Institutions for the New America*, Upper Saddle River, NJ: Pearson-Prentice Hall.

Dryzek, J. S. (2000) Discursive Democracy vs. Liberal Constitutionalism, in Saward, M. (ed.) *Democratic Innovation*, London, Routledge: 78–92.

Electoral Commission (2006a) *May 2006 Electoral Schemes Pilot Schemes: Early voting*, August, London: Electoral Commission.

Electoral Commission (2006b) *Compulsory Voting*, Fact Sheet, December, London: Electoral Commission.

Engelen, B. (2007) Why compulsory voting can enhance democracy, *Acta Politica*, Vol. 42: 23–39. Available at http://www.palgrave-journals.com/ap/journal/v42/n1/full/5500167a.html – aff1 (accessed 11 April 2011).

Fagotto, E. and Fung, A. (2006a) The British Columbia Citizens' Assembly. Available at http://archonfung.net/docs/cases/BCCitizensAssembly0604.pdf (accessed 11 April 2011).

—— (2006b) Empowered participation in urban governance: The Minneapolis Neighborhood Revitalization Program, *International Journal of Urban and Regional Research*, Vol. 30, No. 3: 638–55.

Ferejohn, J. (2008) The Citizens' Assembly Model, in Warren, M. and Pearse, H. (eds) *Designing Deliberative Democracy: The British Columbia Citizens' Assembly*, Cambridge: Cambridge University Press: 192–213.

Fishkin, J. (2006) The nation in a room, *Boston Review*, March/April.

Flintoff, J. P. (2007) Thinking is so over, *The Times* (London), 3 June.

Fung, A. (2001) Accountable autonomy: Toward empowering deliberation in Chicago Schools and Policing, *Politics and Society*, Vol. 29, No. 1: 73–103.

—— (2003a) *Empowered Participation: Reinventing Urban Democracy*, Princeton, NJ: Princeton University Press.

—— (2003b) Deliberative Democracy, Chicago Style: Grass Roots Governance in Policing and Public Education, in Fung, A. and Wright, E. O. (eds) *Deepening Democracy: Institutional Innovations in Empowered Participatory Governance*, London: Verso: 119–39.

—— (2003c) Deliberation where you least expect it: Citizen participation in government, *Connections*, Fall: 30–3.

Fung, A. and Wright, E. O. (2001) Deepening democracy: Innovations in empowered participatory governance, *Politics and Society,* Vol. 29, No. 1: 5–41.

—— (2003) Thinking About Empowered Participatory Governance, in Archon, F. and Wright, E. O. (eds) *Deepening Democracy: Institutional Innovations in Empowered Participatory Governance*, London: Verso: 3–42.

Gerber, E. (1999) *The Populist Paradox: Interest Group Influence and the Promise of Direct Legislation*, Princeton, NJ: Princeton University Press.

Gibson, R. K., Rommele, A. and Ward, S. J. (eds) (2004) *Electronic Democracy*, London: Routledge.

Givel, M. S. (2008) Tobacco industry media efforts to defeat state tobacco control ballot initiatives and referenda, in National Cancer Institute, Monograph 19: *Use of the Media to promote and Discourage Tobacco Use* , Washington. DC: National Cancer Institute.

Goodin, R. E. and Dryzek, J. S. (2006) Deliberative impacts: The macro-political uptake of mini-publics, *Politics & Society*, Vol. 34, No. 2: 219–44.

Gronke, P. (2004) *Early Voting Reforms and American Elections*, Paper presented at the Annual Meeting of the American Political Science Association, Chicago.

Gronke, P., Bishin, B., Stevens, D. and Galanes-Rosenbaum, E. (2004) *Early Voting in Florida*, Paper presented at the Annual Meeting of the American Political Science Association, Washington DC.

Heeks, R. (2003) *Most E-Government-For-Development Fails: How Can Risks Be Reduced?*, Manchester: Manchester University iGovernment Working Papers No. 14.

Held, D. (1987) *Models of Democracy*, Cambridge: Polity Press.

Held, D. and McGrew, A. (1998) The end of the old order?, *Review of International Studies*, Vol. 24: 230.

Held, D. and Pollitt, C. (eds) (1986) *New Forms of Democracy*, London: Sage and The Open University.

Heller, P. (2001) Moving the state: The politics of democratic decentralization in Kerala, South Africa, and Porto Alegre, *Politics and Society*, Vol. 29, No. 1: 131–63.

Hill, L. (2002) On the reasonableness of compelling citizens to vote: The Australian case, *Political Studies*, Vol. 50, No. 1: 80–101.

Inglehart, R. (1997) *Modernization and Postmodernization: Cultural, Economic, and Political Change in 43 Societies*, Princeton NJ: Princeton University Press.

Inglehart, R. and Welzel, C. (2005) *Modernization, and Democracy: The Human Development Sequence*, Cambridge: Cambridge University Press.

International Institute for Democracy and Electoral Assistance (IDEA) (2002) *Voter Turnout Since 1945*, Stockholm: IDEA.

Jefferson, T. (1776) Draft Fragment of the Declaration of Independance, see: http://www.loc.gov/exhibits/jefferson/jeffdec.html (accessed October 2010).

Jennings, K. and van Deth, J. et al. (1990) *Continuities in Political Action*, Berlin and New York: de Gruyter.

Keaney, E. and Rogers, B. (2006) *A Citizen's Duty: Voter Inequality and the Case for Compulsory Turnout*, London: Institute for Public Policy Research.

Keele, L. (2007) Social capital and the dynamics of trust in government, *American Journal of Political Science*, Vol. 51, No. 2: 241–54.

Keen, A. (2007) *The Cult of the Amateur: How Today's Internet Is Killing Our Culture*, New York: Doubleday.

Key, V. O. (1966) *The Responsible Electorate: Rationality in Presidential Voting 1936–60*, Cambridge, MA: Harvard University Press.

Kline, S. J. and Rosenberg, G. (1986) An Overview of Innovation, in Landau, R. and Rosenberg, N. (eds) *The Positive Sum Strategy*, Washington, DC: National Academy Press.

Klug, F., Starmer, K. and Weir, S. (1996) *Three Pillars of Liberty: Political Rights and Freedoms in the UK*, London: Routledge.

Kobach, K. W. (1994) Switzerland, in Butler, D. and Ranney, A. (eds) *Referendums around the World*, Washington, DC: American Enterprise Institute.

Kriesi, H. (2005) *Direct Democratic Choice. The Swiss Experience*, Lanham, MD: Lexington Books.

Lang, A. (2007) But is it for real: The British Columbia Citizens' Assembly as a model of state-sponsored citizen empowerment, *Politics and Society*, Vol. 35, No. 1: 35–69.

LeDuc, L. (2003) *The Politics of Direct Democracy: Referendums in Global Perspective*, Toronto: Broadview Press.

Lowndes, V., Pratchett, L. and Stoker, G. (2001) Trends in public participation: Part 2 – citizens' perspectives, *Public Administration*, Vol. 79, No. 2: 445–55.

Lupia, A. and Matsusaka, J. G. (2004) Direct democracy: New approaches to old questions, *Annual Review of Political Science*, Vol. 7: 463–82.

Magleby, D. B. (1984) *Direct Legislation: Voting on Direct Propositions in the United States*, Baltimore, MD: Johns Hopkins University Press.

Mahrer, H. and Krimmer, R. (2005) Towards the enhancement of e-democracy: Identifying the notion of the 'middleman paradox', *Information Systems Journal*, 15: 27–42.

Mansbridge, J. J. (1983) *Beyond Adversarial Democracy*, Chicago, IL: University of Chicago Press.

Margolis, M. (2007) E-government and Democracy, in Dalton, R. and Klingemann, H.-D. (eds) *The Oxford Handbook of Political Behaviour*, Oxford: Oxford University Press: 765–82.

Matland, R. E. (2007) Electoral Quotas, Frequency and Effectiveness, in Dahlerup, D. (ed.) *Women, Quotas and Politics*, London: Routledge: 275–91.

Meier, P. (2007) Who is who? Defining groups entitled to reserved seats in national legislatures. Available at http://www.paviagroup.be/documents/Meier.07.WhoIsWho.doc (accessed 11 April 2011).

Mendelsohn, M. and Cutler, F. (2000) The effect of referendums on democratic citizens: Information, politicization, efficacy and tolerance, *British Journal of Political Science*, Vol. 30: 687–701.

Millstein, M. (2010) *Limits to Local Democracy: The Politics of Urban Governance Transformations in Cape Town*, Working Paper No. 2, Stockholm: ICLD (Swedish International Centre for Local Democracy).

Minos, D. C. (2002) Porto Alegre, Brazil: A New, Sustainable and Replicable Model of Participatory and Democratic Governance?, in Klyve, R. C. (ed.) *Kampen For En Stemme. Globalisering Sett Fra Sør*, Solidaritet Forlag/ATTAC Norge, Oslo: 3–24.

Moeckli, S. (2007) Direct Democracy and Political Participation from a Cross-National Perspective, in Zittel, T. and Fuchs, D. (eds) *Participatory Democracy and Political Participation*, London: Routledge: 107–24.

Morris, C. (2007) *Lessons in Direct Democracy from New Zealand*, London: Centre for Policy Studies.

Newton, K. (1982) Is small really so beautiful? Is big really so ugly? Size, effectiveness and democracy in local government, *Political Studies*, 30 (June): 190–206.

—— (2006) Political support, social capital, civil society and political and economic performance, Political Studies, Vol. 54: 846–64.

Norris, P. (2002a) *Democratic Phoenix*, Cambridge: Cambridge University Press.

—— (2002b) *E-voting as the Magic Ballot*, Cambridge, MA: Harvard University, John F. Kennedy School of Government.

—— (2004) *E-campaigning and E-democracy*, Cambridge, MA: Harvard University, John F. Kennedy School of Government.

Oates, S., Owen, D. and Gibson, R. K. (2006) *The Internet and Politics: Citizens, Voters, and Activists*, New York: Routledge.

O'Donnell, G. (1999) Horizontal Accountability in New Democracies, in Schedler, A., Diamond, L. and Plattner, M.F. (eds) *The Self Restraining State: Power and Accountability in the New Democracies*, Boulder, CO: Lynne Reinner.

OECD (2001) *Citizens as Partners: OECD Handbook on Information, Consultation and Public Participation in Policy-making*, Paris: OECD.

Offe, C. (1997) Micro-aspects of Democratic Theory: What Makes for the Deliberative Competence of Citizens?, in Hadenius, A. (ed.) *Democracy's Victory and Crisis*, Cambridge: Cambridge University Press: 81–104.

Pratchett, L. (1999) New fashions in public participation: Towards greater democracy?, *Parliamentary Affairs*, No. 52, Vol. 4: 616–33.

—— (2002) *The Implementation of Electronic Voting in the UK*, London: Local Government Association.

Rattila, T. (2000) Deliberation as Public Use of Reason – Or, What Public? Whose reasons?, in Saward, M. (ed.) *Democratic Innovation*, London: Routledge: 66–77.

Renn, O., Webler, T. and Wiedemann, P. (eds) (1995) *Fairness and Competence in Citizen Participation: Evaluating Models for Environmental Discourse*, Dordrecht: Kluwer Academic Publishers.

Reynolds, A. (2005) Reserved seats in national legislatures: A research note, *Legislative Studies Quarterly*, Vol. 30, No. 2, May: 301–10.

Rowe, G. and Frewer L. J. (2004) Evaluating public participation exercises: A research agenda, *Science, Technology, and Human Values*, Vol. 29, No. 4: 512–56.

Sartori, G. (1987) *The Theory of Democracy Revisited*, Chatham, NJ: Chatham House.

Saward, M. (2000) Less Than Meets the Eye: Democratic Legitimacy and Deliberative Theory, in Saward, M. (ed.) *Democratic Innovation*, London: Routledge.

Scarrow, S. (2001) Direct democracy and institutional change: A comparative investigation, *Comparative Political Studies*, Vol. 34: 651–65.

Schmitter, P. and Trechsel, A. H. (2004) *The Future of Democracy in Europe. Trends, Analysis and Reforms*, Strasbourg: Council of Europe.

Schumpeter, J. A. (1942) *Capitalism, Socialism and Democracy*, New York: Harper & Row.

Slater, M. and James, T. (2007) Vote-by-mail doesn't deliver. Available at http://www.tompaine.com/articles/2007/06/29/votebymail_doesnt_deliver.php (accessed 11 April 2011).

Smith, G. (2000) Toward Deliberative Institutions, in Saward, M. (ed.) *Democratic Innovation*, London: Routledge: 29–39.

—— (2005) *Beyond the Ballot: 57 Democratic Innovations from Around the World*, London: Power Inquiry.

Smith, G. and Stephenson, S. (2005) The theory and practice of group representation: Reflections on the governance of race equality in Birmingham, *Public Administration*, Vol. 83, No. 2: 323–43.

Stevens, D. and O'Hara, K. (2006) *Inequality.Com: Power, Poverty and the Digital Divide*, Oxford: Oneworld Publications.

Stoker, G. (2006) *Why Politics Matters: Making Democracy Work*, Basingstoke: Palgrave Macmillan.

Strange, S. (1996) *The Retreat of the State: The Diffusion of Power in The World Economy*, Cambridge: Cambridge University Press.

—— (1997) The erosion of the state, *Current History*, Vol. 96, No. 613: 365–9.

Sunstein, C. (2002) *Republic.com*, Princeton NJ: Princeton University Press.

Svensson, P. (1996) Denmark: The Referendum as Minority Protection, in Gallagher, M. and Uleri, P. V. (eds) *The Referendum Experience in Europe*, London: Macmillan: 33–51.

Van Creveld, M. (1999) *The Rise and Decline of the State*, Cambridge: Cambridge University Press.

Vidich, A. J. and Bensman, J. (1958) *Small Town in Mass Society: Class, Power, and Religion in a Rural Community*, Chicago, IL: University of Illinois Press.

Wisse, E (2006) *Promoting Democracy: An International Exploration of Policy and Implementation Practice*, Amsterdam: Ministry of the Interior and Kingdom Relations, Department of Constitutional Matters and Legislation.

Zimmerman, J. F. (1999) *The New England Town Meeting: Democracy in Action*, Westport, CT: Praeger.

Zittel, T. (2004) Digital Parliaments and Electronic Democracy: A Comparison Between the US House, the Swedish Riksdag and the German Bundestag, in Gibson, R. K., Rommele, A. and Ward, S. J. (eds) *Electronic Democracy*, London: Routledge: 70–95.

Zittel, T. and Fuchs, D. (2007) *Participatory Democracy and Political Participation*, London: Routledge.

8 Impacts of democratic innovations in Europe

Findings and desiderata

Brigitte Geissel

Representative democracies are without doubt under pressure, as all chapters in this volume have already pointed out. These pressures – some authors even speak of diseases, demystification and deconsolidation – are the breeding ground for new democratic procedures. International and supranational organizations, along with numerous politicians and scholars, are convinced that 'the cure for democracies' ills is more democracy' (Dalton et al. 2006: 251). And in fact, most representative democracies invested significantly in democratic innovations. They introduced a variety of new forms in order to involve citizens in decision-making processes (OECD 2005: 10). Following this development, it is striking that up until now, systematic evaluations of democratic innovations are just beginning and a comparative perspective, in particular, is still lacking. This chapter is a starting point for a long-term research project aiming to fill these gaps and in it I will begin to develop a conceptual framework for the evaluation. I will illustrate this by examining examples of European experiences.

After a short description of the term democratic innovation and the innovations under research, the framework for the evaluation will be developed. It will then be applied exemplarily – as an initial step for future evaluation. Despite its preliminary nature, the analysis offers convincing and clear-cut results summarized in my conclusion.

Democratic innovation – use of the term and its meaning in this study

As already pointed out in the introduction to this volume, 'innovation' is a complex term, which is used mostly in technology and economics but attracting increasing interest in the context of politics (Papadopoulos and Warin 2007; Smith 2005; Casper and van Waarden 2005). In technology and economics, about 70–80 per cent of what firms interpret as innovations are not really new for the sector, but are actually imitations or reinvention (Unger 2005: 21). This is also true in the world of politics. An innovation can be new in one country, but well-established in another. Thus, given the fact that, for example, direct democracy is common in Switzerland, direct democratic elements in other countries could be considered as imitation, but also – as in technology – as an innovation (see also Budge in this volume). Accordingly, as a working definition, I refer to democratic innovation as new practice or process consciously and purposefully introduced with the aim of improving the quality of democracy, irrespective of whether the innovation in question has already been tried out in another state.

The literature on democratic innovations covers checks and balances between the branches of representative government, institutions controlling the political elite (for example, Beyme 2003; Offe 2003), or combinations of local and global democracy (Held 1995). However, for the most part, the literature has focused on innovations promoting citizens' participation in processes of political will formation and decision making. This is currently seen as the most important issue and my chapter thus focuses on participatory innovations. Similar political terms, such as 'strong democracy' or 'participatory democracy', refer to analogous developments, but often portray 'more participation' in a normative way, as a desirable project with utopian features. In contrast, my research project aims to evaluate existing participatory procedures empirically.

Which innovations?

Which innovations are now worth considering? Based on a comprehensive literature search conducted at the Social Science Research Center Berlin in 2006, using over 500 publications, the following three main democratic innovations can be identified (see also the introduction to this volume; Smith 2009).

Direct democracy: people express their will or decide by popular vote

Direct democratic procedures can be mandatory, for example constitutionally required, they can be initiated by political representatives ('top down', e.g. by parliament, city council, president, mayor) or by citizens ('bottom up', i.e. 'popular initiative' or 'petition').[1] Citizens' petitions can either function as agenda-setters, forcing the decision-making bodies to address a neglected political issue ('decision promoting'), or attempt to change a political decision ('decision controlling'). Referenda initiated by representatives serve other purposes: representatives often promote a referendum to gain a mandate from the citizens, if decisions are impossible without offending key political actors. The Swedish government, for example, held a referendum on nuclear energy in 1980, because major actors disagreed on the issues and could not find a consensus (see also Kriesi and Budge in this volume). Similar examples include the Spanish referendum on North Atlantic Treaty Organization (NATO) membership in 1986, or the Swedish vote on alternative pension plans in 1957. And, sometimes, a government has held a referendum to demonstrate popular support for its decisions, for example, the French referendum on the Maastricht Treaty in 1994.

In most countries, initiation as well as valid acceptance of a popular vote are subject to strict quora rules. The number of signatures required to launch a citizens' petition (initiation) and the quora for a valid popular vote differ vastly (see also Budge and Kriesi in this volume). Generally, for a valid acceptance a simple majority of yes or no votes is not enough, but first a minimum number of participants casting their votes and second a certain percentage of votes favoring the proposal are required. In cases of high quora, the initiation as well as the valid acceptance of a direct democratic procedure is unlikely, whereas low quora lead to a more intensive use of direct democratic procedures (see Mittendorf 2008).

Direct democratic procedures are more often not binding than binding. However, at the national level they mostly affect the decision-making bodies: 'There has never been a case in West European democracies in which the parliamentary majority has ignored the result of a formally advisory government-initiated referendum' (Setälä 2006: 713).

Co-governance and network governance: political representatives share their decision-making power

According to Smith (2005: 56–60), co-governance is distinguished from other innovations by at least some degree of direct citizen influence over decisions. Other terms used in the literature are 'collaborative governance'[2] and 'empowered participatory governance' (Fung and Wright 2001). In spite of the abundant debates on these new forms of governance, the reality looks quite different. Forms of co-governance, in which the decision-making power is shared between elected representatives and citizens, are still rare (Geißel 2009). Participatory budgeting is one of the few – and famous – examples of co-governance (see for details on co-governance Talpin in this volume).

Consultative–discursive procedures, in which public issues are discussed among non-state actors[3]

Consultative–discursive procedures can have many different facets. On the one side of the continuum – and most widespread – are top-down information-exchanging events with a minimum of discussion, for example public hearings, in which political representatives mainly inform the citizenry about their decisions. On the other side of the continuum, high-quality deliberative procedures can be found, with well-recruited participants, well-prepared background materials, as well as qualified mediators (see Fishkin and Smith in this volume). Furthermore they also differ according to the scale (from neighborhood to supranational level).

Examples of consultative–discursive procedures include '*Planungszellen*' (planning cells), 'Round Tables', 'Cooperative Discourse', 'Citizens' Juries', and 'Focus Groups'. One might assume that these different terminologies reflect clear differences between the different procedures and clear-cut procedural structures. However, this is not the case: similar procedures may be named differently and dissimilar procedures can have the same labels. Citizens' Juries, for example, were developed mainly in the USA and they are similar to *Planungszellen* developed by Peter Dienel in Germany. The model of Consensus Conferences was developed by the Danish Board of Technology. However, the different labels were soon used for several different procedures. For example, the term Citizens' Jury is sometimes used for a form of participatory budgeting.[4] Thus, the field remains chaotic with respect to terminology and semantics.

Consultative–discursive procedures can be initiated for different reasons. They may be intended to develop new ideas and policies, to negotiate compromises in contentious situations, to enhance civic virtues, or to develop, mould, and clarify citizens' preferences. The recruitment of the participants also reflects the varieties. Some consultative–discursive procedures comprise self-selected participants; in other procedures participants are chosen randomly. They can also be recruited to mirror the social composition of the constituency, or to guarantee the involvement of all stakeholders (see also Smith 2009; Ansell and Gingrich 2006; Fung 2003). However, all discursive procedures with citizens have in common that they are consultative and without any decision-making power. They can, in most cases, just generate elaborate advice for decision-making bodies, one of the few exceptions being the British Columbia Citizens' Assembly (see Talpin in this volume).

How to measure the impacts of participatory innovations on the quality of democracy – the framework

Frameworks for evaluating democratic innovations are rarely spelled out. Although Sewell and Philips called for a 'concise research agenda' as early as 1979, few authors followed their call (Abelson and Gauvin 2006; Rowe and Frewer 2004: 521 ff.). These authors applied different approaches: some of them developed criteria by relating to the perspectives of the participants: 'success must be defined and judged by those involved' (Moore 1996: 168). Accordingly, criteria refer to impacts on the participant and the group, for example the improvement of political knowledge and enhancement of civic skills (Carnes et al. 1998: 390; Moore 1996: 156; see also Fishkin in this volume).

In the European context, the criteria 'legitimacy and effectiveness' attracted major attention in the wake of Scharpf's work. In his book *Governing Europe: Effective and Democratic?* Scharpf (1999) argues that the quality of democratic systems can be measured first by input-legitimacy and second by effectiveness. Several European authors refer to these criteria in their evaluation of democratic innovations (for example, Holtkamp et al. 2006).

Other scholars follow a different line, applying criteria such as openness, acceptance, quality of deliberation, publicity, representativeness, access to resources, early involvement, accountability, context, process, transparency, accountability, outcome or resolving conflicts (Papadopoulos and Warin 2007: 455 ff.; Abelson and Gauvin 2006; Dalton et al. 2006: 14; Rowe et al. 2004: 93; Rowe and Frewer 2004; Beierle and Cayford 2002: 6; Renn et al. 1995). Similarly, in this volume, different frameworks and criteria have been applied (see the chapters of Budge, Fishkin and Smith).

Not all, but many of these criteria, however, face five crucial problems: first, they are either too abstract to be used empirically; second, they lack any theoretical background. Whereas, for example, Renn et al. (1995) discussed theoretical questions at length, they addressed practical, operational questions only very briefly. Other authors, such as Moore (1996), seem to have little interest in theoretical reflection. Third, some of the criteria are problematic. For example the criteria 'openness' (Papadopoulos and Warin 2007) is tricky. 'Open' innovations, in which participants recruit themselves, might provide less inclusive participation than 'closed' innovations with selected participants. Or, as Dalton et al. (2006: 262) put it: 'Equality of access is not sufficient if equality of usage is grossly lacking.' 'Publicity' as a criterion is another example. Why should a high level of publicity enhance the quality of democracy (see Smith in this volume)? These examples lead to the fourth problem: *ex ante* and *ex post* impacts are often not differentiated properly. Impacts that are predisposed by design a priori and impacts that can only be measured after the end of the procedure are grouped together. For example, the fact that consultative procedures are just consultative without decision-making competency is part of the design and not an *ex post* impact – it was mostly determined from the beginning that they will have no effect on public policies. Fifth, and this might be the most important problem, criteria for the evaluation of success and prerequisites for success are often confused: for example, criteria such as 'access to resources' or 'early involvement' (see Rowe et al. 2004) might be favorable conditions for a successful participatory procedure. However, they cannot serve as criteria for the evaluation of the impacts of a participatory innovation. Similarly, 'context' (see Abelson and Gauvin 2006) is necessary to identify favorable conditions for successful innovations, but cannot be a criterion to measure success. It is fundamental to distinguish between impacts (or success, in most studies) and prerequisites for success (see Smith in this volume). Without doubt, impacts and prerequisites are linked, but for a clear analysis, both must be scrutinized separately.

Thus, the question arises as to how a framework can be developed without stepping into these pitfalls. It might be helpful to consider not only research on democratic innovations, but more general research on the quality of democracy, since the question of how to measure the quality of democracy has recently gained popularity (for example, Diamond and Morlino 2005). In the debate on the quality of democracy, three lines of argument can be identified. One line in the literature examines the procedural aspect, namely input-legitimacy and democratic process. The second line in the literature adds the outcome of democracy. These authors agree on the notion that democratic input and procedure is not enough and that a democracy must also fulfill collective goals of a constituency (for example, Scharpf 1999). However, a third, often forgotten line, has already been mentioned by Thomas Jefferson (1776). He, like many others, insisted that democracy should also generate an informed, enlightened democratic citizenry (see also Fung and Wright 2001; Dahl 1992).

This classification provides the outline for the framework of this study. I suggest a framework based on the following four dimensions: (1) input-legitimacy, (2) democratic process, (3) effectiveness, and (4) civic education. All aforementioned topics coalesce and relate to these four criteria in one way or another. However, all four criteria are complex concepts and require further explanation, as outlined in the following paragraphs.

Input-legitimacy

Input-legitimacy refers to the input-side of the political system ('government of the people'). In representative democracies, this means that citizens are equally and significantly involved. It was the main promise of representative democracy to provide political equality, expressed as 'one man, one vote'. However, more and more citizens are drawing the conclusion that equal political input via election of representatives is a myth and is not reflected in reality. As mentioned before, many participatory innovations have been established to counter these feelings of political inequality, which are often combined with political distrust and alienation.

In fact, the main arguments for and against participatory innovations focus on the question of inclusive participation: proponents argue that participatory innovations would attract a multitude of citizens who do not get involved in elections and other forms of traditional participation. Opponents reason that only the politically active strata of society engage. So, the questions to be answered are whether participatory innovations guarantee de facto inclusive and equal involvement, or whether participants stem from the 'well-off', already politically active strata of society (see Smith and Talpin in this volume).

Legitimacy can, however, also be measured by a second criterion: legitimacy, which refers to citizens' political support ('perceived legitimacy'). Several proponents of democratic innovations argue that citizens would accept their representatives, the political system and political decisions with more enthusiasm if they were involved in the political process. Thus, one criterion of evaluation should be whether participatory innovations improve 'perceived legitimacy'.

Democratic process[5]

After the so-called 'deliberative turn' (Dryzek 2002), one dimension of the political process moved to be the focus of attention: the quality of deliberation (see Steiner et al. 2005). Deliberation is defined in different ways[6] and means basically the rational, wide-ranging exchange of arguments leading to optimal solutions (see Rucht in this volume). Deliberation is also crucial in theories on representative democracy, where it is located mainly in representative, elected bodies. In contrast, proponents of deliberative democracy focus primarily on deliberation among citizens. They argue that citizens' preferences are poorly grounded without deliberation; thus elections just lead to the aggregation of citizens' 'crude' preferences and do not necessarily result in optimal solutions. As Levine et al. (2005: 274) put it: 'there is a world of difference between a vote that follows rich deliberation and one on which people simply register their "raw" opinion'. From this point of view, it is necessary to improve the unsophisticated aggregation democracy (see Fishkin in this volume). Some authors even argue that it would be dangerous to give citizens more options to make political decisions (e.g. in direct democratic procedures) without providing them with sufficient opportunities for public deliberation. So, the quality of deliberation is an important criterion for the evaluation of participatory innovations. However, the measurement of deliberation is controversial. European authors often refer to Habermas' concept of deliberation, which includes strict rules, for example the rational exchange of arguments among free and equal citizens. In contrast, US proponents apply less high standards and regard most kinds of discussion as deliberation. Recently, some indices to measure the quality of democracy have been worked out (see Fishkin and Rucht in this volume; Steiner et al. 2005; Bächtiger 2005).

Effectiveness

In politics, effectiveness refers to the capacity of a democratic system to achieve the shared, collective goals of a constituency, for example social justice or low criminality. It also refers to the 'substantial' or 'materialist' conception of democracy. From this perspective, one criterion to measure the quality of a democracy is to check whether it effectively promotes and meets the collective goals of the citizens (Scharpf 1999: 6). Accordingly, effectiveness comprises two components: first, the collective goals of a constituency are identifiable and uncontroversial; and, second, a community has the capacity to implement policies effectively in order to reach these collective goals.

However, the collective goals of a community are frequently not evident, but contested. In these cases, collective aims must be identified – or compromised – before they can be 'translated' into policies. Some participatory innovations are designed to support the identification of shared goals. In fact, participatory innovations are often regarded as a 'necessity for establishing what the public interest really is' (Beierle and Cayford 2002: 5). Thus, in order to evaluate participatory innovations, one must ask two questions: are they really helpful in, first, identifying collective goals and, second, reaching those collective goals?

Civic education

Almond and Verba (1963) have already demonstrated the importance of citizens' attitudes, skills and behavior for stable, thriving democracies: democracies can only consolidate if citizens accept democratic principles and act accordingly. Several proponents of participatory innovations have adopted this line of thought and applied it to participatory innovations. They argue that participatory innovations are necessary, because they have the capacity to enhance civic skills. Some authors even consider that 'participating in democratic decisions makes participants better citizens' (Barber 1984: 232; Fung and Wright 2001). Civic skills such as knowledge, or virtues such as tolerance, are assumed to be improved via political involvement. However, it is unlikely that all civic skills and virtues can be enhanced at the same pace and to the same extent. Some skills such as knowledge, for example, might be improved quite quickly and easily, whilst democratic virtues like tolerance might be more difficult to acquire (see also Talpin in this volume).

The discussed criteria are summarized in Table 8.1.

Table 8.1 Framework to evaluate democratic innovations

Input-legitimacy
Inclusive equal participation
Perceived legitimacy
Democratic process
Deliberative quality
Effectiveness
Identification of collective goals
Achievement of collective goals
Civic education
Improvement of knowledge
Improvement of civic skills

Evaluating participatory innovations – exemplifying the framework

In the evaluation research to date, the case study approach prevails and most studies examine the different innovations separately.[7] Until recently, most studies focused on one innovation in one country, but did not compare the impacts of the case with other innovations or countries. Thus, research is still piecemeal. The following exemplary application of the framework therefore cannot provide a full-fledged evaluation of participatory innovations tried out in European states. And it can certainly not take into account and re-analyze all existing case studies. But, it is a start in trying to develop hypotheses pointing at future research.

Participatory innovations in Europe – common trends and specific patterns

Generally, the inclusion of citizens and citizens' associations in political decision making is not new in Europe. In every democracy, the representative bodies decide how to guarantee the flow of input. However, traditions of how to transfer citizens' preferences to the representatives (and back) differ. Some countries traditionally have few formal rules regulating the integration of citizens and citizens' associations into the legislative process, whereas others have strict regulations. In France, for example, with its republican tradition, governmental actors are less interested in involving citizens' groups in legislative decision-making processes, whereas The Netherlands has a long tradition of consultation and negotiation in a relatively formalized way. For example, the so-called *Sociaal-Economische Raad (SER)*, consisting of employers, employees and experts, is an important voice in the Dutch legislative process and the decision-making bodies are legally obliged to ask the *Raad* for advice on socio-economic issues.

In spite of the diverse traditions, changes towards more citizens' participation can be observed within most European states since the 1990s, often at the local level (see, for example, Vetter and Kersting 2003: 335). Most countries have introduced some form of participatory innovation. Most post-socialist states established participatory options in their constitutions at the beginning of the 1990s and also many consolidated democracies passed new laws to enforce participation, such as Great Britain, France and Germany.

Direct democracy

The widespread diffusion of direct democracy is uncontested. Over twenty improvements for direct democracy took place in the Organisation for Economic Co-operation and Development (OECD) countries within the recent decades (Scarrow 2006). Direct democratic procedures found their way into almost all new constitutions of the post-socialist states, with Lithuania, Slovakia and Hungary granting extensive legislative competences to its citizens, and the Czech Republic, Bulgaria and Rumania the least (Walter-Rogg 2008: 253; Scarrow 2006: 58). Today, sixteen European nation states have institutionalized obligatory referenda in their national or regional constitutions – with some variations. In most states, a referendum is only mandatory if the constitution is to be revised completely or in its main parts, whilst in other states smaller changes require a referendum; and in some states the constitutions demand a referendum in specific cases. For example in Switzerland, Ireland, Liechtenstein, Italy, Denmark and many of the post-communist democracies, the government must hold a referendum on several 'mandatory topics'. Often, a referendum is demanded before the nation state can join major international or supranational organizations, or ratify a supranational treaty. For example, the Irish referenda on the European Treaties were constitutionally mandated.

In many European states, citizens may file petitions at the national or sub-national level.[8] Several countries provide initiative rights only at the *national level,*[9] while other countries allow citizens' initiatives only at the *sub-national* level.[10] In Greece, France and Ireland a popular vote can be launched by citizens neither at national nor sub-national level (Walter-Rogg 2008: 255).

Almost no states have the same set of rules concerning direct democratic procedures. For example, the requirements for a popular vote to be binding differ vastly. In Hungary, for a binding popular decision, at least one quarter of the electorate must take part and at least a simple majority of the votes must be in favor of the petition. In Poland, a referendum is only binding if more than half of the electorate takes part in the ballot. In Slovakia, the hurdle is even higher. Half the electorate must have cast a vote in favor of the petition.[11] The role of the government is another example of the differences in the rules. Whereas in Ireland the government must keep a neutral stance and is forbidden to spend money to support one side, many countries do not have such strict rules. Also, the amount of elite control concerning citizens' petitions varies largely. Only in Italy, Slovenia and Lithuania can citizens initiate a popular vote without the approval of the government or the parliament (see also Kriesi in this volume). So, the sheer existence of direct democratic options does not tell much about the real options.

Looking at the *usage* of direct democratic options at the *national* level, Switzerland and Liechtenstein are leaders. They are followed by Italy, which has had 87 referenda since the introduction of this option. France (38), Ireland (29), Denmark (19), Lithuania (18) and Spain (16) are next on the ranking list (Walter-Rogg 2008: 246).[12] Most of these direct democratic procedures have taken place in recent years. This rise was sparked partly by the use of citizen-initiated direct democratic procedures: more than 500 petitions were submitted between 1991 and 2000, which is more than twice the number of any previous decade (see for details Scarrow 2006: 50 ff., 58). Another factor adding to the growth is the European Union. No other issue has activated as many direct democratic procedures as the European Union (EU). Between 1970, when the French voted on the enlargement, and 2005, almost fifty popular votes had been conducted on EU memberships, EU treaties or the euro.

Direct democratic options and usage have not only increased at the national level, but also at the *sub-national* level (local, regional) (Scarrow 2006: 50): many European states allow local popular votes. They are binding in many post-socialist states (such as Slovakia, Poland, Hungary) and in Germany, but in the majority of states they are only advisory.

Research about the usage of direct democratic procedures at the local level is a difficult task, because data are not easily available. What can be said is that – unsurprisingly – the usage depends mainly on the hurdles. In Germany, for example, the number of popular votes varies significantly between the German member states (Mittendorf 2008: 81). Bavaria, which has the lowest hurdles, is the most active state, and in states with higher hurdles, fewer referenda are initiated. However, the numbers do not tell the whole story. Just the threat of a petition often forces local representatives to take citizens' preferences into account and to act in a more responsive way. Direct democratic options often became a striking 'sword of Damocles' (see also Kriesi in this volume).

What is known about the *impacts* of the direct democratic procedures concerning the criteria for evaluation described above? Considering the criteria of inclusive participation, which strata of society cast a ballot? Not many studies are available, but an analysis of German local popular votes reveals interesting patterns (Gabriel and Walter-Rogg 2006: 48). In contrast with most forms of participation, men and women engage to the same degree and there are no significant differences between income groups, though the level of education shows the 'normal' participation bias: people with higher education are more strongly involved. However, people with lower education are more often involved in direct democratic activities than in political party activities (see also Kriesi in this volume).

Perceived legitimacy seems to be higher in states with comprehensive direct democratic options. Citizens of these states are more likely to regard their political system as legitimate (see Kriesi in this volume). Whereas, for example, 88 per cent of the Swiss are politically contented, the European average lies between 50 and 60 per cent (European Social Survey 2004; Bowler and Donovan 2002; Lindner 1999).[13] But trust in politicians and the government is not necessarily improved by the use of direct democratic procedures (see, for example, Gilens et al. 2001). Again, Germany can serve as an example: German citizens, who participate in popular voting, do not necessarily trust politicians more than non-active citizens (Gabriel and Walter-Rogg 2006: 49).

The deliberative quality in the context of direct democratic procedures is, on the whole, rather low (see LeDuc 2006). Direct democratic options do not necessarily lead to well-thought deliberations about the different options. Most citizens stick to 'heuristic cues', as Kriesi has already pointed out in this volume.

Without doubt, direct democratic procedures help to identify collective goals: they inform about the preferences of the majority of the voters. Direct democracy also seems to support the achievement of collective goals more often than not. States providing more direct democratic options seem to achieve a better performance than those with fewer options – at least in the Swiss case (Moeckli 2007: 122). Swiss cantons with more direct democratic options have lower debt rates (per capita), they provide services more efficiently, and their decisions are more often in compliance with the preferences of the population. They also score better when it comes to the fulfillment of welfare-state policies (Vatter 2006; Kriesi in this volume).

In relation to the improvement of political knowledge, most studies show that citizens are better informed about politics when they have direct democratic participation options. For example, citizens in states with EU-related referenda know more about the EU than citizens in states without EU related popular vote (Benz and Stutzer 2007; Kriesi in this volume). However, direct democratic options do not necessarily improve participation in elections: they neither lead automatically to higher nor to lower voter turnout.[14] Considering the improvement of civic skills, comprehensive direct democratic options seem to improve internal efficacy (for example, see Tolbert et al. 2003). But until now, not much is known about the impacts on qualities such as tolerance or the ability to compromise.

Table 8.2 summarizes the impacts of direct democratic procedures.

Table 8.2 Evaluation of direct democratic procedures

Input-legitimacy	
Inclusive equal participation	+
Perceived legitimacy	+ (political system)/ 0 (political representatives)
Democratic process	
Deliberative quality	0
Effectiveness	
Identification of collective goals	+
Achievement of collective goals	+
Civic education	
Improvement of knowledge	+
Improvement of civic skills	0

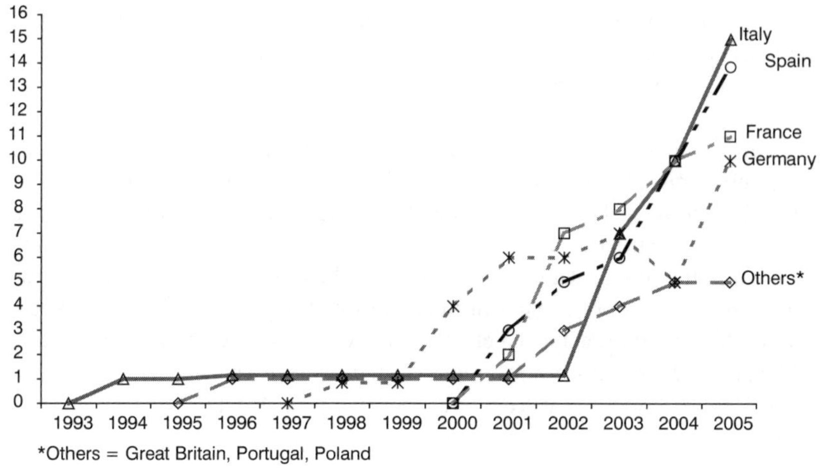

Figure 8.1 Number of participatory budgets in Europe by country (1993–2005)

Source: http://www.buergerhaushalt-europa.de/, May 2008.

Co-governance

As already pointed out, new forms of co-governance with shared decision-making powers between political representatives and non-state actors are still rare. However, there are innovations in this field and one of the most important examples of co-governance is participatory budgeting.[15] The Porto Alegre example provoked tremendous attention and several municipalities all over the world adopted similar procedures. Figure 8.1 shows the development and the spread of participatory budgeting processes in Europe.

Participatory budgeting procedures took place in a variety of contexts, for example in municipalities with high unemployment (such as Cordoba, with over 20 per cent) as well as in cities with low unemployment (such as Salford, with below 5 per cent). Also, the municipal budget per citizen varies vastly from below 50 euros to almost 4000 euros. In Spain, Italy and France, mostly left-wing local authorities introduced participatory budgeting. Germany was an exception, with both conservative and liberal local governments taking up the idea (Sintomer et al. 2005).

What is known about participatory budgeting in Europe? The main empirical source for answering this question is a comparative study by Sintomer et al. (2005), who found that participation in European procedures is seldom inclusive. Participants of European participatory budgeting meetings come mainly from the middle and the upper working class – with country-specific differences (see also Talpin in this volume). In Germany, for example, the middle class prevailed in all procedures and members of the working class barely participated, whereas in other countries, members of other strata of society also took part (Sintomer et al. 2005).[16] What about deliberative quality? The quality of deliberation has varied

Table 8.3 Evaluation of co-governance procedures

Input-legitimacy	
Inclusive equal participation	Depending on recruitment of participants
Perceived legitimacy	?
Democratic process	
Deliberative quality	If adequate prerequisites available
Effectiveness	
Identification of collective goals	Depending on recruitment of participants
Achievement of collective goals	Depending on recruitment of participants
Civic education	
Improvement of knowledge	+
Improvement of civic skills	+

vastly in the different participatory budgeting procedures. Sintomer and his team found that the deliberative quality of most German cases was insufficient – in contrast with Spanish municipalities with high deliberative quality.

Participatory budgeting was per se set up to identify collective goals. However, the question remains: whose goals are identified? Owing to the limited number of participants, procedures of co-governance can never represent the whole citizenry. Which goals are identified is dependent on the recruitment of the participants. Thus, the recruitment of participants has fundamental implications: objectives, which are identified as collective objectives, differ according to the recruitment. If participants are recruited from all social groups, the identified goals reflect collective goals to a higher degree.

And what is known about the impact to achieve shared goals? Municipalities that applied participatory budgeting often improved their services (Sintomer et al. 2005). However, the impacts vary: Sintomer et al. (2005) concluded that participatory budgeting procedures had the least effect in the German municipalities. In Great Britain and France the effects were moderate, especially at the neighborhood level, while in Spain and Italy the effects were strongest.

Political knowledge of the participants was improved in all processes, and comprehension of local budgets was enhanced substantially. 'Political culture' within the municipalities applying participatory budgeting was also advanced – greatest in Spain and Italy and the least in Germany (Sintomer et al. 2005).

Table 8.3 summarizes the evaluation of co-governance procedures.

Consultative–discursive procedures

Several forms of consultative–discursive procedures have been established in Europe since the 1990s. However, until now, most research has focused on US or Canadian experiences (for example, Smith 2009; Beierle and Cayford 2002). However, in Europe too, several consultative–discursive procedures have been tried out. Many European governments have passed regulations to enforce consultative–discursive procedures, particularly in Scandinavia, The Netherlands and the UK (Ansell and Gingrich 2006: 174–5). In The Netherlands, for example, urban 'interactive policy making', promoting citizen participation has been *en vogue* since the 1990s. Finland began a 'Participation Project' in 1997 to enhance participation in local affairs and Norway engages in 'joint consultations' (see also OECD 2005). In addition, the EU has intensified its consultation process and the European Commission is particularly active in this field.[17] In spite of all these developments, systematic, comparative analyses on Europe are just beginning. For the following evaluation, I have summarized the findings of several case studies.

The inclusiveness of participation is dependent on the recruitment of the participants. In most procedures with self-selection, the less educated, immigrants and the lowest classes are either entirely absent or considerably under-represented. And if they do attend meetings, they tend to be marginalized in the debate: the 'usual suspects' generally dominate when self-selected recruitment is applied. However, specific forms of recruitment have been tried out in many consultative–discursive procedures in order to avoid the social bias – with randomly selected citizens, stakeholder invitation or recruitment according to social characteristics (see, for example, Fishkin, Smith and Talpin in this volume).

The impacts of consultative–discursive procedures on perceived legitimacy are seldom scrutinized, though a research team from Harvard Kennedy School has examined two consultative–discursive procedures launched by the EU: the European Citizens' Consultation and Tomorrow's Europe. These public engagement projects have not improved the perceived legitimacy of EU institutions (Culpepper et al. 2008; similar: Geissel 2009).[18] However, Fishkin in this volume has shown that perceived legitimacy was enhanced within the group of participants. Different research results can be explained partly by different interview questions applied by research teams. Systematic meta-analysis of the findings is still lacking.

What about the quality of deliberation? Mansbridge (1983) has already pointed out that successful deliberation is most likely in groups that share common interests as well as social bonds, and when the problem can be solved in a univocal, amicable way. If underlying interests differ, if social bonds are missing and if a univocal, amicable consensus is unlikely, deliberation is often problematic and needs specific support. Unsurprisingly, deliberative quality was excellent in those consultative–discursive procedures that provided adequate prerequisites such as an experienced organizer and moderator, thoughtful recruitment of participants and preparation of background material (see also Smith in this volume).

Consultative–discursive procedures are often similar to procedures of co-governance launched to identify collective goals – and the recruitment of participants plays the same crucial role as discussed in the chapter on co-governance. The impacts on the achievement of shared goals depend largely on access to the decision-making bodies. Impacts of consultative–discursive procedures are, in most cases, relatively small and indirect (see, for example,

Table 8.4 Evaluation of consultative–deliberative procedures

Input-legitimacy	
Inclusive equal participation	Depending on recruitment of participants
Perceived legitimacy	?
Democratic process	
Deliberative quality	+ If adequate prerequisites available
Effectiveness	
Identification of collective goals	Depending on recruitment of participants
Achievement of collective goals	Depending on and access to decision-making bodies
Civic education	
Improvement of knowledge	+
Improvement of civic skills	+

Frewer and Rowe 2005). Most procedures pass without much attention from decision-making bodies (see also Smith and Talpin in this volume). However, there are also positive examples. In a few cases – the Danish Consensus Conferences, for example – the elected representatives took the advice into account. In addition, longitudinal analyses of the consultative–discursive procedures 'Local Agenda 21' (LA 21) revealed clear impacts (Joas 2000). The forerunner municipalities, which had started LA 21 processes early in the 1990s, showed better results concerning environmental policies than the latecomers and the communities without the LA 21 process. Clearly, the LA 21 processes had substantial impact in achieving the shared goal of sustainability. But, again, there are country differences. Estonian, Russian, Latvian and Lithuanian municipalities with LA 21 processes improved their environmental performance far less than municipalities in Denmark or Germany.

The impact on knowledge is unequivocal. Participants of consultative–discursive procedures improve their knowledge on the specific topic significantly (similarly for the USA: Beierle and Cayford 2002). In the above-mentioned LA 21 forerunner municipalities, for example, the attitudes of the local government as well as the whole community have shifted towards a more environmentally conscious direction (Joas 2000). Of all innovations under research, consultative–discursive procedures seem to have the most impact on civic skills, such as tolerance or the ability to compromise (Delli Carpini et al. 2004: 324, 326).

Table 8.4 summarizes the evaluation of consultative–deliberative procedures.

Discussion, outlook and some concluding remarks

Political science has several tasks and one of the most important challenges is to find remedies for the current democratic malaise. This chapter focuses on participatory innovations as the currently most debated recommendations, that is, direct democracy, co-governance and consultative–discursive procedures. The intention is not to provide conclusive results, but to be a starting point for future evaluation of participatory innovations from a comparative perspective.

The study reveals several strengths and weaknesses of all innovations under research. Thus, many hopes concerning democratic innovations can only be fulfilled if participatory innovations are combined in such a way that their weaknesses and strengths can be balanced (see also Smith in this volume). Some examples illustrate this idea: one of the disadvantages of consultative–discursive procedures is the small number of participants who can be involved: they may be able to deliberate sophisticated suggestions, but they cannot make any decisions. With popular votes, the problem is the reverse: a large number of people, in fact the entire electorate, may take part. However, the simple aggregation of citizens' preferences might not be the best solution, as the preferences are not well thought out and may be based on insufficient information. Thus, neither consultative–discursive procedures nor the aggregation of preferences ('voting') are optimal. However, the combination and 'sequencing' (Smith 2009) of different innovations could mitigate some of the weaknesses of each innovation (similarly, see Saward 2000). For example, participants of discursive procedures might discuss different options to solve a problem and their suggestions are subsequently decided on via direct democracy. The British Columbia Citizens' Assembly on Electoral Reform is one of the rare examples of the combination: selected citizens discussed, in the context of a consultative–discursive procedure, whether and how the electoral system in British Columbia should be reformed, and their advice was then put to a popular vote (see Talpin in this volume). This sequence could serve as a blueprint for the future.

In terms of a future research agenda, the study reveals, first, the need for an analysis that takes different designs of democratic innovations into account. For research on direct democracy, for example, this means to evaluate the different forms separately – for example, binding and non-binding procedures, bottom-up and top-down initiatives, as well as decision-promoting and decision-controlling features – in order to discover the strengths and weaknesses of each of these forms.

Second, the context must be considered in a comparative perspective. In spite of the general trend towards participatory innovations, the national context is crucial. The impacts of participatory innovations depend – besides their respective designs – on long-established institutions and traditions. Or, as Schmitter and Trechsel (2004: 73) put it, the points of departure are different from state to state. It might, for example, not be a surprise that Consensus Conferences started in Denmark, a country well known for its tradition of consensus-oriented decision making and direct engagement with citizens. Taking the different contexts into account, it is also obvious that innovations do not produce the same effects in all countries. Whereas, for example, participatory budgeting seems to work well in some states, other states provide less successful results. Furthermore, political levels play a role: experiences on a small scale can not necessarily be implemented on a larger scale – a problem discussed on several occasions in this volume (and also Levine,

Fung and Gastil 2005: 275; Schmitter and Trechsel 2004: 75). Innovations that might be successful at the local level, might not work at other political levels. However, it is not a certainty that participatory innovations have different impacts at different levels, but a matter that requires empirical research – something that is still lacking.

Third, the study demonstrates the need for comprehensive methods. Case studies have prevailed so far and these studies are necessary and useful because of their depth. However, in the next phase of research, combinations of multiple methods are needed (for a similar comment, see Delli Carpini et al. 2004: 336). Methodological variety including quantitative methods will provide more comprehensive knowledge on participatory innovations than is available today. The findings will then help political actors select the best participatory innovation suited to solving the specific problem within a certain context, hopefully enhancing input-legitimacy, deliberation, effectiveness and civic skills of the citizenry.

Notes

1 The terminology used in the literature is rather blurred. Some authors use the term 'referendum' for all forms of direct democratic procedures including popular initiatives (e.g. Setälä 2006); other authors differentiate between popular initiatives and referenda initiated by representatives (see Kriesi in this volume).

2 The term 'collaborative governance' is sometimes also used for consultative procedures (e.g. Ansell and Gingrich 2006).

3 Some authors also include private–public interrelationships such as lobbying, petitioning, or even clientelism, patronage or bribes. However, none of these phenomena are democratic innovations and thus not of interest here.

4 This was the case for a Citizens' Jury in Berlin. It was assigned a monetary budget to be spent on local projects.

5 The quality of the democratic *process* is also often regarded as a criterion to measure the quality of democracy. The indicator is, mostly, whether democratic rules are applied. However, in most participatory innovations in Europe democratic rules are applied *de jure* and de facto. Thus, this criterion is less useful for the evaluation.

6 See for a comprehensive discussion on the different meanings of the term 'deliberation': Delli Carpini at al. 2004: 316–319.

7 Some articles provide an overview, for example on direct democracy (Freitag and Wagschal 2007) or on consultative–discursive procedures (Delli Carpini et al. 2004). Some publications report on specific fields, for example the local level (Abelson and Gauvin 2006; *Policy Studies Journal*, 2006, vol. 34, no. 4; *European Journal of Political Research*, 2006, vol. 46, no. 4; Beierle and Cayford 2002).

8 Hungary, Italy, Lithuania, Slovakia, Slovenia, The Netherlands, Poland, Spain, Liechtenstein and Switzerland.

9 Latvia, Austria, Portugal, Albania, Macedonia, Croatia, Romania, Moldavia, Andorra, Serbia and San Marino.

10 Belgium, Czech Republic, Estonia, Finland, Germany, Sweden, Great Britain, Norway and Bulgaria.

11 In Slovakia most referenda fail. Only the referendum on EU membership reached a participation rate of 52 per cent with 92 per cent yes votes.

12 In Belgium, Germany, Greece and Bulgaria no national referenda have taken place in the last eighteen years (Walter-Rogg 2008: 246–51; Moeckli 2007).

13 Studies on the USA show similar results: Bowler and Donovan (2002) showed that citizens living 'in states that use more initiatives tend to have more positive views of their own political abilities' (389).

14 Data on different countries, e.g. Switzerland, France, Italy, Denmark, Ireland and Liechtenstein, show that the number of referenda does not directly correlate with the average voter turnout (Moeckli 2007: 111).

15 Some new forms of co-governance at the local level refer to social improvements, e.g. the British National Strategy for Neighbourhood Renewal and the New Deal for Communities or the French 'politique de la ville', an initiative targeting impoverished urban areas (Sintomer and Maillard 2007; see also Talpin in this volume).

16 The impacts on perceived legitimacy cannot be described adequately, because there is too little research available.

17 See http://www.european-citizens-consultations.eu/14.0.html.

18 Studies on consultative–discursive procedures within the USA point in the same direction: perceived legitimacy, measured for example with the indicator 'trust in political institutions', is not enhanced by involvement in consultative–discursive procedures (e.g. Beierle and Cayford 2002).

References

Abelson, J. and Gauvin, F.-P. (2006) *Assessing the Impacts of Public Participation: Concepts, Evidence and Policy Implications*, Ottawa: Canadian Policy Research Networks.

Almond, G. A. and Verba, S. (1963) *The Civic Culture: Political Attitudes and Democracy in Five Nations*, Newbury Park, CA: Sage Publications.

Ansell, C. and Gingrich, J. (2006) Reforming the Administrative State, in Cain, B. E., Dalton, R. J. and Scarrow, S. E. (eds), *Democracy Transformed?* Oxford: Oxford University Press: 164–91.

Bächtiger, André (2005) *The Real World of Deliberation. A Comparative Study of its Favorable Conditions in Legislatures*, Bern: Paul Haupt.

Barber, B. (1984) *Strong Democracy*, Berkeley, CA: University of California Press.

Beierle, T. C. and Cayford, J. (2002) *Democracy in Practice: Public Participation in Environmental Decisions*, Washington, DC: Resources for the Future.

Benz, M. and Stutzer, A. (2007) Direct Democracy and Citizens' Information about Politics, in Pallinger, Z. T. et al. (eds), *Direct Democracy in Europe*, Wiesbaden: VS Verlag: 125–42.

Beyme, K. von (2003) Demokratiereform als Reform der parlamentarischen Parteiendemokratie, in Offe, C. (ed.) (2003) *Demokratisierung der Demokratie,* Frankfurt a.M. and New York: Campus: 27–42.

Bowler, S. and Donovan, T. (2002) Democracy, institutions and attitudes about citizen influence on government, *British Journal of Political Science* 32: 371–90.

Carnes, S. A., Schweitzer, M., Peelle, E. B., Wolfe, A. K. and Munro, J.F. (1998) Measuring the success of public participation on environmental restoration and waste management activities in the U.S. Department of Energy, *Technology in Society* 20: 385–406.

Casper, S. and van Waarden, F. (2005) *Innovations and Institutions*, Cheltenham: Edward Elgar.

Culpepper, P. D., Fagotto, E., Fung, A. and Lee, T. (2008) *Can Deliberative Democracy Reduce the EU's Democratic Deficit?*, Paper presented at the Annual Meeting of the American Political Science Association, Boston MA.

Dahl, R. A. (1992) The problem of civic competence, *Journal of Democracy*, 3(4), 45–59.

Dalton, R. J., Cain, B. E. and Scarrow, S. E. (2006) Democratic Publics and Democratic Institutions, in *Democracy Transformed?,* in Cain, B. E., Dalton, R. J. and Scarrow, S. E. (eds), Oxford: Oxford University Press: 1–23 and 250–75.

Delli Carpini, M. X., Lomax Cook, F. and Jacobs, L. R. (2004) Public deliberation, discursive participation, and citizen engagement: A review of the empirical literature, *Annual Review of Political Science*, 7: 315–44.

Diamond, L. and Morlino, L. (2005) *Assessing the Quality of Democracy*, Baltimore, MD: Johns Hopkins University Press.

Dryzek, J. S. (2002) *Deliberative Democracy and Beyond*, Oxford: Oxford Scholarship Online Monographs.

European Social Survey (2004) See http://www.europeansocialsurvey.org/ (accessed January 2004).

Freitag, M. and Wagschal, U. (eds) (2007) *Direkte Demokratie*, Berlin: Lit Verlag.

Frewer, L. J. and Rowe, G. (2005) Evaluating Public-Participation Exercises, in *Evaluating Public Participation in Policy Making*, OECD Publications, 85–108.

Fung, A. (2003) Survey article: Recipes for public spheres: eight institutional design choices and their consequences, *The Journal of Political Philosophy*, 11(3): 338–67.

Fung, A. and Wright, E. O. (2001) Deepening democracy: Innovations in empowered participatory governance, *Politics and Society* 29(1): 5–41.

Gabriel, O. W. and Walter-Rogg, M. (2006) Buergerbegehren und Buergerentscheide, *DfK*, 2: 39–56.

Geißel, B. (2009) Effektive und legitime Governance mit Zivilgesellschaft? Dynamiken am Beispiel der Europäischen Kommission und der Lokalen Agenda 21, in Botzem, S., Hofmann, J., Quack, S., Schuppert, G. F. and Straßheim, H. (eds) *Governance als Prozess*, Baden-Baden: Nomos.

Gilens, M., Glaser, J. and Mendelberg, T. (2001) *Having a Say: Political Efficacy in the Context of Direct Democracy*, Paper presented at the American Political Science Association Meeting, San Francisco, CA.

Held, D. (1995) *Democracy and the Global Order. From the Modern State to Cosmopolitan Governance*, Stanford, CA: Stanford University Press.

Holtkamp, L., Bogumil J. and Kissler, L. (2006) *Kooperative Demokratie. Das politische Potenzial von Bürgerengagement*, Frankfurt and New York: Campus.

Joas, M. (2000) Effects on Local Environmental Administration – A Comparative Cross-Time Analysis, in Joas, M. (ed.), *Local Agenda 21 – Models and Effects*, Åbo Akademi: 97–112.

LeDuc, L. (2006) *Referenda and Deliberative Democracy*, Paper prepared for presentation at the International Political Science Association, Fukuoka.

Levine, P., Fung, A. and Gastil, J. (2005) Future Directions for Public Deliberation, in Gastil, J. and Levine, P. (eds), *The Deliberative Democracy Handbook*, San Francisco, CA: John Wiley and Sons, Inc.

Lindner, W. (1999) *Schweizerische Demokratie. Institutionen, Prozesse, Perspektiven*, Bern: Haupt Verlag.

Mansbridge, J. (1983) *Beyond Adversary Democracy*, Chicago, IL: University of Chicago Press.

Mittendorf, V. (2008) Auswirkungen von Quoren und Themenrestriktionen bei kommunalen Bürgerbegehren im Ländervergleich, in Vetter, A. (ed.), *Erfolgsbedingungen lokaler Bürgerbeteiligung*, Wiesbaden: VS Verlag, S: 73–103.

Moeckli, S. (2007) Direct democracy and Political Participation from a Cross-national Perspective, in Zittel, T. and Fuchs, D. (eds), *Participatory Democracy and Political Participation*, New York: Routledge: 107–24.

Moore, S. A. (1996) Defining successful environmental dispute resolution: Case studies from public land planning in the United States and Australia, *Environmental Impact Assess Review*, 16: 151–69.

OECD (2005) *Evaluating Public Participation in Policy Making*, OECD Publications.

Offe, C. (ed.) (2003) *Demokratisierung der Demokratie. Diagnosen und Reformvorschläge*, Frankfurt a.M. and New York: Campus.

Papadopoulos, Y. and Warin, P. (2007) *European Journal of Political Research*, 46, Special Issue.

Renn, O., Webler, T. and Wiedemann, P. (1995) *Fairness and Competence in Citizen Participation: Evaluating Models for Environmental Discourse*, Dordrecht: Kluwer Academic Publishers.

Rowe, G. and Frewer, L. J. (2004) Evaluating public-participation exercises: A research agenda, *Science, Technology, and Human Values*, 29(4): 512–56.

Rowe, G., Marsh, M. and Frewer, L. J. (2004) Evaluation of a deliberative conference using validated criteria, *Science, Technology, and Human Values*, 29(1): 88–121.

Saward, M. (ed.) (2000) *Democratic Innovations*, London and New York: Routledge.

Scarrow, S. E. (2006) Making elections more direct?, in Cain, B. E., Dalton, R. J. and Scarrow, S. E (eds), *Democracy Transformed*, Oxford: Oxford University Press, 44–58.

Scharpf, F. W. (1999) *Regieren in Europa. Effektiv und demokratisch?*, Frankfurt a.M.: Campus.

Schmitter, P. and Trechsel, A. H. (2004) *The Future of Democracy in Europe: Trends, Analyses and Reforms*, Green Paper for the Council of Europe.

Setälä, M. (2006) On the problems of responsibility and accountability in referenda, *European Journal of Political Research*, 45: 699–721.

Sewell, D. and Philips, S. (1979) Models for the evaluation of public participation programmes, *Natural Resources Journal*, 19: 337–58.

Sintomer, Y. and Maillard, J. de (2007) The limits to local participation and deliberation in the French 'politique de la ville', *European Journal of Political Research*, 46: 503–29.

Sintomer, Y., Herzberg, C. and Röcke, A. (eds) (2005) *Participatory Budgets in a European Comparative Approach – Perspectives and Chances of the Cooperative State at the Municipal Level in Germany and Europe*, Final report, Volume II, Berlin: Centre Marc Bloch.

Smith, G., (2005) *Beyond the Ballot: 57 Democratic Innovations from around the World.* Available at http://www.makeitanissue.org.uk/Beyond%20the%20Ballot.pdf (accessed 8 April 2011).

—— (2009) *Democratic Innovations: Designing Institutions for Citizens Participation*, Cambridge: Cambridge University Press.

Steiner, J., Bächtiger, A., Spörndli, M. and Steenbergen, M. R. (2005) *Deliberative Politics in Action. Analysing Parliamentary Discourse*, Cambridge: Cambridge University Press.

Tolbert, C. J., McNeal, R. S. and Smith, D. A. (2003) Enhancing civic engagement: The effect of direct democracy on political participation and knowledge, *State Politics and Policy Quarterly*, 3:23–41.

Unger, B. (2005) Problems of Measuring Innovative Performance, in Casper, S. and van Waarden, F. (eds), *Innovations and Institutions*, Cheltenham: Edward Elgar: 19–51.

Vatter, A. (2006) *Direkte Demokratie in der Schweiz: Entwicklungen, Debatten und Wirkungen*, Paper presented at the Conference 'Direkte Demokratie. Bestandsaufnahmen und Wirkungen im internationalen Vergleich', Heidelberg, 5–6 May.

Vetter, A. and Kersting, N. (2003) Reforming Local Government, in Kerstin, N. and Vetter, A. (eds), *Reforming Local Government in Europe*, Opladen: Leske und Budrich: 333–49.

Walter-Rogg, M. (2008) Direkte Demokratie, in Gabriel, O. W. and Kropp, S. (eds), *Die EU-Staaten im Vergleich*, Wiesbaden: VS Verlag: 236–67.

9 When democratic innovations let the people decide

An evaluation of co-governance experiments

Julien Talpin

Introduction

Can the people govern? Are the people sufficiently competent and responsible to make wise collective decisions shaping public policies? In what circumstances can individuals effectively share a part of the political power of which they are supposed to be the legitimate holders? Co-governance innovations across the globe try precisely to offer institutional answers to these crucial questions that have animated democratic theory debates for centuries. While deliberative and participatory experiments have mushroomed in the last two decades, in both Western democracies and in the global South (for good reviews see Fung and Wright 2003; Smith 2005, 2009), only a few of them grant a direct decision-making power to lay citizens. The most prominent of these co-governance innovations will be presented and analyzed here. In a co-governance institution, citizens and public authorities share political power. They can be defined, following Smith (2005: 56–7), by three main features, distinguishing them from other deliberative and participatory innovations: (1) they are granted part of the decision-making authority, (2) they also have a degree of agenda setting power, and, therefore, a form of autonomy from the politicians who created them, and finally (3) they are ongoing forms of engagement, meeting regularly over months or even years, rather than snapshot events, like deliberative polls, citizens' juries or consensus conferences (Fishkin et al. 2002; Smith and Wales 2000; Goodin and Niemeyer 2003; Sintomer 2007). Co-governance innovations also differ from direct legislation, in the sense that power is shared between citizens and elected officials, and require an institutionalized and iterated public deliberation before taking the decision.

The aim of this chapter is first of all to present some of the most successful cases of co-governance, namely participatory budgeting, with the paradigmatic example of Porto Alegre, the Citizens' Assembly, and especially the one that took place in the Canadian state of British Columbia in 2004, and finally specific forms of community organizing, such as the community policing of the city of Chicago and decentralized planning in Kerala, India. How does co-governance work in practice? Why did they appear in these specific contexts? Do these experiences have anything in common? After having presented the empirical cases, I will answer these questions by tackling four of the most salient issues concerning co-governance innovations that will form the last four sections of this chapter. First of all, what is the public of co-governance innovations? Is it the 'usual suspects' from the articulate middle class or can people from the working class be integrated into the process too? The different institutions reviewed offer alternative solutions to these crucial dilemmas, from random selection to community mobilization. In any case, it appears that the direct decision-making power of co-governance institutions makes them more attractive for poorer people than other participatory arenas. Thus, our second consideration: if subaltern publics participate, are they capable of making sensible decisions about politics? Are co-governance institutions opening the door to amateurism and the expression of private interests in the public sphere? We will review the different ways in which empowered democratic innovations solve these issues, from offering formal lectures to citizens, to the more diffuse learning made possible by repeated participation.[1] This learning process nevertheless tears engaged citizens away from the general population, the former becoming increasingly expert and specialized and, therefore, cut off from the needs of the grass roots. Finally, do co-governance practices also have a redistributive impact towards the most needy in society? We will observe that the inclusion of modest and non-professional actors in the decision-making process can have a decisive impact on public policies, different actors promoting alternative needs and taking different decisions.

Co-governance innovations and representative democracy: a new division of political labour?

Whilst co-governance institutions share many features, they take very different procedural forms. Three will be presented here; each embodying a paradigmatic example of empowered innovation. The three institutional forms, despite the differences of context, were all created and supported by strong political will on the part of elites. They could also count – when they were successful – on the decisive mobilization of civil society organizations, working as a 'countervailing power' (Fung and Wright 2003), insuring a greater autonomy to these institutions.

Participatory budgeting: empowered urban democracy

A participatory budget (PB) can be defined as the institutionalized inclusion of lay citizens and civil society organizations in the budget decision-making process of a public administration (typically at municipal level, although it has been implemented by a small number of regions). PB, therefore, shifts decisions over the investment side of the budget from the city's elected officials to a system of neighbourhood and city-wide popular assemblies. Sharing some features with town meetings (Mansbridge 1983; Bryan 2004), participation is more formalized in PBs and the link with decisions more direct, as embodied in a voting procedure in most of the cases. PB's paradigmatic experiment emerged in Brazil. Since

1989, the city of Porto Alegre, led by the (then recently elected) left-wing Workers' Party, has implemented a very ambitious mechanism of participatory budgeting. Created as a top-down innovation, by liberal political elites aiming at 'democratizing democracy', the creation and institutionalization of PB owes a lot to the pressures coming from civil society, asking for greater participation and democracy. Procedurally, the PB process is divided among different institutions at the neighbourhood, district and municipal levels (Abers 2000; Avritzer 2002; Gret and Sintomer 2005; Baiocchi 2005). Popular assemblies are organized at the neighbourhood level, and are open to all volunteers. People can make proposals, which are then ranked through popular vote. Delegates – for the district and city levels – are also elected to promote the priorities of the neighbourhood at the higher stages. Through a complex system of socio-demographic criteria, the most marginal neighbourhoods and categories of the population tend to receive more public funding than others, following a form of 'territorial affirmative action'. Whilst its impact will be evaluated later on, it can nevertheless be stressed that PB's ability to involve an impressive number of citizens in its assemblies, and especially from the poorest classes, as well as its impact on public policies – its ability to 'invert priorities' towards the most deprived neighbourhood of the city – has captured the imagination of both social scientists and political activists, who have then tried, with varying success, to export the model.

Since its successful establishment in Porto Alegre, PB has spread widely, first in Brazil, then across Latin America, and more recently in Europe. The World Social Forum – created at the initiative of the anti-globalization movement to coordinate actions and share experiences (Della Porta et al. 2006; see Rucht in this volume) – organized in Porto Alegre since 2001, played a great role in the diffusion of the experience (Sintomer et al. 2008a). By 2008, several hundreds of cities in the world had adopted a participatory budgeting mechanism. Apart from Porto Alegre, several hundred PBs have been created in Latin America in the last decade and more than a hundred in Europe. Porto Alegre's paradigmatic example goes far, however, in encompassing all the procedural diversity of participatory budgets across the world – so well that Sintomer et al. (2008a) constructed six ideal types to describe the European cases.[2] It must be stressed that in contrast to Porto Alegre's case, European PBs only deal with a fraction (1–20 per cent) of the administration's budget. The 'Porto Alegre PB adapted for Europe' model follows, to a great extent, the Brazilian city procedural design, and is well represented in Spain (where about twenty PBs are currently functioning), and to a lesser extent in Italy. The cities of Cordoba and Seville (which embodies the biggest European PB experiment in this city of 700,000 inhabitants), with the emphasis they put on social justice and the allocation of funds towards the most deprived neighbourhoods, are good examples of this model. The 'proximity participation' PB model is mainly present in France (with about ten cases)[3] and in Italy. In these cases, PBs are less autonomous from the administration, with direct participation of elected officials in the process, and decisions taken by consensus rather than vote. Here, the aim is mostly to bridge the gap between politicians and citizens and thus to solve the 'crisis of representation'. As a consequence, some of these experiments are merely consultative, with elected officials 'cherry-picking' the ideas and proposals they find interesting. 'Consultation on public finances' is the most common PB model in Germany. It mainly consists of information and transparency on the city's budget and financial decisions. Citizens can give suggestions – usually made individually rather than through collective deliberation – on how to modernize public services. Finally, 'community funds at the local level' is the most common PB model in the UK, with examples in cities such as Bradford and Salford. In this case, local authorities generally engage non-governmental organizations (NGOs) and community organizations to allocate financing coming from urban renewal programmes (Lavan, 2007). PB has indeed generated a great deal of interest in the last decade in the UK. During the Blair administration, the then Secretary for Communities and Local Government, Hazel Blears, promoted the establishment of PBs – mostly understood as in the 'community fund' model – across most British local authorities.

The overall development of PB has been impressive in the last decade, with the World Bank even recommending this democratic innovation as a model of 'good governance' to be encouraged, especially in Asia and Africa. PBs appear in some regards as embodying one of the most widespread experiences of co-governance innovation across the globe. From this perspective, it seems that despite the variations of PB's procedural form according to the context, it is adaptable to very different circumstances and mostly depends on the political will of its initiators.

The Citizens' Assembly model: mixing mini-public and direct democracy

By mixing different participatory and deliberative designs, the Citizens' Assembly model arguably offers the most ambitious form taken by co-governance innovations in recent years. In submitting the results of a mini-public deliberation to a referendum process, it connects deliberative quality with binding public decisions for the first time (Lang 2007; Warren and Pearse 2008). The most prominent experience took place in the Canadian state of British Columbia (it has since then been replicated in Ontario and The Netherlands). From January to November 2004, 160 randomly selected Canadian citizens – one man and one woman from the 79 provincial electoral districts plus two Aboriginal members – met regularly to recommend an electoral reform. Its inception resulted from a shared appraisal among the political elites that the Single Member Plurality system had led at best to 'awkward' or at worst, to 'unfair' results, the translation of votes into seats being largely disproportionate.[4] The political class being divided about the best alternative electoral system – and appearing as both judge and jury in such a decision – it therefore decided to organize a Citizens' Assembly, whose recommendations would go to a referendum.

The Citizens' Assembly was organized in three phases, spread out over a year: a learning phase, a public hearing phase and a deliberation phase. Citizens first of all learned about the variety of voting procedures around the world, with their respective advantages and drawbacks, receiving formal lectures by political scientists every other weekend over three months. Then, the public hearing phase allowed the Citizens' Assembly participants to listen and consult supporters and opponents of the different electoral systems all over the province, any citizen or organization being able to make a presentation in one of the fifty local meetings that were organized. Finally, the citizens met again to deliberate collectively about which electoral system was the best. They opted for a Single Transferable Voting (STV) system.[5] Their agreed position was then proposed by a referendum to all the citizens of the State, but did not pass, since it failed to reach the quorum of 60 per cent of the electorate.

Despite this final failure, this participatory experience appears extremely appealing, as it combines random selection, information and deliberation phases, and was granted a high degree of autonomy and hence empowerment. Interestingly, the British Columbia Citizens' Assembly (BCCA) was a top-down experience – created by political leaders – to tackle an issue on which politicians where both biased and incapable of reaching a compromise. From this perspective, citizens' assemblies could be organized on other contentious issues, like campaign financing, constitutional reforms (Fung 2007; Lang 2007), or subjects dangerous for political leaders (abortion, death penalty, pension system) who do not want to take sides (or decisions) on issues when their electorate is divided (Ferejohn 2008). Whilst its creation stemmed from a strong political will of enlightened political elites, it must be stressed that some of the limits – in both practice and theory – of the Citizens' Assembly model came from the lack of civil society and bottom-up mobilization. The failure of the British Columbia referendum can be attributed to insufficient debates in the public sphere. With greater media coverage and civil society mobilization, the referendum could have passed (see for more details Smith in this volume). From a theoretical perspective, deliberation in the public sphere appears also crucial for the Citizens' Assembly model. While the randomly selected participants had the chance to get information and deliberate intensively on the virtues and limits of each electoral system, the greater public did not have such an opportunity. Referendums have the same limits as aggregative democracy: those who decide – the people – have little knowledge about the issues at stake. Hence the importance of organizing a dense deliberation phase between the Citizens' Assembly and the referendum – or even to set up a deliberation day (Ackerman and Fishkin 2004) in the state – where both the media and civil society discuss the proposals of the Citizens' Assembly and where the general public can be informed. This is crucial to link democratic deliberation in a mini-public to deliberative democracy in the public sphere (Chambers 2009; Geissel in this volume).

While the Citizens' Assembly embodies a unique model, another hybrid co-governance experiment can be evoked, namely Berlin citizens' juries, which only existed from 2001 to 2003. Based on random selection of lay citizens, like any citizens' jury (see Smith's chapter in this volume), but also composed (at 49 per cent) of local association representatives, they were annually granted 500,000 euros to finance local development projects. They therefore appeared as a mix between mini-publics and participatory budgeting at the local level (Röcke and Sintomer

2005). Taking place in seventeen of Berlin's most deprived neighbourhoods, these citizens' juries allowed any resident or local association to present a project, which was then discussed among the jurors to decide whether or not to finance the project according to its 'usefulness' and general quality (the final decision usually taken through a secret vote). On average, the juries met about fifteen times throughout the year to evaluate about seventy-two projects, half of them in the end being financed (see Koehl and Sintomer 2002; Sintomer 2007). Created by the Berlin senate, coordinated and facilitated by public functionaries, this co-governance innovation disappeared with the change of the municipal majority, which again indicates the importance of political support for such innovations.

Community organizing, neighbourhood development and decentralized planning: sectoral co-governance

Other co-governance innovations take place in specific policy sectors, from schooling and housing, to policing and economic development. It therefore offers coordination platforms between lay citizens and public functionaries in defining common problems, identifying priorities and evaluating results.

Since 1995, the Chicago Police Department has held monthly community meetings in 285 neighbourhood beats across the city (Fung 2004). In these beat meetings, police officers and local citizens discuss how to improve public safety in the neighbourhood. Following a problem-solving method, the neighbourhood meetings define priorities and strategies for action and review progress. Successful strategies often involve coordinated action by local citizens and police officers. Community policing is particularly interesting, as there is a strong incentive for disadvantaged citizens to attend. Evidence shows that this innovation reverses the typical participation bias – citizens from within poor and less well-educated neighbourhoods (which suffer from higher levels of crime) turn out at higher rates.

The Chicago participatory reform was implemented in order to solve the problems created by an increasingly inefficient Weberian-type bureaucracy. Emanating from the Chicago Police Department's own reflections, as well as from progressive community organizations, the participatory reform of the city's policing was also supported by the Mayor, who saw in it a way to demonstrate the administration's innovative spirit to fight crime. Participatory democracy appeared as a way to modernize public services by including citizens in the decision-making process. Following a German union motto, it could be said: 'Making public services efficient to avoid privatizing them.' Transparency and efficiency seems indeed to result from such participatory procedures, as will be seen later on.

The US also has a great deal of experience of participatory procedures at the neighbourhood level. Many large cities have, for instance, created neighbourhood councils (Berry et al. 1993). While most of them are consultative, some experiments are more empowered, allowing the co-governance of neighbourhood development plans. The Minneapolis Neighborhood Revitalization Program (NRP) has, for example, been granted US$400 million, to be spent over twenty years, to develop local project plans (Fagotto and Fung 2006). In the first part of the process, neighbourhood associations gather information about the concerns and priorities of residents (through surveys, door-to-door and focus groups, and discussions during neighbourhood meetings). These priorities then coalesce into a neighbourhood action plan that details neighbourhood needs and lists concrete actions to achieve these objectives. The plan must finally be ratified in a general assembly involving the whole neighbourhood, and obtain approval from Minneapolis City Council. Despite low participation, and an overwhelming representation of homeowners, this innovation had a substantial redistributive impact, as will be seen later on.

In a completely different context, the decentralized planning process in Kerala, India, created highly empowered institutions that gathered an impressive number of lay citizens. When the Left Democratic Front returned to power in Kerala in 1996, the State government rapidly launched the 'People's Campaign for Decentralized Planning'. It first of all consisted of administrative decentralization, with local government receiving new powers and being brought under the authority of local elected bodies. Second, fiscal decentralization took place, 40 per cent of all developmental expenditures being allocated to the Local Self-Governing Institutions. Third, there has been a decentralization of political power, elected local representatives now having the possibility to define, finance and implement development plans and projects (Isaac and Heller 2003). These plans take shape through a multi-stage participatory process of iterated deliberation, between elected representatives, government officials, activists and lay citizens. In keeping with the principle of subsidiarity it is supposed to embody, the process begins in ward-level assemblies, open to all volunteers, in which participants discuss collective problems and identify development priorities. Projects are progressively refined by task forces meeting regularly in development seminars. The aim is to prepare detailed project proposals, including a definition of the objectives, criteria for beneficiaries or areas, a time frame, an identification of funding sources, a review of the social and environmental impact, and so on. Projects are then submitted to the municipal councils that set priorities and budgets for local plans. A comprehensive local development plan is thus constructed, consisting of hundreds of projects, addressing a variety of local needs and problems.

Whilst being a top-down decentralizing movement initiated by elected representatives, the Kerala People's campaign is also the product of twenty-five years of local experimentation by NGOs. The campaign stemmed from a collective reflection on the limitations of the traditional command-control model of development, relying a lot on political parties' motivations. Reform appeared necessary at the time, as the increased climate of sectarian and partisan divisions had become an obstacle to development. The Peoples' campaign, therefore, replaced the conventional system of vertical accountability to political parties and bureaucracies, with horizontal forms of cooperation between different sets of actors.

Sectoral co-governance appears in policy areas that are facing either inefficiencies or patronage problems. The participation of the public can, therefore, appear as a way to modernize public services, making them more efficient through a problem-solving process. It also increases the transparency of public decision making, the number of people having an eye on the process, rendering corruption and clientelism almost impossible. In the end, most of these reforms have stemmed from a positive cooperation between enlightened political elites willing to launch ambitious democratic reforms, allowing a better allocation of public resources, and active civil society organizations that pushed for greater empowerment and autonomy from local governments. These democratic innovations have shown, as will now be seen, a great deal of popularity, attracting high numbers of participants, especially among the most deprived factions of society.

Activating the inactive and the marginalized

Participatory democracy aims at opening up the institutional machinery of political decision making to the citizens. Through the organization of public meetings, assemblies and working groups, citizens are offered the opportunity to have their say and eventually to have an impact on public decision-making processes. Despite the high expectations and incantatory discourses of both political philosophers and the promoters of democratic innovations, participation rates in public arenas remain on average fairly low (Verba et al. 1995; Ryfe 2005). Those who get involved in participatory politics appear in this regard as either 'a happy few' or new local elites. What types of actors are ready to dedicate their time and energy for the community's welfare in co-governance arrangements? Are co-governance innovations more inclusive than other participatory designs? Is the decision-making power they are granted enough to reach marginalized citizens? These questions are pivotal as they lie at the core of the legitimacy of democratic innovations.

Co-governance institutions, like most democratic innovations, stem from a critique of representative government. At the very roots of representation lies a desire to filter the passions of the masses and to let competent and enlightened people decide (Manin 1997). Two main criticisms are addressed to representative government by participatory democrats. First, there is the question of the tyranny of powerful minorities (Fung 2007), which raises problems of the democratic legitimacy of the representative government's decision-making processes. This issue is all the more salient today with the decline of participation rates in representative elections. Second, representative government appears to some participatory democrats as a hurdle to social justice (Pateman 1970; Barber 1984). Those in charge of political decision making emanating from a certain elite – allegedly cut off from the economic and social necessities biasing the judgement of the masses – tend to promote their private interests in the name of a defence of the common good. Far from embodying the whole population, most representatives are white males, relatively old, who went to the same universities and come from the upper economic groups of society. Generally implying an adequacy between individuals' interests and preferences, participatory democrats therefore fear the orientation of public policies in the interests of the dominant elite. They push forward the idea of a 'politics of presence' (Phillips 1995; Goodin 2004) or 'mirror representation', forms of participatory democracy providing for the inclusion of social, ethnic or gender groups generally excluded from public decision making (Young 2000).

To what extent are co-governance institutions able to answer these criticisms? The most successful experiences, presented above, even if they remain the exception rather than the norm in the field of participatory democracy, manage to gather either a high number of people (when they rely on open participation mechanisms) or a representative sample of the population through random selection. These two procedural devices – self-selection and lot – and their consequences will be presented in turn.

Porto Alegre's participatory budget, as well as Chicago's community policing and Kerala's decentralized planning, managed to gather large numbers of participants, especially among the poorest, who generally do not participate in other political forums. Kerala's popular assemblies managed, for instance, to gather over two million people in 1997, with an average of 180 persons per ward meeting, representing 11.4 per cent of the voting population, and about one out of four households (Isaac and Heller 2003: 102). After ten years of existence, 8.4 per cent of Porto Alegre's population declared to have participated in the PB assemblies at some point in the previous five years.[6] Each year, more than 10,000 people participated in the neighbourhood assemblies. The very procedural design of the experiment creates an incentive for participation, since the number of delegates in the district and city assemblies is proportional to the number of participants in the neighbourhood assemblies. If people want to see their proposals passed, they must first of all mobilize in the local assemblies. Porto Alegre's PB also managed to include the poorest sections of the population. In 2003, the twentieth percentile of the population accounted for 30 per cent of the participants in the neighbourhood assemblies.[7] Interestingly, the number of people on lower incomes decreases when representative mechanisms are reintroduced, dropping to 20 per cent for forum delegates and 15 per cent for councillors.[8]

In Chicago, on average between seventeen and twenty-one citizens attend each beat meeting, which equates to a city-wide attendance of approximately 80,000 citizens each year (Fung 2004: 56). According to surveys, 14 per cent of the citizens attended at least one meeting in 1997, and 79 per cent of the population was aware of the programme (Fung 2003: 139 and 121). Whilst within neighbourhoods, wealthier residents and homeowners participate more than others, participation rates are overall higher in poorer neighbourhoods that suffer higher levels of criminality (Ibid.: 129–31). Participation rates are, however, lower in most American and European co-governance experiences, which also appear less attractive to poor people and immigrants. Apart from the French region Poitou-Charentes high-school participatory budget, gathering between 7 or 8 per cent of all the invited population, most European PB experiences gather between 1 and 2 per cent of the population. In Rome's 11th District PB, only 1500 people participated in 2004, that is, a little more than 1 per cent of the district population.[9] Whilst women participate as much as men – which is true for most PB cases in both Europe and Latin America – elderly people, activists and the middle classes are clearly overrepresented in European PB assemblies. In 2003, in Rome's PB, 44 per cent of the participants were over fifty, 61 per cent were homeowners, 40 per cent members of an association and 20 per cent members of a political party.[10] Similarly, Minneapolis NRP only gathers 2,000 persons every year, that is, 2 per cent of the neighbourhood's population on average, with a large majority of homeowners (Fagotto and Fung 2006: 644). Overall, European and American co-governance experiences – because they are granted limited decision-making power and community organizations are less active in mobilizing the population – fail to involve the people for whom they had been created in the first place, that is, those generally excluded from traditional processes of political participation.

From this perspective, random selection appears as an attractive alternative mode of selection, capable of involving those who do not participate spontaneously. Whilst random selection does not give everyone an equal opportunity of participation, it offers an equal probability of being selected for the participatory process (see Fishkin, Geissel and Smith in this volume). There is, however, a dilemma affecting mini-publics: they cannot constitute a statistically representative sample of the population, because the number of participants would then be too high to allow a rich and intensive deliberation to take place. The initiators of randomly selected institutions, therefore, predefine a set of criteria they deem important for the selection process. In the case of the BCCA, the organizers wanted as many men as women, and two people from each electoral district. They also realized that having some Aboriginal participants would be necessary: two were therefore selected, even if this category of the population remained under-represented. The British Columbia example highlights the fact that random sampling requires a form of 'manipulation' by the organizers, in order to arrive at a group of people mirroring the general population.

Even if embodying the diversity of the population, a randomly selected group has, however, problems of legitimacy and accountability: can 160 persons, unrelated to the general population, take a binding decision in its name? Where is the popular control required by any form of democratic process? How can a group of people leaving their office after a year be made accountable for the decisions they have made? These crucial dilemmas explain why most mini-publics remain consultative, decisions being taken ultimately by legitimately elected representatives. The Citizens' Assembly offered, however, an innovative solution: by organizing a referendum, the burden of legitimacy and accountability did not lie on the mini-public, but on the general public, deciding through a direct democracy procedure.

Whilst they sometimes manage to gather impressive numbers of participants and appear more effective than most democratic innovations to activate marginalized actors, co-governance experiments do not reach the majority of the population. However, the minority participating actively in these institutions do it intensively – so well that they find the experience enriching, thus affecting them significantly.

Learning democracy: how citizens become competent by participating

According to their promoters, democratic innovations have the potential to re-enchant politics, by including large sections of the population. State-sponsored initiatives of participation could, therefore, appear as spaces of political socialization, allowing non-politicized individuals to get their first public experience and thus to be able to participate more effectively in the public sphere in the future. Whilst the limited knowledge of the political system, the difficulty to locate candidates and programmes on a left/right spectrum, the instability and incoherence of individual preferences, have been largely demonstrated by now and are accepted by most social scientists (Converse 1964; Bourdieu 1979), and sometimes conceptualized as 'cognitive incompetence' (Sartori 1987), the more marginalized individuals seem, nevertheless, capable of political reasoning in different contexts, and especially in small-group discussions (Gamson 1992; Duchesne and Haegel 2007). While certain people are unable to talk about politics in public, they can express genuine political arguments in more private or intimate contexts (Eliasoph 1998). The question of the role of the (social, institutional and political) context in shaping individuals' political practices should, therefore, be put at the forefront, in order to be able to understand how and when individuals can become enlightened citizens. The idea that individuals can become better citizens by participating actively in the polity has indeed been at the centre of debates in political theory, from its Greek origins to classical republicanism and civic humanism theorists, before being reformulated by theorists of participatory democracy and partly renewed by writers on deliberative democracy (Mansbridge 1999). People could learn new skills and habits, become competent or even 'better citizens' (Ibid.) by participating, with intensive engagement allowing individuals to reach surprising levels of expertise on rather technical issues. Participation is in itself a source of learning for individuals. Most empirical research indicates that when appropriately organized, co-governance innovations represent enriching experiences for participants, who become increasingly knowledgeable and competent through time (see also Geissel in this volume). What do people learn in these empowered democratic institutions?

Participation, first of all, allows individuals to learn to speak in public in an appropriate manner, to manage a meeting, to facilitate a discussion, to increase self-confidence amongst the less competent speakers, to set up an agenda, to mitigate between different interests and sensibilities, and even sometimes to organize a negotiation between irreducible positions. Talpin shows for instance how, in some Roman neighbourhood assemblies, people learnt to deliberate, to listen to each other's arguments and to speak in a non-aggressive manner, after weeks of messy and unproductive discussions, thanks to the positive influence of facilitators and, as people, became more aware of the inefficiencies of their ways of relating to one another (Talpin 2011). As Fung argues about the participatory school councils he studied in Chicago: 'After six months ... they began to behave cordially to one another and, more importantly, to deliberate about substantive school improvements rather than using meetings as occasions for political manoeuvring' (Fung 2003: 135). In the Chicago beat meetings, residents and police officers received formal training in the problem-solving orientation of community policing deliberation. Participation, therefore, teaches groups to deliberate effectively, but also teaches individuals to speak up. As Fung writes of one Chicago resident: 'For the first few months of our acquaintance, she was so shy that she refused to be interviewed. When I finally spoke with her, I asked her why she had avoided me for so long. She said that: "It took me a while to get confidence to speak [to you]. I have learned from [other community-policing activists] how to speak up." By the end of the observation period, Mrs. Rivers had become one of the most active community-policing participants in Central Beat' (Fung 2004: 156–7).

It is through trial and error, to answering problems faced in certain situations (such as a shared analysis of the inefficiencies of discursive messiness), and thanks to the positive influence of enlightened facilitators stressing the importance of simple organization procedures, that a collective learning mechanism can take place.[11] Far from being a purely cognitive, discursive or rational process, the learning of democracy firstly requires mastering certain ways of doing, which can only happen in interaction.

Even if co-governance institutions are generally not highly technical institutions – to avoid excluding the most culturally and educationally deprived individuals – participation can nevertheless allow the learning of some technical skills that were, until this point, the privilege of experts. In the BCCA, participants met for six weekends, when they received lectures on the different electoral systems. At the end of that phase, they had basically taken a graduate course in electoral system design (Lang 2007). Participants' levels of expertise on a rather obscure issue – most of the participants initially did not know that competing voting procedures existed – therefore increased drastically, thanks to participation.

Similarly, in PBs, people learn the organization of a public budget (composed of different taxes and sources, requiring an equilibrium, and so on), and as PBs often deal with urban planning issues, participants can learn through discussion technical skills on how to build a road or a public park, the nature of technical and juridical rules, and so on (Talpin 2011). From this perspective, participatory engagement seems capable of reducing the gap between experts and amateurs in designing public policies. Co-governance organizers sometimes devolve large resources for training, as in the Kerala experience: 'In the first year, in seven rounds of training at state, district and local level, some fifteen thousand elected representatives, twenty-five thousand officials, and seventy-five thousand volunteers were given training. ... Separate handbooks and guides, amounting to nearly four thousand pages of documentation, were prepared and distributed for each round' (Isaac and Heller 2003: 83).

Finally, it seems that empowered participation has the potential to increase individuals' political sophistication. This concept is generally defined as the capacity to understand the political system, to locate politicians and ideas on a left/right spectrum, and is therefore measured through survey answers (Luskin

1990). Participatory arenas are not detached from the local political system, since such participation is a way to increase one's knowledge of the political game. Being in regular interaction with elected officials, participants can more easily identify their political orientation (which was far from being the case for most of them at the beginning), learn to negotiate with elected officials, to play off the rivalries between parties to get things done. Participants also discover the way the administrative machine works, the distribution of competences among different public bodies, as well as the conflicts between different institutions. The discourse voiced by certain activists can sometimes appear as lectures on the local power relationships or on the way the municipal institution really works, thus embodying a great deal of knowledge for apparently uninformed citizens. Political parties' members evoke the latest municipal decisions, housing rights militants tackle the homeless situation problems of the city, environmentalists share their knowledge on questions such as global warming or urban planning. This increased political knowledge might, however, result in a greater cynicism from the citizens if they end up disappointed by their participatory experiences (Talpin 2011).

Even if the increase of individuals' political competence might not have a direct impact on public policies, it can nevertheless be understood as a positive externality of co-governance innovations. As they often manage to gather people with little political experience, co-governance institutions can play a role of political socialization for lay citizens. This might re-boost civil society – by nurturing new members for civic organizations or fostering the creation of new associations (see Baiocchi 2005, in the case of Porto Alegre) – and it could have a wider effect on the political system, transforming non-voters into active citizens. The electoral consequences of participatory democracy remain, however, a contested issue in the literature (see Anduza et al. 2008; Sintomer et al. 2008a).

Whilst the issue of citizens' capacities is crucial for determining the democratic quality of co-governance institutions, it appears that it is only through repeated participation that citizens become competent enough to take binding decisions. Repeated participation is a condition for learning, but it has also the side effect of closing up groups on themselves: highly active, integrated and expert participants appearing increasingly distant from the grass roots.

The emergence of a new local elite

Despite the will to build inclusive institutions, embodied in different selection mechanisms – random or self-selection – it must be stressed that co-governance innovations always face a similar dilemma: since they require repeated participation over time, a small core of participants always ends up assuming the lion's share of the work in mobilizing the population, refining proposals, negotiating with elected officials, monitoring project implementation. Institutions based on random selection gather, by definition, a small group of people, who become increasingly specialized and expert over time. Similarly, institutions based on open participation at the grass roots level either reintroduce representative mechanisms at the higher stages (as in participatory budgets, for instance) or let people with more time and energy (often retired people, housewives, students) have a more decisive role in the participatory process. It has, indeed, been shown that biographical availability is a decisive factor explaining participatory engagement (Talpin, 2011).

As a consequence, all co-governance experiments based on self-selection mechanisms end up with a small in-group of highly active citizens. In some cases, the in-group is even institutionalized, as in Seville's PB, where they created 'motor groups', seen as the pillars of the participatory process. The existence of a new sub-elite in co-governance institutions appears all the more evident, since turnover rates are high in these institutions. Whilst data are scarce on this issue, we know that in Rome's 11th district PB, for instance, more than 50 per cent of the 2003 participants did not take part in the 2004 PB cycle. Despite the diversity of the reasons explaining citizens' withdrawal from the process, this reinforces the centrality of the few actors who participated regularly and repeatedly over time, appearing increasingly as the core of the institution.

Theoretically, rotation procedures should prevent the emergence of a new sub-elite at the local level. Most PB institutions and neighbourhood councils follow a rule of rotation of the delegates, impeding a former delegate to run for office two years in a row. In practice, however, the most committed actors continue to participate in one way or another (prevented from running for PB council, they might serve in the monitoring commissions for instance) – which appears necessary to the survival of the experiment, given the low participation rates.

Furthermore, the learning processes that have been observed transform the few highly active participants into experts. They acquire skills and competences, a form of expertise that they are able to reinvest in other civic organizations, from local associations to political parties. Trajectories of notabilization have thus been observed (Talpin 2011), with some highly integrated participants becoming locally elected representatives. This raises a crucial dilemma for co-governance innovations: while repeated participation always ends in closing up the groups on themselves, thus jeopardizing the legitimacy of participatory institutions, it also allows learning processes to take place (Fagotto and Fung 2006), the level of citizens' capacities appearing crucial for determining the democratic quality of co-governance institutions. Such processes could recall the 'iron law of oligarchy' highlighted by Michels in the case of political parties, with delegates becoming increasingly competent and specialized and thus cut off from the language, needs and interests of the masses (Michels 1914). Similarly, ordinary citizens could feel betrayed by participatory democracy institutions' insiders, who reproduce the traditional delegation mechanisms they were supposed to overcome in the first place. Such criticisms have not been frequently observed in the case of co-governance experiments, however, simply because most citizens ignore the existence of these participatory institutions or do not care about them. The closing up of co-governance experiments on themselves makes the enlargement of participation harder, as it appears increasingly difficult for newcomers to integrate into an institution ruled by certain implicit norms, routines and shared assumptions, only known to the regular and specialized participants.

The closing up of co-governance experiments on themselves raises another dilemma for participatory democracy: if participants increasingly become a new sub-elite, to what extent can such institutions promote innovative public policies, alternative to those of the traditional elite? Whilst one of the justifications of participatory democracy is precisely the inclusion of non-specialized actors in the policy cycle, does it lose its *raison d'être* when the public gains expertise and gets professionalized? The policy impact of empowered democratic innovations appears contrasted from this perspective.

The impact of co-governance innovations: how can lay citizens sometimes take better decisions than elites?

The main specificity of co-governance institutions, in comparison with other democratic innovations, is their level of empowerment. The question remains as to whether citizens' participation in the decision-making process of public authorities makes a difference. Does it lead to different decisions from those that traditional elites would have taken? Are those decisions better, being more rational or more just as hypothesized by deliberative theory? Whilst being exceptional, some of the cases reviewed here show remarkable effects on public policies, with co-governance more directly taking into account the will and needs of the most marginal citizens.

When given sufficient autonomy and leverage, co-governance institutions take different decisions from those of traditional elites. The BCCA example is quite telling from this perspective. As Lang (2007) argued, several expert panels had advocated a Mixed Member Proportional System. The choice of the STV system by lay citizens was linked to the fact that they saw it as a system designed to curtail the power of political parties. Citizens simply had different criteria than had experts for defining what constitutes a good electoral system. They especially valued 'local representation', while discarding the importance of having a 'stable government', which is generally the most important aim of constitutional or electoral systems designs for political scientists. Including non-professional actors in the policy process can clearly produce different decisions.[12] As long as democratic innovations are empowered enough and granted sufficient autonomy from public authorities – something that remains exceptional, especially in North America and Europe – the inclusion of the public has an impact on public policies. The question remains open, however, as to whether these decisions are better.

One of the answers to this crucial question on the efficiency of democratic mechanisms is that co-governance innovations have the potential to increase the pool of knowledge available before taking a decision, by integrating lay citizens' local knowledge in the policy cycle (Fischer 2000), who thus take better decisions. The value of local knowledge was highlighted by Aristotle and has been reinterpreted recently by prominent democratic theorists and tested empirically by social scientists (Mendelberg 2002).[13] Usage and practice would thus be the conditions for sound judgment, as John Dewey argues: 'The man who wears the shoe knows best that it pinches and where it pinches. ... A class of experts is inevitably so removed from common interests as to become a class with private interests and private knowledge, which in social matters is not knowledge at all' (Dewey 1927: 207). Empirical evidence of the virtues of local knowledge is plenty, as Fung argues in the case of Chicago's beat meetings: 'Invariably, the officers responded that residents usually know crime situations better than police', that often police surveillance revealed that resident complaints 'were accurate, and that they were glad to have this kind of help' (Fung 2004: 159). Local knowledge is particularly useful for pointing out problems that experts and technicians, supposedly cut off from the field, could have missed. Very often in European PB assemblies, participants draw the attention of the public to important issues: safety in a Roman public park, cold in a deprived neighbourhood primary school in Seville, or indecent living conditions in the dorms of a high school in Poitou-Charentes. Technicians themselves learn to value the practical knowledge of users, as testified by a Poitou-Charentes functionary: 'I remember this high-school director who found it pointless to freshen up the dorms, saying that at his time pupils were raised tough. ... The PB allowed pupils to express their needs, and the dorms were renovated. PB allows the expression of needs that we did not hear before, as the decision makers are different' (see Sintomer and Talpin 2011). Local knowledge is generally shared through anecdotes or testimonies, illustrating the nature of a particular problem; hence the importance of the mobilization of emotions and personal stories in co-governance deliberations (Young 1996; Sanders 1997).

Beyond local knowledge, it seems that decisions taken in co-governance institutions can be more impartial than those taken in representative bodies. In the case of the Citizens' Assembly, it was especially designed to solve a conflict of interest, political parties being necessarily biased in the reform of an electoral system. But citizen participation might also have a positive impact in increasing transparency and limiting patronage. Porto Alegre appears exemplary from this perspective, PB reform having substantially diminished patron/client relationships, which used to be the rule – especially in the area of construction. Even if relying on self-reporting (which casts doubt on the reliability of such findings in sensitive issues like corruption), several studies highlighted the decrease of patronage after the creation of the participatory budget. While 18 per cent of community leaders declared their engagement in client/patron exchanges of benefit to political support prior to PB, this dropped to only 2 per cent after the creation of the co-governance mechanism (Baiocchi 2005: 45). Forty-one per cent of associations received funding from clientelistic relationships before 1989, whereas none relied on such a personalized system after the creation of PB (Avritzer 2002: 37). The transparency in the allocation of public resources, as well as in the choice of private contractors, simply made patronage and corruption more difficult (Gret and Sintomer 2005). Contrary to some sceptics' expectations, the devolution of political power to citizens did not translate into increased clientelism, because the politicization of decision-making processes impeded such corrupted practices. Co-governance institutions appear, from this perspective, particularly effective in countries where corruption levels are high.

The impact of empowered innovations in developing countries can sometimes be impressive. In Kerala,

> from 1997 to 1999, 98,494 houses have been built, 240,307 sanitary latrines constructed, 50,162 wells dug, 17,489 public taps provided, and 16,563 ponds cleaned. A total of 2,800,179 individual beneficiaries received support from the plan for seedlings and fertilizers. 8,000 kilometres of roads were built. These figures far outspace public construction from previous comparable periods.
>
> (Isaac and Heller 2003: 100)

Similarly, in Porto Alegre,

> each year, the majority of the 20 to 25 kilometres of new pavement has gone to the city's poorer peripheries. Today, 98 per cent of all residences in the city have running water, up from 75 per cent in 1988; … in the years between 1992–1995, the housing department offered housing assistance to 28,862 families, against 1,714 for the comparable period of 1986–1988; and the number of functioning municipal schools today is 86, against 29 in 1988.
>
> (Baiocchi 2001: 48)

In Chicago, community policing led to decreasing crime rates, even if the latter fell nationally at the same time, thus making the origin of the process hard to identify (Wacquant 2005).

Not only are these co-governance institutions efficient, allowing the pace of economic and social development to quicken, but they can also be instruments of social justice, resulting in priority being given to allocating resources towards the most needy groups and areas. In the Indian People's Campaign,

> local bodies have accorded much greater priority to basic needs such as housing, drinking water, and sanitation. ... In contrast to past patterns, investment priorities in special plans prepared for scheduled castes and tribes differed significantly from the overall investment patterns. The low income, asset, and skill position of these marginalized communities has been taken into account.
>
> (Isaac and Heller 2003: 99)

In Porto Alegre, the redistributive impact of the system is encapsulated in the rules of the game, as poorer and more populated areas received more funds, following the will of the Workers Party to 'invert priorities' towards the more needy. Similarly, Minneapolis NRP 'systematically favored disadvantaged neighborhoods through a progressive funding allocation formula that included factors such as neighborhood size, poverty level and dwelling units' condition' (Fagotto and Fung 2006: 647). The social justice effect of co-governance is, therefore, neither the product of the altruism of enlightened citizens, nor of other-regarding deliberation – most of the participants mobilizing for the interest of their own communities – but of rules of the game designed by progressive political elites. This is further evidence of the crucial role of the political will of the elected representatives when they design co-governance institutions in the first place.

The same conclusion can be drawn from the study of European cases, where the absence of redistributive effects is first of all the result of a more moderate political will. As this elected official says in one of the nevertheless most empowered French PBs: 'The investment choices made by the citizens were pretty much those we [town representatives] would have made. And it was really reassuring for us' (Talpin 2007). Contrary to the Brazilian or Indian experiments, and despite the fact that most European co-governance innovations are led by politicians on the left of the political spectrum, they do not directly aim at fostering social justice through participation.

As the most comprehensive study on European PB concludes, most cases have at best moderate redistributive impacts (Sintomer et al. 2008b: 306–15). Primarily, the reason for this limited impact is the financial dimension of European PBs. Whilst in Porto Alegre, the whole investment side of the budget was allocated through a PB, only a small percentage is decided by citizens in European cases. In the small Italian cities of Pieve Emmanuele and Grottamare, where 10 per cent of the budget is allocated by citizens, the PB nevertheless permitted the rehabilitation of the most deprived neighbourhoods. This was made possible, owing to the massive mobilization of the residents of these areas. Some Spanish experiences, influenced by Porto Alegre's model, set up 'social justice criteria', aimed at allocating more resources for the most deprived areas and the most marginal segments of the population, but with little result. In Seville, the social justice criteria resulted in only 70,000 euros of 'bonus' for the most deprived zone of the city (Ibid.: 309), a marginal amount in comparison to the 12 million euros of the PB (which only represents 1.2 per cent of the total city budget).

The comparison of co-governance experiments indicates that five conditions are necessary for democratic innovations to have a social impact: (1) a clear political will to promote social justice from the initiators of the participatory procedure; (2) a significant level of empowerment, allowing citizens to decide on high-stakes issues; (3) a certain transparency, making the evaluation of the social impact of public policies possible; (4) distribution criteria aimed at maximizing the condition of subaltern classes; and (5) a mobilization of civil society organizations to defend the interests of marginalized groups (Ibid.: 314). While these conditions were often present in the Brazilian and Indian cases, they were absent most of the time in those of Europe and North America.

Conclusion

What makes co-governance institutions unique in the universe of democratic innovations seems to be at the root of their political and social success. Iterated participation allows citizens to become competent enough to take wise decisions, more directly in their interest. The empowered nature of co-governance attracts more directly subaltern groups, which fulfils both the will of participatory democrats to include the traditionally politically excluded, and to foster social justice. The question remains, however, as to the impact of these generally local democratic innovations on the wider political system (Chambers 2009; Geissel in this volume). Whilst they were initially designed to answer the democratic malaise faced by representative government, a reflection on the connection between micro and macro politics appears necessary.

When participatory democracy is promoted by national political leaders, like French former presidential election candidate Ségolène Royal, or Hazel Blears in the UK, they generally remain vague in their definitions of the concept and elusive in the degree of empowerment they are ready to grant to new institutional designs. Whilst democratic innovations have mushroomed across the globe in the last two decades, participation embodying 'the new spirit of democracy' (Blondiaux 2008), it is not certain whether dramatic transformations will result from such changes. The vast majority of democratic innovations remain consultative, and co-governance institutions – while sometimes having a decisive impact locally – are not sufficiently numerous to have an aggregated impact on national policies. At the macro level, they might, nevertheless, have a more diffuse impact on the political culture of a country. In Brazil, where they are the most widespread, state/civil society relationships have been partly reconfigured in the last decade (Baiocchi 2005). Similarly, the learning of new skills and competences made available to low-income and depoliticized individuals can also have an impact on political culture, by nurturing a more competent citizenry. The importance of these transformations will depend on the political will of elites and the mobilization of civil society organizations in making co-governance institutions either instruments of legitimation of traditional policies, or tools fostering social justice and a more vibrant democracy.

Notes

1. The terms co-governance institutions and empowered innovations will alternate here, as the latter, conceptualized by Archon Fung, share the main features of the former (Fung 2004).
2. Only the four more common ones are presented here, however.
3. A law on 'proximity democracy' was passed in France in February 2002, that made neighbourhood councils compulsory in all cities with over 80,000 residents. These democratic innovations cannot be considered co-governance institutions, however, as they are essentially consultative. This law nevertheless embodies the meaning of participatory democracy in this country, primarily understood as a way to increase proximity between politicians and citizens, which has a direct impact on French co-governance experiments like PBs.
4. In 1996, the British Columbia Liberal Party received fewer seats than the New Democratic Party, despite winning the majority of votes, and was therefore shut out of government for five years. Leaders of the party therefore decided at the time to change such an unfair electoral system and to organize a Citizens' Assembly when they returned to power. In 2001, the Liberals returned to power with 58 per cent of the votes and won all but two seats – another perverse election result!

5 The STV system is organized around multi-member electoral districts, and uses a preferential ballot, where voters have to rank-order candidates in each district. As a consequence, different candidates from the same party can run for office in the same district, the STV system thus undermining the power of political parties. The STV system is used in Ireland, Malta, and some US cities. It can also be noted that back in the 19th century John Stuart Mill had advocated for a STV system, which was better at reflecting the intensity of voters' preferences.

6 Rebecca Abers, 'Learning Democratic Practice: Distributing Government Resources Through Popular Participation in Porto Alegre, Brazil', in *Cities for Citizens*, ed. Mike Douglass and John Friedmann (Chichester and New York: Wiley, 1998), p. 49.

7 Harvard University Center for Urban Development Studies, *Assessment of Participatory Budgeting in Brazil* (Washington: Inter-American Development Bank, 2003), p. 10, quoted by G. Smith, *Beyond the Ballot*, 2005, p. 64.

8 Sources: Ibid.

9 E. D'Albergo (ed.) (2005) *Pratiche partecipative a Roma. Le osservazioni al piano regolatore e il bilancio partecipativo*, Rome: Università La Sapienza.

10 Sources: Ibid.

11 On the importance of facilitation for deliberation see Smith, this volume. We want to stress here that facilitation also allows the learning of certain discursive styles, by imitation of what is defined as a good collective deliberation.

12 Even if in this case it was not enacted considering the results of the referendum in British Columbia.

13 Rawls makes a similar argument: 'We normally assume that an ideally conducted discussion among many persons is more likely to arrive at the correct conclusion than the deliberations of any one of them by himself. … No one of them knows everything the others know, or can make all the same inferences that they can draw in concert. Discussion is a way of combining information and enlarging the range of arguments', in Rawls, J. (1971) *A Theory of Justice,* Cambridge, MA: Harvard University Press, pp. 358–9.

References

Abers, R. (2000) *Inventing Local Democracy: Grassroots Politics in Brazil*, Boulder, CO: Lynne Rienner.

Ackerman, B. and Fishkin, J. (2004) *Deliberation Day*, New Haven, CT: Yale University Press.

Anduza E. et al. (2008) The Electoral Impact of Direct-Democratic Practices, *International Journal of Urban and Regional Research*, vol. 32, n°2: 473–91.

Avritzer, L. (2002) *Democracy and the Public Sphere in Latin America*, Princeton, NJ: Princeton University Press.

Baiocchi G. (2001) Participation, Activism, and Politics: The Porto Alegre Experiment and Deliberative Democratic Theory, *Politics & Society*, vol. 29, n°1, March.

Baiocchi G. (2005) *Militants and Citizens: The Politics of Participatory Democracy in Porto Alegre*, Princeton, NJ: Princeton University Press.

Barber, B. (1984) *Strong Democracy, Participatory Politics for a New Age*, Berkeley, CA: University of California Press.

Berry J. M., Portney K. E. and Thomson K. (1993) *The Rebirth of Urban Democracy*, Washington, DC: The Brookings Institution.

Blondiaux, L. (2008) *Le nouvel esprit de la démocratie. Actualité de la démocratie participative*, Paris: Seuil.

Bourdieu, P. (1979) *Distinction: A Social Critique of the Judgement of Taste*, Harvard, MA: Harvard University Press.

Bryan, F. (2004) *Real Democracy: The New England Town Meeting and How It Works*, Chicago, IL: Chicago University Press.

Chambers, S. (2009) Rhetoric and the Public Sphere: Has Deliberative Democracy Abandoned Mass Democracy?, *Political Theory*, 37 (3): 323–350.

Converse, P. (1964) The Nature of Belief Systems in Mass Publics, in Apter, D. (ed.) *Ideology and Discontent*, New York: Free Press: 206–61.

Della Porta, D., Andretta, M., Mosca, L. and Reiter, H. (2006) *Globalization from Below: Transnational Activists and Protest Networks*, Minneapolis, MN: University of Minnesota Press.

Dewey, J. (1927) *The Public and its Problem*, Athens, OH: Ohio University Press.

Duchesne S. and Haegel F. (2007) Avoiding or accepting conflict in public talk, *British Journal of Political Science*, vol. 37, n°1: 1–22.

Eliasoph, N. (1998) *Avoiding Politics. How Americans Produce Apathy in Everyday Life,* Cambridge: Cambridge University Press.

Fagotto, E. and Fung, A. (2006) Empowered participation in urban governance: The Minneapolis Neighborhood Revitalization Program, *International Journal of Urban and Regional Research*, vol. 30, n°3: 638–55.

Ferejohn, J. (2008) The Citizen Assembly Model, in Warren, M. and Pearse, H. (eds) *Designing Deliberative Institutions. The British Columbia Citizen Assembly*, Cambridge: Cambridge University Press.

Fischer, F. (2000) *Citizens, Experts, and the Environment: The Politics of Local Knowledge*, Durham: Duke University Press.

Fishkin J., Luskin R. and Jowell R. (2002) Considered opinions: Deliberative polling in Britain, *British Journal of Political Science,* vol. 32, July.

Fung, A. (2003) Deliberative Democracy, Chicago Style: Grass-Roots Governance in Policing and Public Education, in Fung, A. and Wright, E. O. (eds) *Deepening Democracy*, London: Verso: 111–43.

Fung, A. (2004) *Empowered Participation*, Princeton, NJ: Princeton University Press.

Fung, A. (2007) Democratic Theory and Political Science: A Pragmatic Method of Constructive Engagement, *American Political Science Review*, vol. 101, n°3, August, 443–58.

Fung, A., Wright, E. O. (2003) Countervailing Power in Empowered Participatory Governance, in Fung, A., Wright, E. O. (eds) *Deepening Democracy, Institutional Innovations in Empowered Participatory Governance*, London: Verso: 259–89.

Gamson, W. (1992) *Talking Politics*, Cambridge: Cambridge University Press.

Goodin, R. (2004) Representing Diversity, *British Journal of Political Science*, vol. 34 n°3.

Goodin, R. and Niemeyer, S. (2003) When Does Deliberation Begin? Internal Reflection versus Public Discussion in Deliberative Democracy, *Political Studies*, vol. 51: 627–49.

Gret, M. and Sintomer, Y. (2005) *The Porto Alegre Experiment: Learning Lessons for a Better Democracy, New York: Zed Books.*

Isaac, T. H. and Heller, P. (2003) Democracy and Development: Decentralized planning in Kerala, in Fung, A. and Wright, E. O. (eds) *Deepening Democracy*, London: Verso: 77–110.

Koehl, E. and Sintomer, Y. (2002) *Les jurys de citoyens berlinois,* Paris: Rapport final pour la Direction Interministérielle de la Ville.

Lang, A. (2007) But Is It for Real? The British Columbia Citizens' Assembly as a Model of State-Sponsored Citizen Empowerment, *Politics and Society*, vol. 35, n° 1: 35–69.

Lavan, P. (2007) *Participatory Budgeting in the UK. An Evaluation from a Practitioner Perspective*, Manchester: The PB Unit.

Luskin, R. (1990) Explaining Political Sophistication, *Political Behaviour*, vol. 12, n°4: 331–61.

Manin, B. (1997) *The Principles of Representative Government*, Cambridge: Cambridge University Press.

Mansbridge, J. (1983) *Beyond Adversary Democracy*, New York: Basic Books.

Mansbridge, J. (1999) On the Idea that Participation Makes Better Citizens, in Elkin, S. and Soltan, K. (eds) *Citizen Competence and Democratic Institutions*, Philadelphia, PA: The Pennsylvania University Press: 291–325.

Mendelberg, T. (2002) The Deliberative Citizen: Theory and Evidence. In Delli Carpini, M.X., Huddy, L., and Shapiro, R.Y. (eds). Research in Micropolitics, vol.6: Political Decision Making: Deliberation and Participation, New York: Elsevier Press, 151–193.

Michels, R. (1914) *Political Parties: A Sociological Study of the Oligarchical Tendencies of Modern Democracies*, New York: Free Press.

Pateman, C. (1970) *Participation and Democratic Theory*, Cambridge: Cambridge University Press.

Phillips, A. (1995) *The Politics of Presence*, Oxford: Clarendon Press.

Röcke, A. and Sintomer, Y. (2005) Les jurys citoyens berlinois et le tirage au sort: un nouveau modèle de démocratie participative?, in Bacqué, M.-H., Rey, H., Sintomer, Y. (eds) *Gestion de proximité et démocratie participative: les nouveaux paradigmes de l'action publique, Paris:* La Découverte: 139–60.

Ryfe, D. (2005) Does deliberative democracy work? *Annual Review of Political Science*, vol. 8., 49–71.

Sanders, L. (1997) Against Deliberation, *Political Theory*, vol. 25, n°3: 347–76.

Sartori, G. (1987) *The Theory of Democracy Revised*, Chatham, NJ: Chatham House.

Sintomer, Y. (2007) *Le pouvoir au peuple. Jury citoyens, tirage au sort et démocratie*, Paris: La Découverte.

Sintomer, Y. and Talpin, J. (eds.) (2011) *La démocratie participative au-delà de la proximité. Poitou-Charentes et l'échelle régionale*, Rennes: Presses Universitaires de Rennes.

Sintomer, Y., Herzberg, C. and Röcke, A. (2008a) Participatory Budgeting in Europe: potentials and Challenges, *International Journal of Urban and Regional Research*, vol. 32, n°1, March: 164–78.

Sintomer, Y., Herzberg, C. and Röcke, A. (2008b) *Démocratie participative et modernisation des services publics: des affinités électives? Enquête sur les expériences de budget participatif en Europe*, Paris: La Découverte.

Smith, G. (2005) *Beyond the Ballot: 57 Democratic Innovations from around the World*, London: Power Inquiry.

Smith, G. (2009) *Democratic Innovations*, Cambridge: Cambridge University Press.

Smith, G. and Wales, C. (2000) Citizens' Juries and Deliberative Democracy, *Political Studies*, vol. 48, n°1: 51–65.

Talpin, J. (2007) Who Governs in Participatory Budgeting Institutions? The Impact of Citizen Participation in Municipal Decision-Making Processes in a Comparative Perspective, in Dewitt P. et al. (eds) *Towards DIY-Politics. Participatory and Direct Democracy at the Local Level in Europe*, Bruges: Vanden Broele: 103–25.

Talpin, J. (2011) *Schools of Democracy? How Ordinary Citizens (Sometimes) Become Competent in Participatory Budgeting Institution*, Colchester: ECPR Press.

Verba S., Lehman Schlozman K. and Brady, H. E. (1995) *Voice and Equality: Civic Voluntarism in American Politics*, Cambridge: Harvard University Press.

Wacquant, L. (2005) *Parias urbains. Ghetto, banlieues, Etat,* Paris: La Découverte.

Warren, M. and Pearse, H. (eds) (2008) *Designing Deliberative Institutions. The British Columbia Citizen Assembly*, Cambridge: Cambridge University Press.

Young, I. M. (1996) Communication and the Other: Beyond Deliberative Democracy, in Benhabib, S. (ed.) *Democracy and Difference. Contesting the Boundaries of the Political,* Princeton, NJ: Princeton University Press: 120–35.

Young, I. M. (2000) *Inclusion and Democracy*, Chicago, IL: Chicago University Press.

Conclusion

Democratic innovations

Theoretical and empirical challenges of evaluation

Brigitte Geissel

Without doubt representative democracy, as we know it today, is transforming. There is a high level of consensus that established democracies 'attend to their own gathering problems of public dissatisfaction and … disillusionment', as Diamond and Morlino (2005: ix) put it. Thus representative democracy, giving citizens only the option to elect their representatives, is increasingly complemented with participatory innovations. These innovations are expected to solve at least some of the problems described by the authors in this volume.

The question, whether and how democratic innovations actually cure the democratic malaise, runs through all chapters as a leitmotif. It goes without saying that one book cannot cover every aspect. However, this volume is a big step towards answering the question by combining, for the first time, the work of *experts on different democratic innovations*. The authors provide comprehensive overviews, farsighted perspectives and gather the main findings in the field.

By scrutinizing the potentials and failings of democratic innovations, the chapters demonstrate two main theoretical and empirical challenges of evaluating democratic innovations: the yardsticks by which innovations may be judged and the empirical methods of doing so. In this conclusion I will focus on these two theoretical and empirical challenges:

1. The *yardsticks* authors apply for evaluation and preliminary findings. Democratic innovations are expected to fulfill a wide variety of hopes, some of them contradictory. Actors involved expect participatory innovations to solve a mixture of problems, such as enhancing citizens' competence, cutting back the budget of a municipality or providing more redistributive and sustainable policies. Considering these manifold objectives, it might not be surprising that there is no – and will probably never be – consensus about the yardsticks for the evaluation.
2. The *empirical methods* authors apply to gather and to analyze facts and figures. The second main challenge is empirical: for most innovations the data are insufficient and a variety of methods have to be used to gather information and analyze it.

The names in brackets refer to the authors in this volume.

Yardsticks and findings

The preceding chapters use a variety of yardsticks to evaluate democratic innovations. However, in spite of the differences, we can identify recurring criteria. The following are notable:

- inclusive, equal participation
- improvement of citizens' democratic skills
- impact on public policies
- other, but less frequently mentioned, criteria are: quality of deliberation, political satisfaction, legitimacy and transparency.

Most authors refer in one way or another to *inclusive and equal participation*. They use different terms such as political equality, participatory range, representativeness, inclusiveness in presence and voice (e.g. Beetham, Geissel, Smith, Talpin), or equal chance of participation (Fishkin, Kriesi, Rucht) – but they all refer to the same idea of inclusive and equal participation. It seems that political equality is a crucial criterion, no matter which forms of direct or deliberative innovations are scrutinized.

Political equality has always been a goal of modern democracy, epitomized in the notion of 'one person one vote'; and many authors consider political equality as one of the main yardsticks for measuring the quality of any kind of democracy – and also for the evaluation of democratic innovations. In fact, equal and inclusive participation is one of the main arguments of proponents of participatory innovations. Participatory innovations, so goes the argument, provide more input options – especially for those citizens who are not engaged in traditional forms of participation. However, opponents of democratic innovations claim that representative democracy is the best guarantor of political equality and that the new, participatory forms undermine inclusive and equal participation. Participatory innovations will be used – and misused – by politically active citizens, i.e. the well-off and better-educated strata of society, especially middle-aged and middle class males. This possibility cannot be ignored. As Kriesi, Fishkin, Geissel and others in this volume demonstrate, there is always a danger of unequal participation being generated by participatory innovations. However, most experts on participatory innovations show an awareness of this problem and search for solutions. Many contributors in this volume describe the often complex procedures applied to ensure political equality – equal opportunities to participate and to be heard. In cases of innovations based on predefined groups, i.e. discursive procedure such as for example citizens' juries or planning cells (Smith, Geissel), two forms of recruitment are often applied: random selection[1] – with or without stratification of the sample and sometimes combined with incentives (Fishkin) – and inclusion of stakeholders (see e.g. Smith). Considering participatory innovations without predefined groups, such as direct democratic procedures, 'activating the inactive' is often mentioned as means to encourage equal and inclusive participation (Newton, Talpin). Although the success of such attempts is promising, most chapters in this volume demonstrate that efforts must be maintained. Democratic innovations, per se, do not guarantee equal, inclusive participation. Quite the contrary: without special and continued endeavors democratic innovations are likely to result in exclusive and unequal participation. Without persistent efforts to guarantee inclusive and equal participation, opponents of democratic innovations are likely to be right – participatory procedures would mainly benefit the politically active strata of society.

The second criterion mentioned by most of the authors is the *improvement of citizens' democratic skills*. Authors discuss, for example, the impacts on participants (Beetham), civic education (Geissel), making better citizens (Newton), improved public spiritedness (Fishkin), and the enhancement of civic competence (Talpin). It appears that the improvement of citizens' democratic skills is viewed as a major asset when democratic innovations are implemented. The biggest effect seems to be the improvement of knowledge. Most participatory innovations lead to an increase of citizens' knowledge about the issue involved and about politics as a whole (e.g. Fishkin). This is especially true for group-based innovations, where citizens engage intensely in a political topic. But other innovations show similar results. Kriesi demonstrates, for example, that campaigns in the context of direct democratic procedures 'raise the general level of issue-specific competence in the electorate'. Enhancement of citizens' democratic skills or 'becoming a better citizen' seem to be another story. As Fishkin shows, 'public spiritedness' can be enhanced, especially via deliberation (see also Rucht and Smith). If at all, 'becoming a better citizen' takes place mainly in deliberative procedures that provide sufficient support in the shape of mediators and facilitators.

The third criterion several authors refer to is *impact on public policies*, put into terms like effectiveness (Geissel), transformation of citizen preferences into public policy (Budge), performance 'for the economy and for the citizens' personal situations in everyday life' (Kriesi), improved 'popular control' (Smith), social justice or just 'better decisions' (Talpin). Authors focusing on direct democracy stress that democratic innovations can lead to more effective policies in the sense that they bring policies 'closer to median voter preferences' (Budge). Empirical findings on performance are clear-cut – at least for the home country of direct democracy, Switzerland: 'direct-democratic institutions have mainly positive effects with regard to the economy' (see for details Kriesi, Geissel). Authors evaluating deliberative procedures have a slightly different emphasis. They often address the hypothesis that high quality of deliberation will lead to better policies (Beetham, Geissel, Smith). However, proof of this is difficult and up to now theoretical arguments are more convincing than the sparse empirical findings.

So far, many participatory innovations have had little or even no impact on public policies. Direct democratic procedures are often just consultative. Deliberative procedures only have some impact on public policies if they are connected to political decision-making bodies – but this is seldom the case. In this context an interesting debate has started (also discussed in this volume by Newton) complaining that participatory innovations are often window dressing and symbolic action. Is it wrong that participatory innovations have little or no effect on public policies? From my point of view this question is somewhat beside the point. Many outcomes of participatory procedures may not be worth implementing. For example if a participatory innovation is designed badly and includes just the well-off strata of society, it might not necessarily guarantee common welfare. As long as we know so little about the outcomes of participatory innovations with all their different designs we should be careful about complaints of window dressing. It is still an open question whether the decisions made by innovatory procedures are in fact better[2] – with exception of the Swiss direct democracy discussed above (Kriesi).

Other evaluation criteria referred to less often by the authors in this volume are the quality of deliberation, political satisfaction, legitimacy and transparency.

The *quality of deliberation* is raised in several chapters, namely 'deliberative modes' (Beetham, Rucht), 'thoughtfulness' and 'considered judgement' (Fishkin, Smith). These authors focus on the question whether deliberation is possible at all (Rucht) and what requirements are necessary to support deliberative quality (Smith, Fishkin). Rucht looks at deliberation within selected progressive movements. He defined deliberation as symmetric discussion without 'hard power' among actors who consider each other as equal ('weak form of deliberation') and traces the development of deliberation within progressive movements – from the relatively non-deliberative labour movement to the highly deliberative Global Justice Movement. Deliberation turns out to be a more recent development: although talk and discussions have become more widespread since the 1960s, the idea of equality among participants was not an essential component. This has changed in the last decade, when more emphasis was put on symmetric discussion. He also shows that in Global Justice Movements today 'weak versions of deliberative democracy' actually take place – not always and all the time, but more often than critics assume. Fishkin's results look very similar. The idea of deliberation is not utopian; deliberation is not necessarily dominated by male university graduates and it does not always result in polarizing group dynamics (Fishkin). Facilitators, small group designs, specific rules and other settings, described by Smith, turned out to be crucial for providing the supportive environment for deliberation (see for details Smith and also Rucht).

Political satisfaction and the feeling of *legitimacy* (Kriesi, Geissel) are without doubt two important features within any democracy. Political decisions should satisfy citizenry – at least in the long run all decisions should benefit the public. And as research on political culture has shown, a system is more stable if its citizens are convinced of its legitimacy. States with comprehensive direct democratic options seem to score better in these categories – again at least in the Swiss case (Kriesi, Geissel). Switzerland achieves satisfaction and legitimacy to a higher degree than most other democracies. And direct democracy is a main actor explaining these positive attitudes (Kriesi). Whether the same is true for deliberative procedures can be doubted. Since there is no 'home country of deliberative procedures', it is difficult to make final statements. However, research on German Local Agenda 21 processes show that neither satisfaction nor legitimacy have been enhanced significantly by deliberative innovations. The opposite was the case: in many municipalities, which have adopted Local Agenda 21 processes, participants developed a feeling of political frustration because most of their suggestions were ignored (Geissel 2009). In other words, participatory innovations might also have negative impacts on perceived legitimacy and political satisfaction, if their suggestions are ignored systematically and without justification by political representatives.

Some authors also mention *transparency* as a criterion for judging innovations (Talpin). Enhancing transparency is often stressed as an objective when implementing democratic innovations. Especially in states with vast corruption problems this target gains relevance. Transparency was for example an important reason for implementing participatory budgeting in Porto Alegre, Brazil. Findings on this criterion are mixed – and it is surely no surprise that the design of the innovation is crucial. Most deliberative mini-publics for example might be transparent concerning their own collective will formation, but if they are cut off from governmental processes they will surely not enhance the transparency of any political decision making. Only if they gain access to and influence over governmental decision making can transparency be enhanced.

Empirical methods

Democratic innovations are *en vogue* and thus it is not surprising that empirical evidence is increasing rapidly. However, sufficient data does not yet exist to evaluate all innovations. We have a comprehensive body of data for direct democracy in Switzerland and some US states. These data are copious and detailed and can be easily used for statistical calculation – at least for most aspects of direct democracy (Kriesi). The situation looks very different for deliberative procedures, where case studies still prevail (e.g. Rucht, Talpin). Thus, the methods applied by authors in this volume reflect the methodological state of the art: research in direct democracy is often quantitative and conducted statistically to test hypotheses, whereas research on deliberative procedures is qualitative, case-study based and aimed at generating hypotheses.

Recently, reviews of literature on democratic innovations have tried to shed more light on existing research gaps by accumulating and comparing existing figures and reports. Some of the chapters in this volume follow this line (e.g. Beetham, Geissel). These chapters draw on empirical literature, gathering qualitative as well as quantitative evidence. What is still missing is a comprehensive data set combining available data systematically. However, even if a comprehensive data set became available, two main problems will continue to challenge research on participatory innovations. These two main challenges are heterogeneity and multi-collinearity.

The first major methodological difficulty is *heterogeneity*, i.e. the diverse variety of participatory innovations (Geissel). Concerning direct democratic procedures, for example, mediated and unmediated direct democratic procedures interrelate in different ways with representative democracy and they have very different impacts (Budge, Kriesi). Thus, evaluating 'direct democracy' is like measuring the speed of cyclists by taking all kinds of cyclists – from toddlers to racers, in different contexts, from lowland to alps – into account and calculating the arithmetic mean. It is obvious that the arithmetic mean, or any other average value, does not contain much information and gives at most a very vague idea about the impacts of direct democracy (Budge, Kriesi). The same is true for discursive procedures – showing even more varieties (e.g. Beetham, Smith). The only solution to this problem is to find out the most significant differences and to take them all into account. Such differentiated and sophisticated analyses are without doubt intricate and time-consuming. They require not only theoretically and empirically meaningful differentiations, but also a large amount of case studies to allow insightful and robust conclusions. Work has just started and this volume reveals the current state-of-the-art.

Multi-collinearity, i.e. strong correlations between explaining variables, is the second major problem. It is in many cases impossible to single out and prove that a change of attitudes, policies, skills or whatever is due to a particular innovation. One way to approach this problem would be to compare *ex ante* and *ex post* situations. However, 'before and after studies' are still rare. For example, political legitimacy before and after a participatory procedure is seldom analyzed – with one exception, namely research on citizens' preferences. Several studies have scrutinized whether citizens change their preferences and attitudes whilst participating in a participatory procedure. Fishkin's research on deliberative polls is the best known and probably also the most advanced in this field.

When starting this book we hoped to find out whether and which democratic innovations might cure the current democratic malaise. While all the chapters of the book provide enlightening and instructive findings, clear and definitive answers to our questions are few and far between. There is no fast track to evaluating democratic innovations and there is much more work to be done.

Notes

1 See for instructive discussions of different forms of random sampling Fishkin and Smith in this volume.
2 The most elegant definition of 'better' is given by Budge, who suggests that policies made by direct democracy are at least closer to the median and thus the majority voter preference – no matter whether these policies are more sustainable, redistributive or in any other sense 'better'.

References

Diamond, L. and Morlino, L. (eds) (2005) *Assessing the Quality of Democracy*, Baltimore, MD: Johns Hopkins University Press.
Geissel, B. (2009) Participative Governance: Hope or Danger for Sustainable, Effective, and Legitimate Policies? A Case Study of Local Agenda 21, *Local Government Studies*, Vol. 35, No. 4: 401–14.

Index